I0810023

IMAGES
of America

SUPERIOR AND QUEEN VALLEY

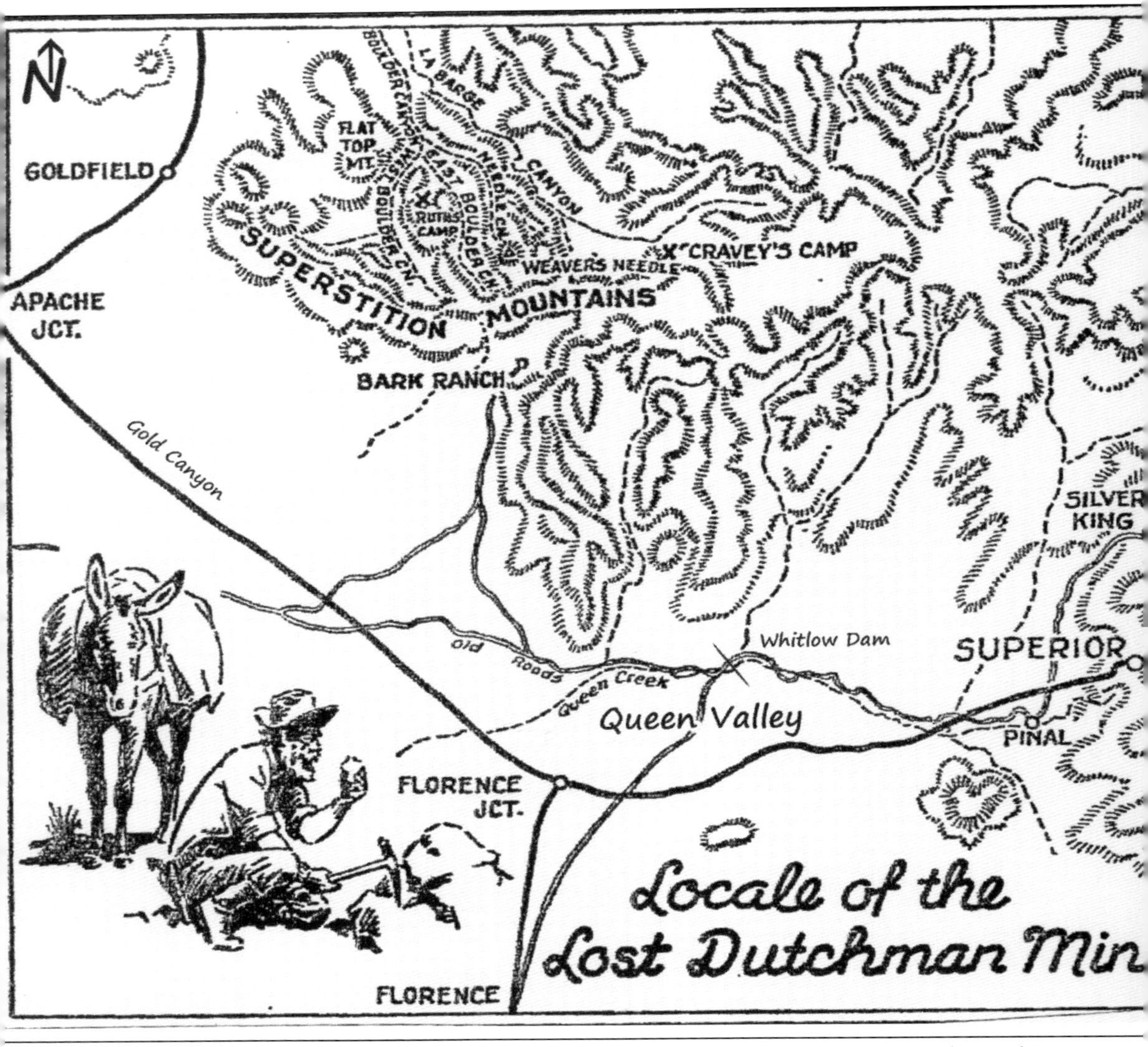

This map of the Superstitions from Sims Ely's book *The Lost Dutchman Mine* shows the areas discussed in this book. Phoenix is approximately 40 miles west of Apache Junction, and Globe is approximately 24 miles east of Superior. Florence is 18 miles south of Florence Junction, and Queen Valley is 4 miles north and slightly east of Florence Junction. (Sims Ely and Jack San Felice.)

ON THE COVER: Often believed to be the Silver King Mine due to its nearby location, this is actually identified by archeologists for the Silver King Mining District as the Monarch of the Sea. There were lone, reclusive prospectors, like the Superstition Mountain's Lost Dutchman Mine, but this unidentified group of family and friends in the 1920s exhibit more prevalent methods of mining, which meant everyone involved shared the work and the rewards.

IMAGES
of America

SUPERIOR AND QUEEN VALLEY

Carol A. Schumacher and
Danielle M. Tomerlin

ARCADIA
PUBLISHING

ISBN 978-0-7385-7965-8

Published by Arcadia Publishing
Charleston, South Carolina

Printed in the United States of America

Library of Congress Control Number: 2010934684

For all general information, please contact Arcadia Publishing:
Telephone 843-853-2070
Fax 843-853-0044
E-mail sales@arcadiapublishing.com
For customer service and orders:
Toll-Free 1-888-313-2665

Visit us on the Internet at www.arcadiapublishing.com

We would like to thank our husbands, Larry Schumacher and Jason Tomerlin, who provided technical and moral support, most of the time very willingly. Writing this book has reminded us that we need to leave not only a healthy planet but also a historic legacy for our future generations. Thus, we dedicate this book to Connor, Lily, James, and Jared.

CONTENTS

Acknowledgments

The authors are grateful for the many resources in the community that made this book possible. The process of capturing the histories of these two towns included many delightful opportunities to chat with the fascinating men and women with roots in these towns. There are too many to mention all by name, but we would like to especially thank the following major contributors: Chip Calamaio and Pat Walsh, amateur historians; Robert King, archeologist; Bill Moser; Manny Ruiz; Cecil Fendley; and descendants of the Whitlow, Mullins, Brown, and Gorham families.

We would also like to thank the following organizations for their assistance: the members of the Queen Valley Historical Society, including president and treasurer Steve and Phyllis Joyce; the Superior Chamber of Commerce, particularly Mila Lira and Mike McKee; Glendon Collins of the Public Lands Foundation; H. Christine Reid of the Pinal County Historical Society Museum; Nyal Niemuth and Diane Bain of the Arizona Department of Mines and Mineral Resources; Greg Davis of the Superstition Mountain Historical Museum; Mark Siegwarth, Paul Wolterbeek, and Lacey Pacheco of the Boyce Thompson Arboretum; the *Superior Sun*; Resolution Copper Company; the Superior Facebook group; and especially historic author and lecturer Jack San Felice.

Our editor Jared Jackson of Arcadia Publishing was a pleasure to work with. He answered our questions with grace and provided guidance and gentle reminders throughout our journey.

Images in this volume appear courtesy of the Queen Valley Historical Society (QVHS), Pinal County Historical Society Museum (PCHSM), Arizona Department of Mines and Mineral Resources (ADMMR), Superstition Mountain Historical Museum (SMHM), Boyce Thompson Arboretum (BTA), Superior Facebook group (SF), U.S. Army Corp of Engineers (ACE), National Archives (NA), Bureau of Land Management (BLM), and others as identified. All unidentified pictures appear courtesy of the authors.

INTRODUCTION

Most ghost towns in Arizona are former mining boomtowns. Once the mines played out, the towns were simply abandoned as miners moved on to hunt for treasure elsewhere. Arizona's early towns were generally set up to serve as central locations for the miners, to act as military camps for troops, or to provide stops as people traveled on supply routes; few were conducive to creating sustainable communities. It was not until miners began bringing their families and reliable routes were established that towns began to be situated in locations that were suitable for permanent habitation.

Early explorers used major waterways to discover the best routes to the West. Through their maps and tales that were passed down, the early pioneers were able to follow those same routes in order to pursue their dreams, which were not always of finding riches but of simply finding good land and a better life. Estimates are that over a million wagons crossed the Allegheny into the prairies and western deserts between 1830 and 1880. In numerous places on the Oregon Trail, wagon ruts bear evidence of the 50,000 wagons that used that route. In the 20 years of Oregon Trail travel, over 20,000 people died on the way. Most were deaths from extreme weather, starvation, lack of water, childbirth, and accidents such as drowning while crossing the rivers. Contrary to popular belief, less than 2 percent of the deaths were attributed to Native Americans.

Many pioneers were traveling to California to join the Gold Rush in 1848. Some were hearty adventurers looking for a new place to call home in the famed West, responding to the opportunity to own what had formerly been public land. However, Arizona was not necessarily their planned final destination. Some people who decided to stay and not continue their journey were attracted to the beauty and grandeur of the deserts and mountains of Arizona. But for the most part, many adventures who chose to stay there were under the belief that they could strike it rich.

Some pioneers were escaping religious persecution or intolerable living conditions in the big cities back East. Brigham Young sent Mormons in the late 19th century to the West to settle Utah and Arizona. Mormon towns were quickly settled across Arizona including Queen Valley in 1915.

In examining the towns of Superior and Queen Valley, several things are made clear about the sustainability of these two communities. They both had the two things every town must have to exist, water and commerce. Having started as a mining town, Superior had the potential of becoming a ghost town when the nearby silver mines played out and the U.S. monetary standard was changed from silver to gold. Fortunately, miners in the area looking for silver and gold also found copper. With the founding of the Magma Mine, Superior began life as a mining camp. The miners of the Silver King Mine and other mines nearby brought their families to the site with them, as shown in the cover photograph and others throughout the book. This factor played heavily in the permanent establishment of the town. Just as important was the fact that the town was located with Queen Creek running through it. With a seasonally reliable and nearby water supply, the town could build an infrastructure that could sustain its growth. Water systems, piped in from nearby Florence, were also added to guarantee year-round water for the town.

The town continued to grow with the influx of capital from a wealthy owner, named Boyce Thompson. This allowed for the mine shafts to be drilled even deeper and for the extraction operations to be expanded. During the hundred years of Superior's existence, merchants, ranching, and mining families built schools, formed clubs and professional associations, completed community projects, and made lifelong friendships. These activities were the bonding agent that kept the community alive through the mine closure in the 1980s until the reopening of the mines in the 1990s. The town's future is secure; those that love the town will live nowhere else. Sometimes those that have grown up there will leave temporarily, but oftentimes, many return to their beloved hometown and commute to jobs nearby or retire there. The town is full of successful former and current business people, many of whom are descendents of the original settlers. Many of the town's inhabitants can claim 30 to 40 years of service to the mining industry that fuels the State of Arizona, the United States, and the world at large with its great mineral wealth.

Queen Valley and Superior share historical roots and modern ties. Founded by a farmer selling produce to Superior miners, Queen Valley continued its commerce with milk and goat farms, as well as cattle ranches. These goods were sold to Superior and Florence families. For its first 40 years, Queen Valley remained a small community along the banks of Queen Creek, home to a few homesteading families. These families and those that settled nearby in Hewitt Station were very supportive of each other's farming and ranching enterprises. Many of the homesteading documents are witnessed by family members from the nearby homes. Some even grew up to marry sons and daughters of neighbors across the towns of Queen Valley, Hewitt Station, and Superior. It was not until the late 1950s that Queen Valley began to grow and become the semi-retirement community it is today. When the original homesteader retired to Superior, his land was sold to a developer, and Queen Valley began its second life as a resort golf community. Several of the remaining homesteads were sold for land to create the Queen Valley Golf Course. Golfing is the focal point of tourism and social activity for the town. It is unlikely that the town would have developed in the first place had it not been a direct commerce and travel route from New Mexico to California, along Queen Creek. It is also likely it may not have been sustainable without the right combination of events: the building of custom homes, a golf course, and the development of close bonds between the people that call this peaceful valley home.

The future is very bright for both of these very special towns. They continue to share community ties with residents from each town having businesses or jobs in the other. They share social and economic ties, as well as a desire to hold onto the lifestyle that has attracted and maintained these towns from their inceptions. As Pinal County and the Copper Corridor are more fully developed in the years to come, more people will no doubt visit these two towns and understand the draw that put and kept these towns on the map. Some will move here for the same reasons the founders did, while others will move here for reasons that are entirely their own. But what is clear is that if planners are careful about planning for the growth, future newcomers to these towns will have the same high quality of life that those who make these towns home now enjoy.

One

Native American Settlers

Superior and Queen Valley have many Native American prehistoric and historic sites. Their strategic position along Queen Creek, between the eastern foothills of the Superstition Mountains and the western edge of the Pinal Mountains, provided many benefits to the earliest settlers. Along with the near year-round water supply, there were abundant game and plant food sources.

The Hohokam settled the desert valley floors in the Gila and Salt River areas around 300 AD but were in decline by 1,000 AD. Surveys done in 1986 in Queen Valley have identified the Hohokam occupation.

The Pueblos appeared around 1,000 AD and were located as far south as the Salt and Gila Rivers. The Pueblo culture is the only one that has survived with an unbroken cultural continuity for the last two millennia and into the last quarter of the 20th century. These people had an agricultural lifestyle, building great canal systems that are still in use today. Pueblo members were gone by the 1400s, which was likely due to water shortages.

The Salado culture was building and occupying stone shelters on mountaintops or in cliff sides from 1050 AD through approximately 1450 AD. They settled around the current Roosevelt Lake area and in Globe, not far from Superior.

The Western Apaches arrived in the 1700s and were nomadic and opportunistic, rather than agricultural. From the Mogollen Rim, they roamed across Arizona to the south into what was, at the time, Mexico, located just south of Florence and the Gila River.

As Mexican and Anglo settlers began moving into the areas previously occupied by Native Americans, preservation of America's ancient treasures became imperative. The Antiquities Act of 1906 provided protection for the "historic landmarks, prehistoric structures, and other objects of historic or scientific interest on public lands." Within 10 years, 35 natural areas and prehistoric sites ranging from half of an acre to 300,000 acres were preserved. The National Parks Service, created in 1916, became the guardian. The nearest protected prehistoric site to Superior is Besh-Ba-Gowah, and to Queen Valley, it is the Casa Grande National Monument.

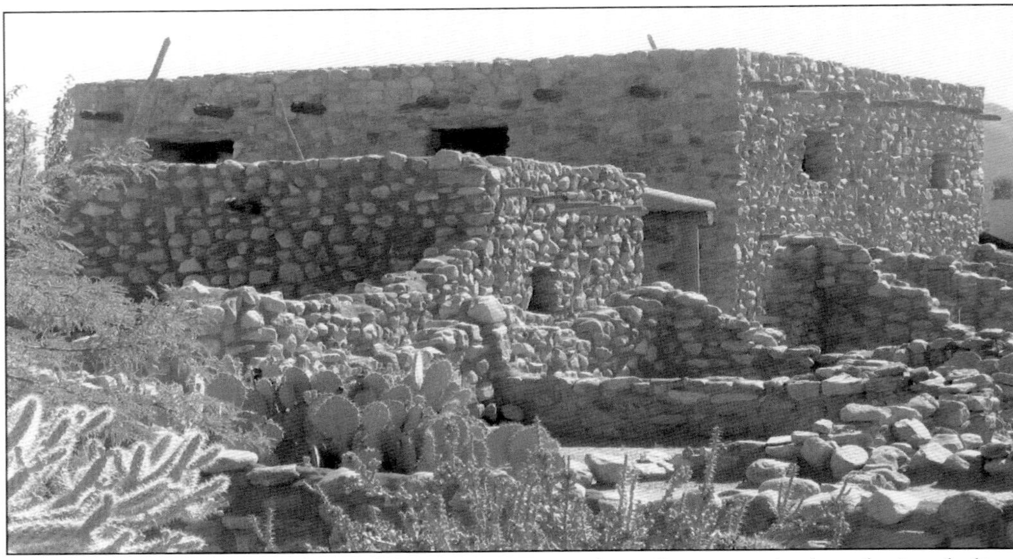

Besh-Ba-Gowah is located in Globe, just minutes from Superior. Archaeologists believe Besh-Ba-Gowah was a Salado Indian ceremonial, redistribution, and food storage complex. The Salado culture is identified as the cultural period from 1150 AD to 1450 AD in the Tonto Basin, around Globe. The name comes from the Western Apache and means "house for metal," which is likely a reference to the ore mining in Globe.

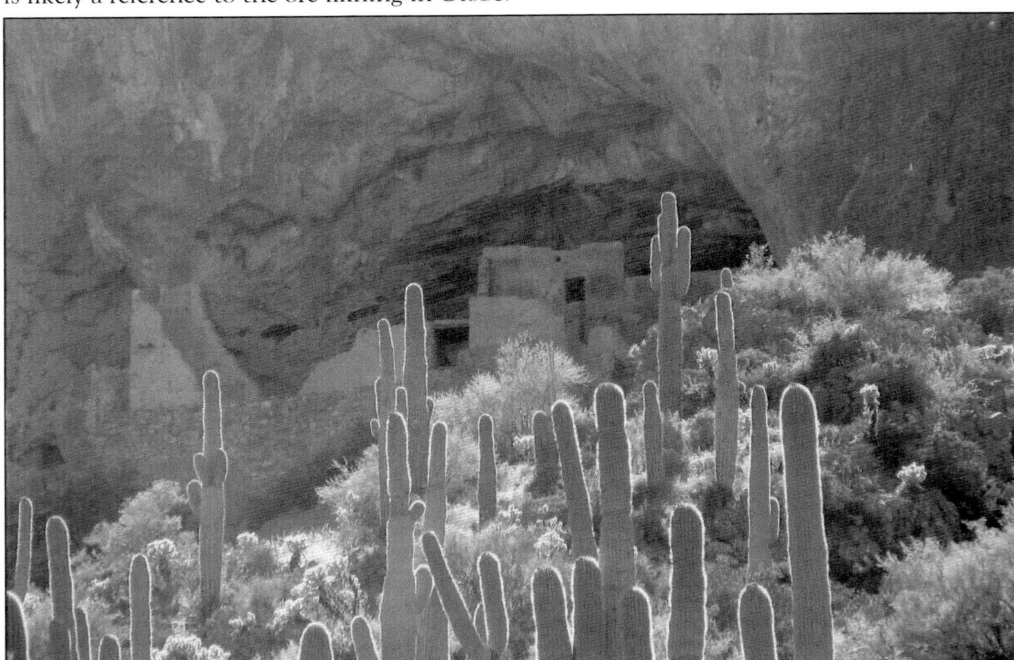

Tonto National Monument is one of many prehistoric treasures saved by the Antiquities Act of 1906. From about 1050 AD until approximately 1450 AD, the Salado culture thrived in this valley where the Tonto Creek joins the Salt River, northwest from Superior and Queen Valley. Around 1300, members of the Salado spread out from the valley onto hillside slopes, plateaus, and caves. Trade and hunting likely brought them through both towns.

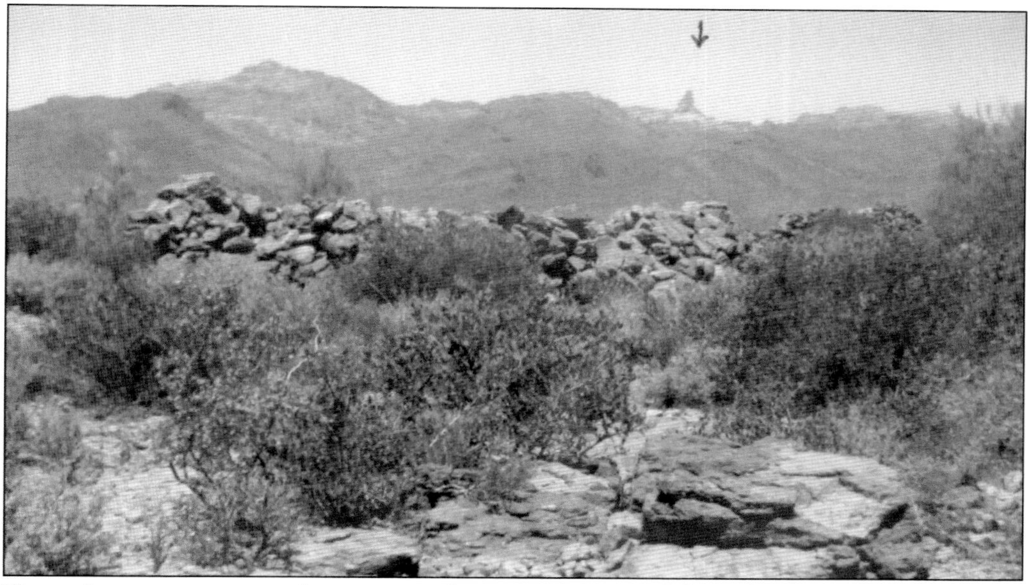

Shown here are remnants of a mountain that was once part of the archaic, and later Hohokam, settlement overlooking Queen Creek, as it travels through the town of Queen Valley. Notice Weaver's Needle in the background (indicated by an arrow). This strategic position provided water, game, edible plants, and defensible protection. These ruins and artifacts were discovered when houses were being built. These artifacts are accompanied by untold stories of the first settlers to Queen Valley. (Jack San Felice.)

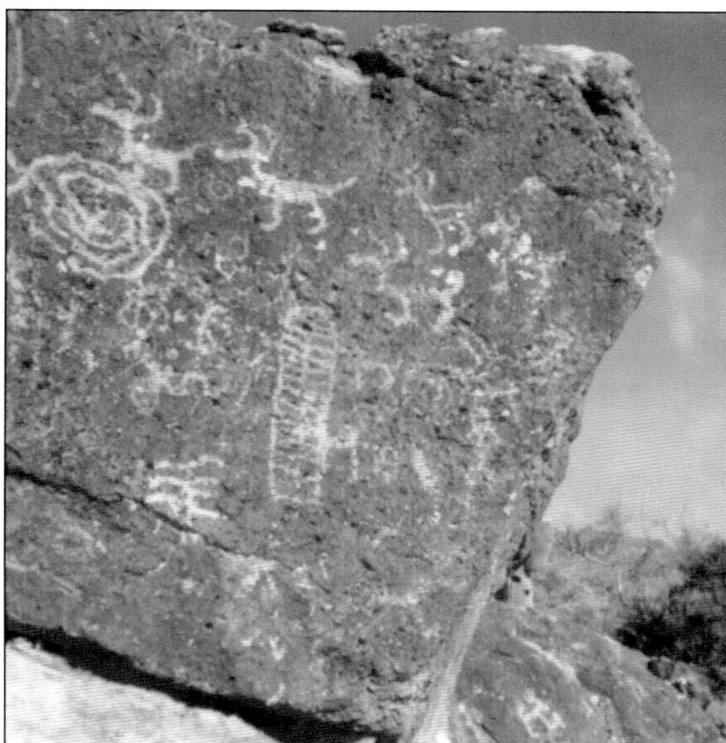

The prehistoric Hohokam culture flourished in the desert, along the Gila and Salt Rivers. They adapted well to the searing landscape, where their impressive waterworks systems allowed agricultural development. The agricultural Pimas and River Yumans who inhabited their land successively are likely descendants of the Hohokam. This Hohokam petroglyph is on Elephant Butte in Queen Valley. (Lund family collection.)

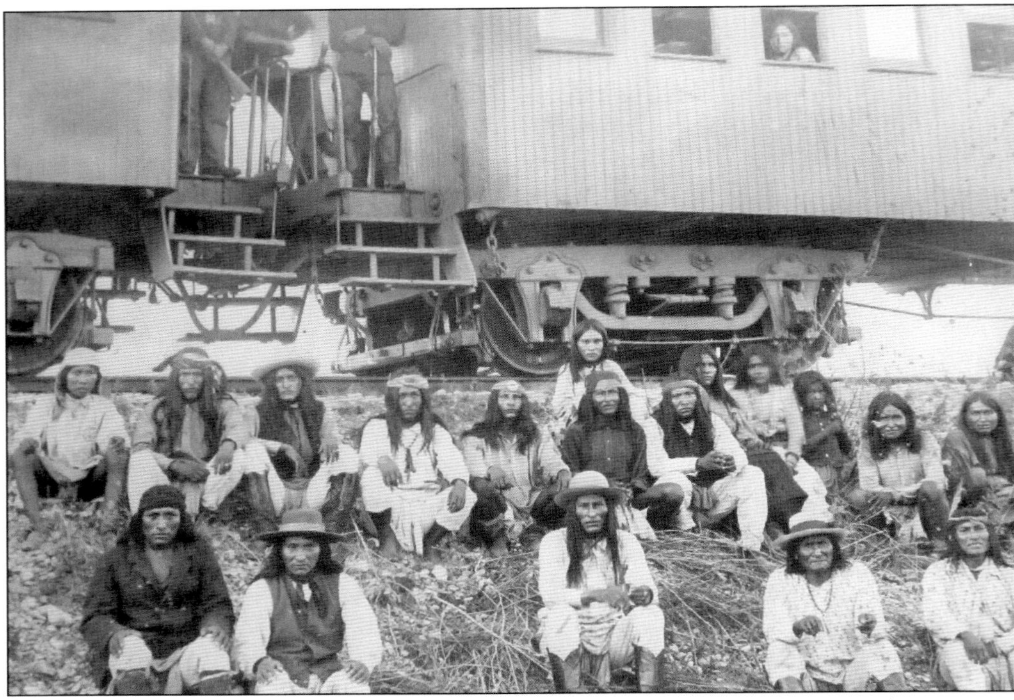

Western Apaches used horses that were introduced by Francisco Vásquez de Coronado to increase raiding ranges. Contrary to legend, their raids on Mexican settlers and Pima Indians were mainly for livestock and equipment. Their raids extended deep into Mexican territory, south of the Gila River. The Indian Wars put an end to this practice, and Western Apaches were taken by train to reservations. Geronimo and Nachez are located in the first row. (NA.)

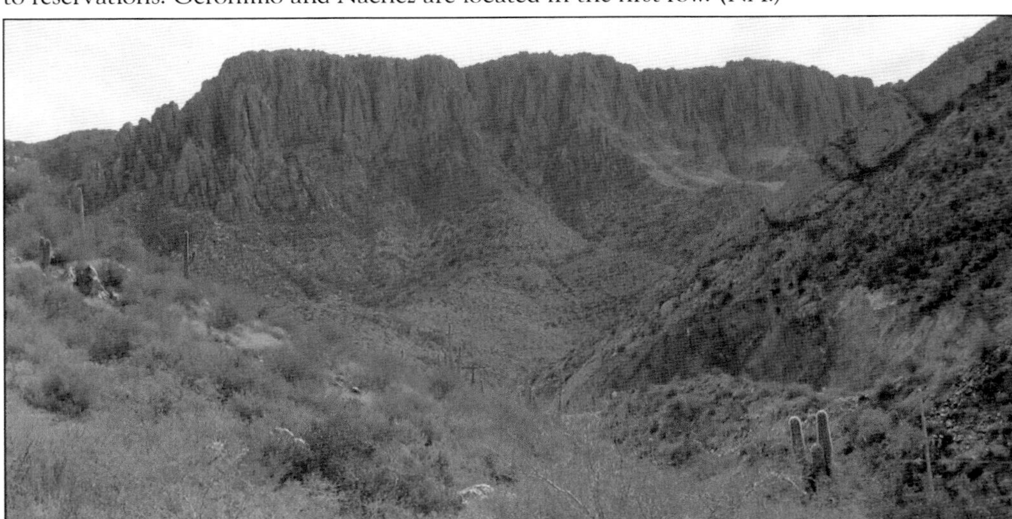

Apache Leap in Superior gets its name from a battle between Apaches in the mountaintop stronghold and a group of Mexicans, Pimas and Maricopa Indians, and a few whites from Florence, led by J. D. Walker. Legend says that Apache survivors, rather than being captured, chose death by leaping over the edge. Legend also associates obsidian stones, called "Apache Tears," with the mourning for loved ones lost in the battle.

Two

EXPLORERS

Spanish explorers were crisscrossing Arizona from 1534 to 1776. The first recorded entry into Arizona was that of A'lvar Nuñez Cabeza de Vaca in 1534. In 1539, Friar Marcos de Niza came searching for *Cibola*, the "Seven Cities of Gold." Although unsuccessful, his reports caused the Spanish viceroy to send Francisco Vásquez de Coronado with 200 horsemen, 100 soldiers, and 1,000 Native American carriers to search for Cibola. Coronado entered through the San Pedro Valley and, by 1542, had traveled up to the area around the convergence of the Santa Cruz, San Pedro, and Gila Rivers. Coronado's records and other evidence show that Spanish and other explorers traveled through the area east of Superior and Queen Valley.

During the Spanish rule of North America, Spain wanted to civilize the native population and convert them to Christianity. They used military presidios and ecclesiastical missions to that end. Some early Spanish explorers were accompanied by priests, but it was not until Fr. Eusebio Francisco Kino arrived in 1687 that missionary work began in Arizona.

Father Kino, who was actually Italian, was the most notable explorer sent by the Spanish government to pass through this area. His route followed a number of rivers in Arizona, including the nearby Gila and very possibly Queen Creek.

Spanish occupation was encouraged by Spain through large land grants that were available to those willing to settle there. Mexico instituted the same policy. Most of Arizona's petitions for land grants were filed between 1820 and 1833 and were vaguely described and surveyed. This led to serious problems of ownership.

The Gadsden Purchase of 1854, named after James Gadsden who recommended a southern route for a proposed railroad, required proof of ownership for land grants with Mexico. Of the 21 land claims made, 11 were approved and 10 rejected. The Peralta-Reavis claim of 11,280,000 acres, located between Phoenix and Safford, was ruled fraudulent, and James Addison Reavis went to prison for forgery.

The first recorded entries by Anglo-Americans into Arizona were the fur trappers or "mountain men" coming out of New Mexico. Soon the area was teeming with traders and military encampments.

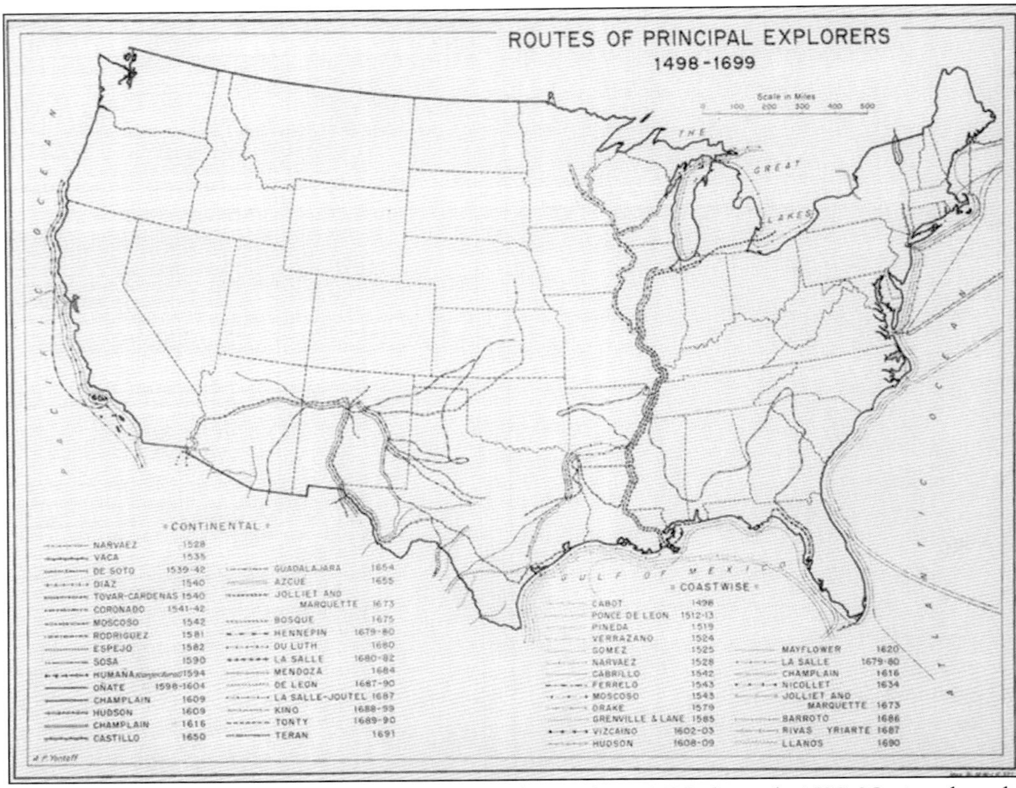

This map shows the routes of the principle explorers from 1498 through 1699. Notice that the explorations generally followed rivers and water sources across the continent. The detailed notes of these early explorers made it possible for those that followed to continually build on the body of knowledge that was utilized in mapping the country from coast to coast. (BLM.)

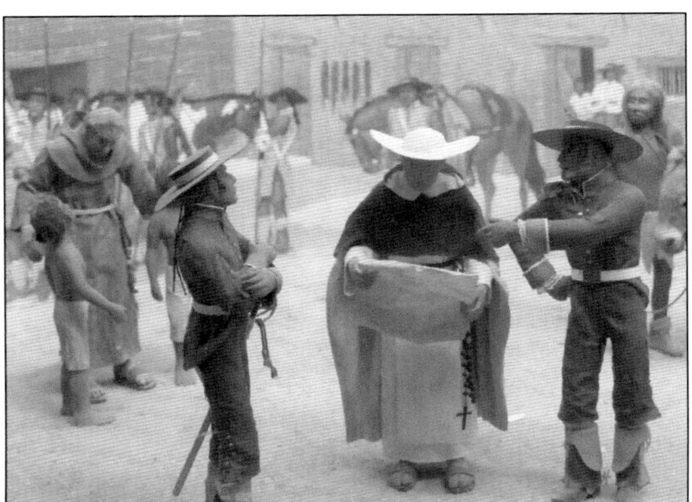

The first known contact with Native American tribes along the lower Colorado River was in 1540. Hernando de Alarco'n, the commander of a supply ship, had been sent to support Coronado's army and traveled up the Colorado River as far as Yuma when he encountered Native Americans. (NA.)

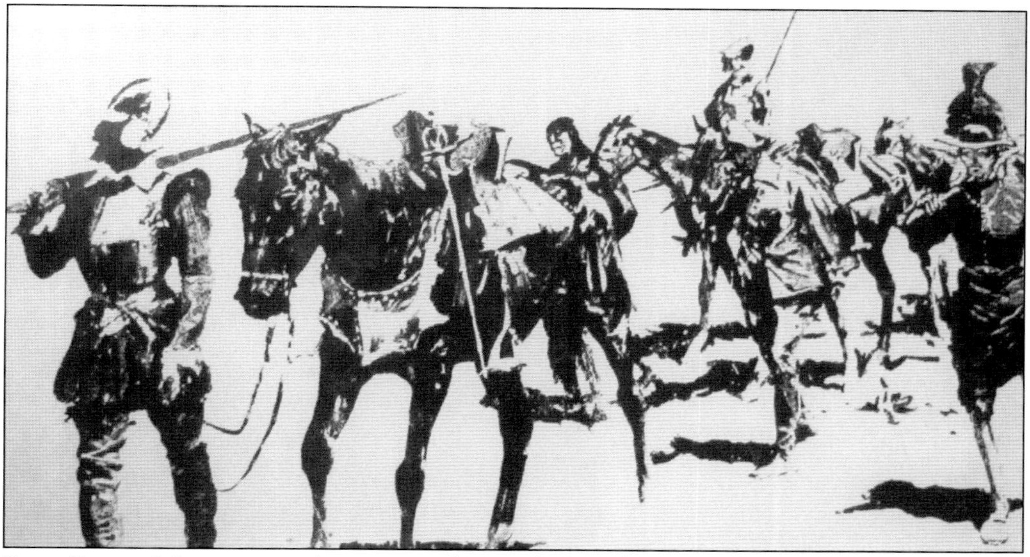

From Coronado's entry into Arizona in 1540 until 1542 when he returned once again, the land between the Gila and the Little Colorado Rivers was known as the *Despolbado*, the "Uninhabited Land." By 1775, that same area was one of the strongholds of the Western Apaches, who continually raided the settlements of the Native Americans along the Gila and San Pedro Valleys. (NA.)

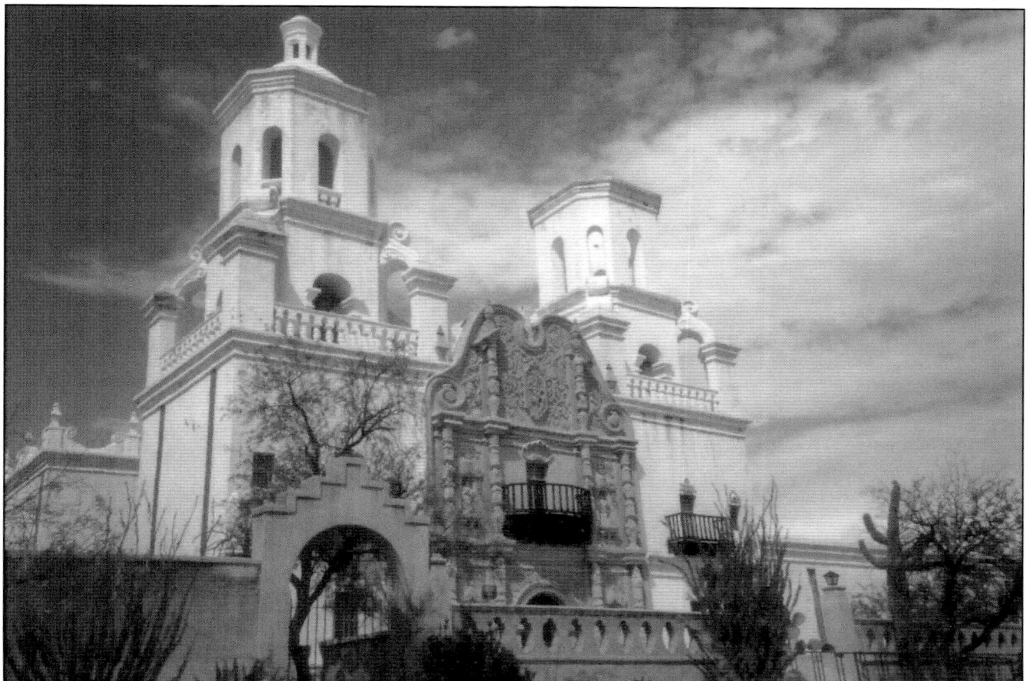

Father Kino's travels across Arizona are documented from 1687 to 1701. He said Mass and helped build houses for the natives and missions for the church. San Xavier del Bac, located near Tucson, is one of the few remaining examples of those early settlements by missionaries. Built in 1699 by Kino, the mission burned in Apache raids in 1770 and was rebuilt in 1797. Franciscans still actively serve the native community nearby.

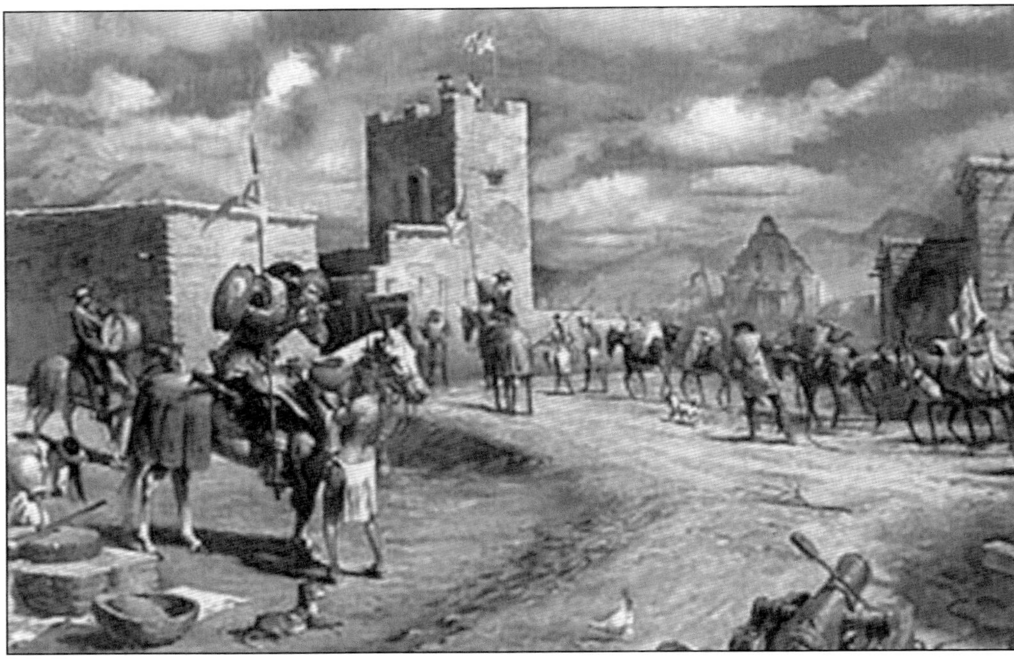

Father Kino brought cattle, sheep, horses, vegetables, and fruits from Europe into Arizona. Following Kino's death in 1711, the missions were inactive for the next 25 years, while Spain was involved in Europe's War of Spanish Succession. When the Jesuits were expelled from the Spanish Empire in 1767, the Franciscans took over and began a revival of missionary work across Arizona. (NA.)

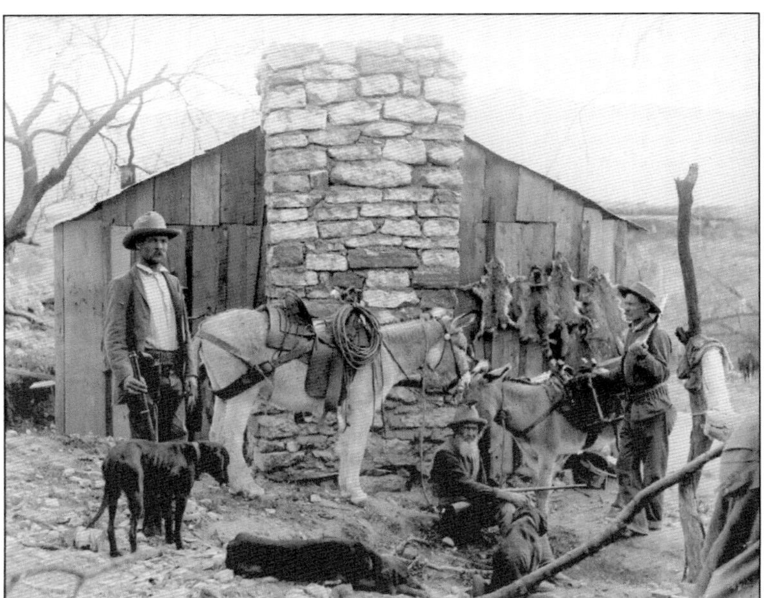

Beginning in 1825, Sylvester Pattie and his party trapped the Gila, Salt, Verde, and Colorado Rivers. Mountain men often served as guides to the military. Kit Carson, who arrived with the Young party, guided General Kearney, and Pauline Weaver guided General Cooke's Mormon battalion. Shown is the Crab family in 1908 in the Four Peaks area. (NA.)

Three

Opening the Public Lands

When exploring the history of America's towns, most people don't realize that all the land now held by private citizens and corporations once belonged to either individual states or the U.S. government. Being a country set up "by the people and for the people," those lands were designated as salable to the public for private use or held in trust as public lands to be shared by all. There is a legacy of governmental acts and laws that were established to guarantee those two outcomes. The following acts and laws were critical to the settlement of Superior and Queen Valley: Land Ordinance of 1785; Land Act of 1796; Louisiana Purchase, 1803; Homestead Act, 1862; Mining Law of 1866; Desert Land Act, 1877; Mineral Leasing Act, 1920; Recreation and Public Protection Act, 1926; Taylor Grazing Act, 1934; Classification and Multiple Use Act, 1964; National Environmental Protection Act, 1970; and Federal Land Protection and Management Act, 1976.

When selling public lands, Secretary of State Thomas Jefferson and Treasurer Alexander Hamilton agreed that selling public lands should continue to retire Revolutionary War debt. However, they did not agree on who should be allowed to buy it. Hamilton wanted the top prices that capitalists and land companies could pay, but Jefferson wanted cash-poor farmers to be accommodated. The Land Act of 1796 offered a compromise that set up the survey township configuration that is still in use today. It also allowed purchase with credit, which was extended to those who needed it.

Occasionally, free land was offered in regions that the government wanted settled. This was done for the New Mexico Territory and parts of Arizona. Development of this area later became crucial as a shipping and commerce route that went into Arizona and California. Industrial supplies from the East were shipped West, and livestock from the West was shipped to the East.

Superior and Queen Valley are surrounded by State Trust Land, Bureau of Land Management, Tonto National Forest, and Superstition National Wilderness lands. Modern-day ranchers are still able to have their herds graze near both Superior and Queen Valley.

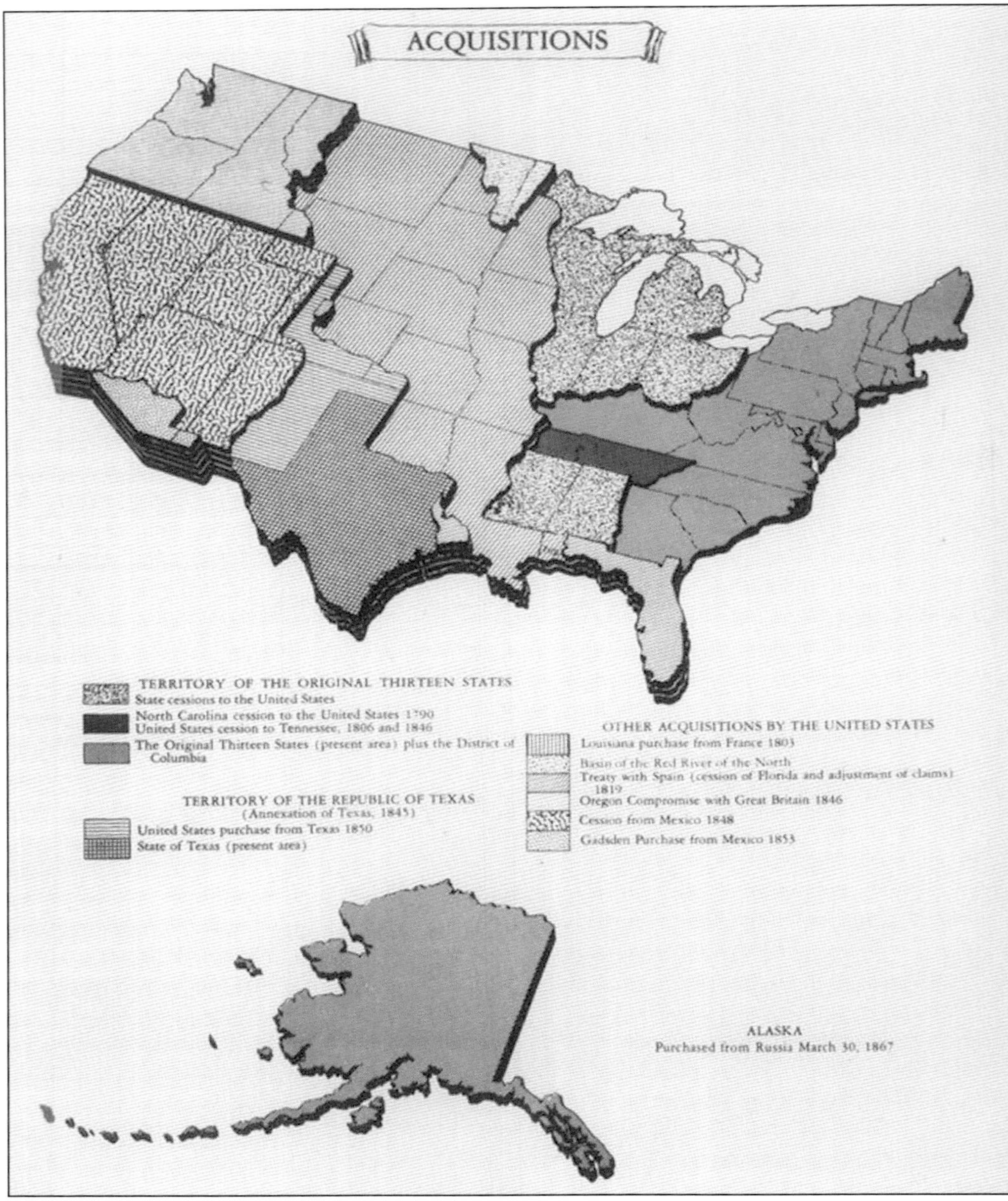

Acquisition of public domain lands began in 1776, when seven Eastern states that held claims to land in the West were called upon to cede their claims to the newly formed central government. Views were that states having conflicting claims to the Western lands, which were not yet inhabited by American settlers, could threaten their relations with each other. They also agreed that the lands should be used to reward soldiers who served in their regiments against the British, but many agreed that these delegations should be federal, not state, land grants. These acquisitions led to an intense acquisition process for obtaining land from other countries that held claims in North America. This chart, which is courtesy of the BLM, depicts those acquisitions from 1776 through the purchase of Alaska in 1867.

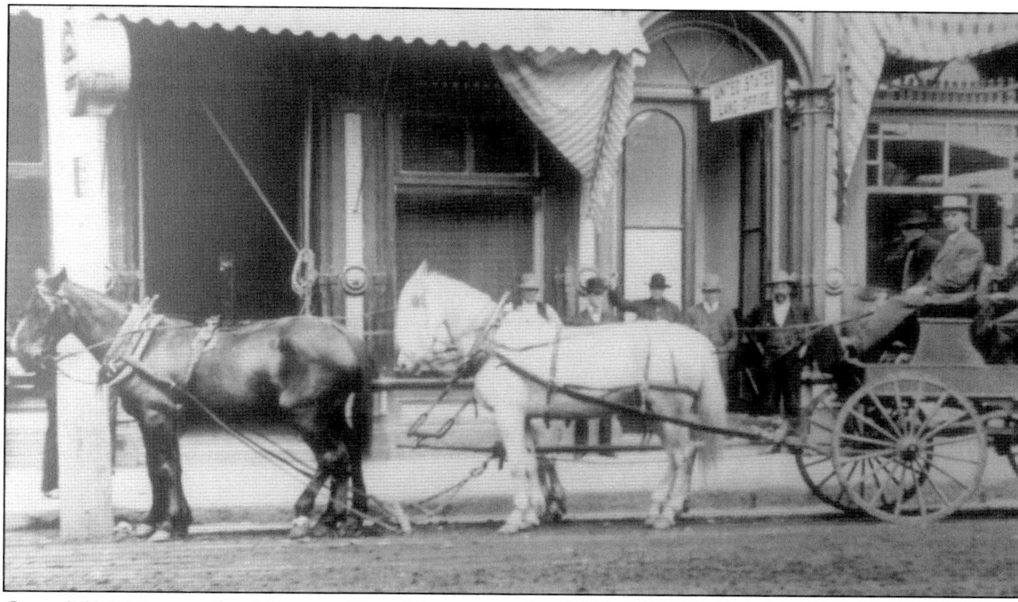

Over 750,000 acres had been sold at $2 per acre by 1802. The Land Law of 1804 extended the repayment for credit purchases and reduced minimum size from 320 to 160 acres. In response to rapidly growing public land business, the responsibility shifted from the Department of the Treasury, War Office, and State Department to the new General Land Office, created in 1812, under the Treasury Department. (BLM.)

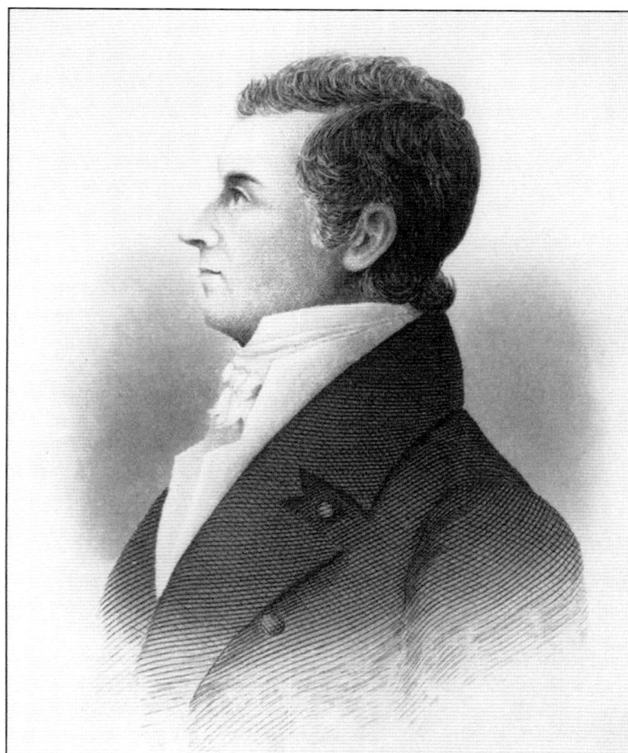

The first commissioner, Edward Tiffin, a former senator, physician, and farmer, set about the task of consolidating the land records that spread throughout Washington. After the War of 1812, land auctions boomed with 1.5 million acres being auctioned off by 1815. Responsibility for land sales shifted in 1849 to the new Department of the Interior, which is where it remains. (BLM.)

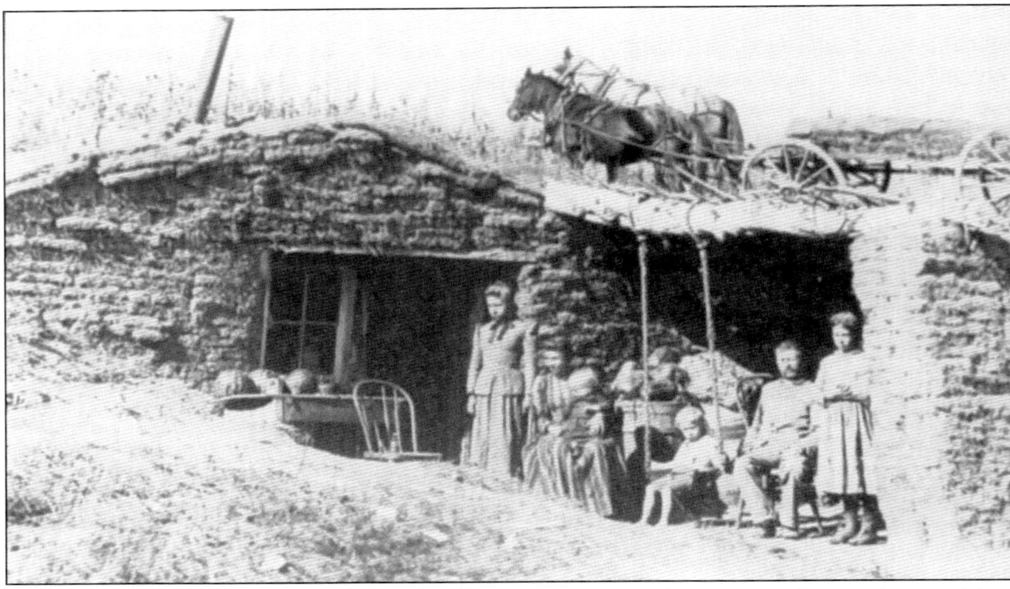

At public auctions, farmers were at a disadvantage, compared to moneyed capitalists and land speculators. Many began to move West, build homes, clear land, and eke out what living they could on un-surveyed public lands. The policy of orderly settlement did not allow this squatting process, and an 1807 law provided for removal, fining, and imprisonment for trespassers. However, this law did little to discourage the squatters. (BLM.)

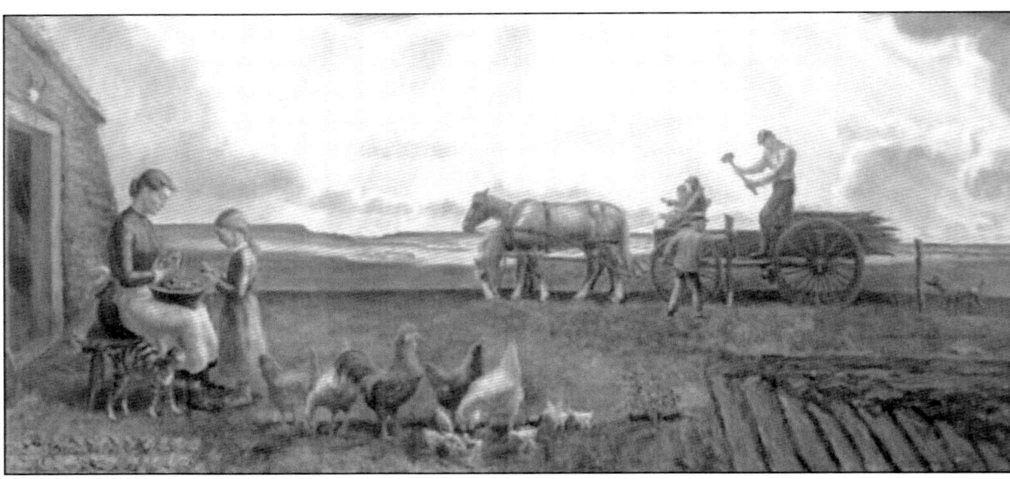

Due to increased public pressure, the government began extending preferential rights to individuals over land speculators to purchase land at a minimum price that he or she had improved. The first general grant of preemption came in 1830 for previously settled land. Under this grant, squatters could purchase 160 acres at the minimum price within one year of the law's passage. This law became permanent in 1841. (DOI.)

In 1860, Congress passed a measure allowing purchase of 160 acres at 25¢ per acre, if resided on and cultivated for five years. President Buchanan vetoed the legislation, fearing it would reduce public land revenues. President Lincoln signed the 1862 Homestead Act allowing heads of households, widows, and singles over 21 to apply for up to 160 acres, subject to entry under the preemption law. (BLM.)

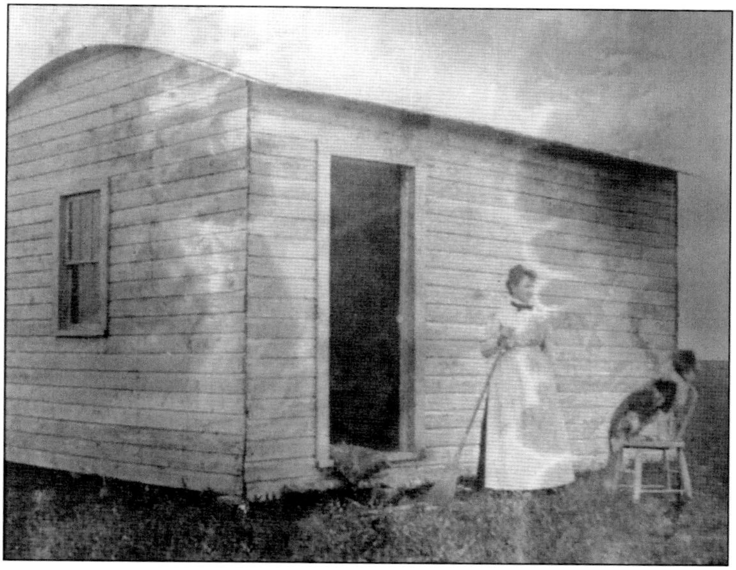

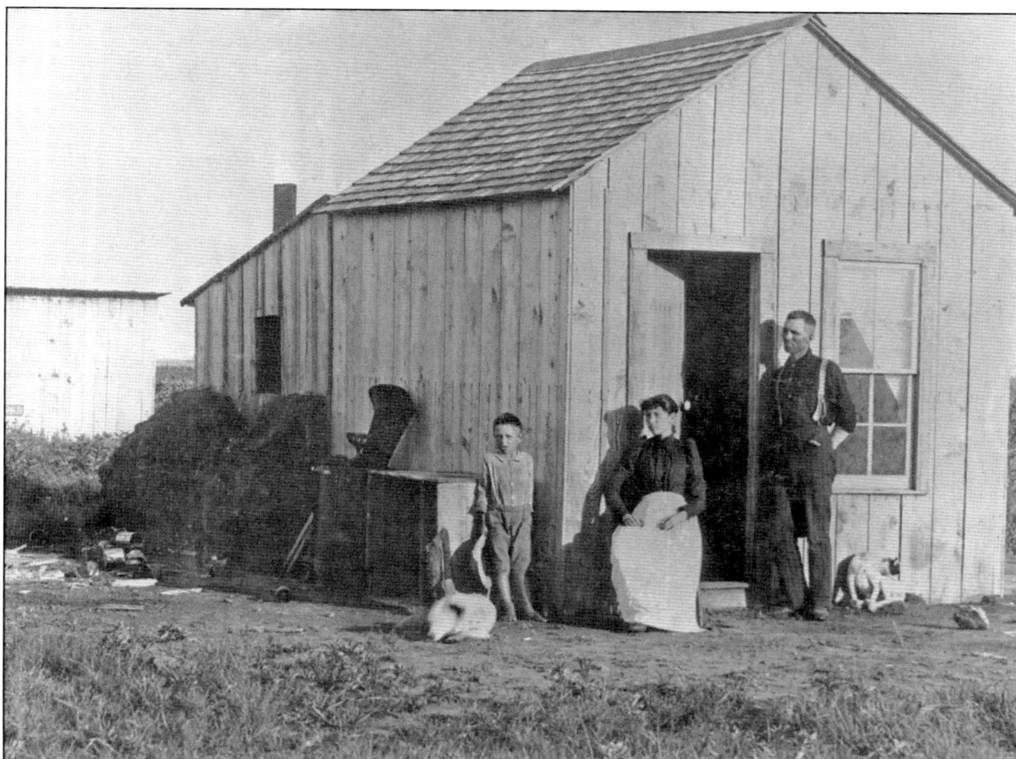

The Homestead Law was a great democratic measure to help settle America. It was, however, a means to an end. While land was offered free, the building of a home and the cost of agricultural or grazing operations took capital. Environment, local climate, and conditions defeated the dreams of many. Of the more than 1.3 million homesteads filed before 1900, only half of them were patented. (BLM.)

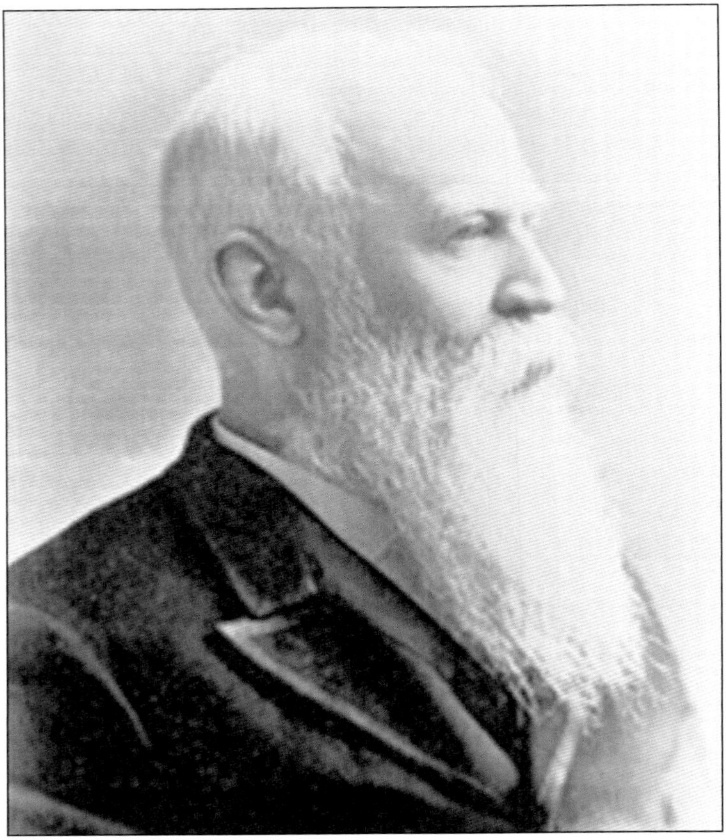

William Morris Stewart is considered the father of the mining law. Having received his law degree from Yale, he caught gold fever and joined the California Gold Rush. Using his mining experience, he became attorney general of California in 1854 and litigated the Comstock Lode as senator of Nevada. He passed laws recognizing the governance set up by mining districts in the remote West and helped enact the 1866 National Mining Act. (BLM.)

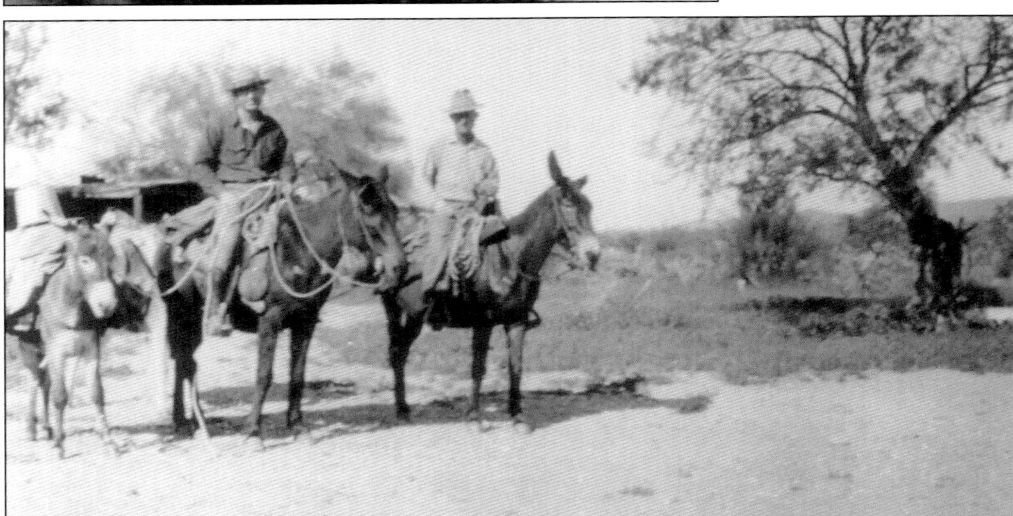

On May 10, 1870, Stewart helped Congress pass a law allowing preemptive rights to lode claimants for the lode and land flanking it. Claims could be as little as 10 acres, and the patent was set at $2.50 per acre. The General Mining Law of 1872 further defined ownership and the recognizable size and quality of improvements required for patents. Here the Mullins family heads for their mine. (Fran Olson Harkey.)

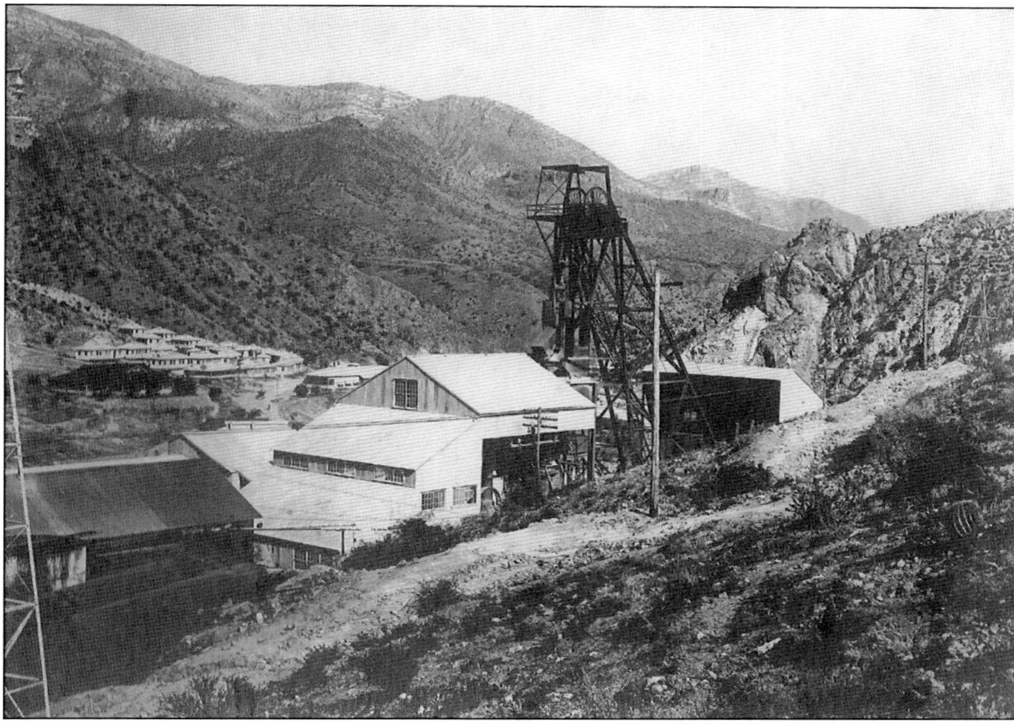

Congress passed the General Mining Law in 1872, declaring "valuable mineral deposits" open to exploration and purchase. This law is a major reason that mining operations in the town of Superior became viable. It set limits on lode location and limited claims to 20 acres for individuals and 160 for associations. Miners paid $100 yearly in assessment work and $500 in improvements that were required for patenting. (ADMMR.)

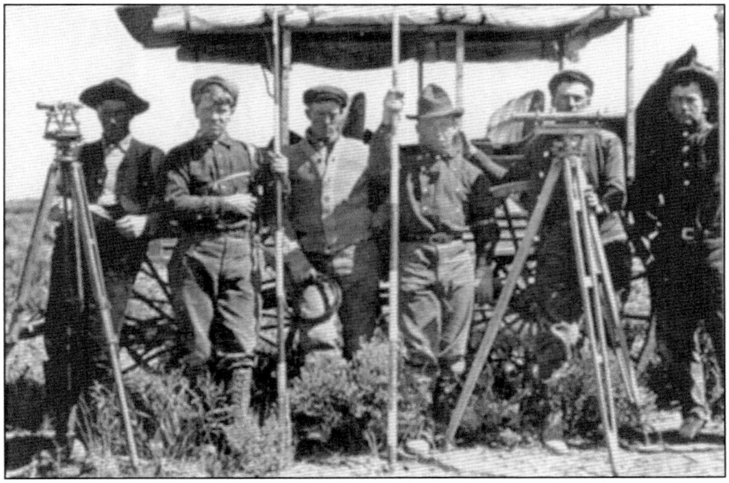

After the Civil War, Congress began funding scientific and geologic explorations of the West to further encourage mineral development and the settlement of the public lands. The men employed by the General Land Office to survey the public lands in the 1800s faced grave dangers during unprecedented journeys to explore and map the western frontier. (BLM.)

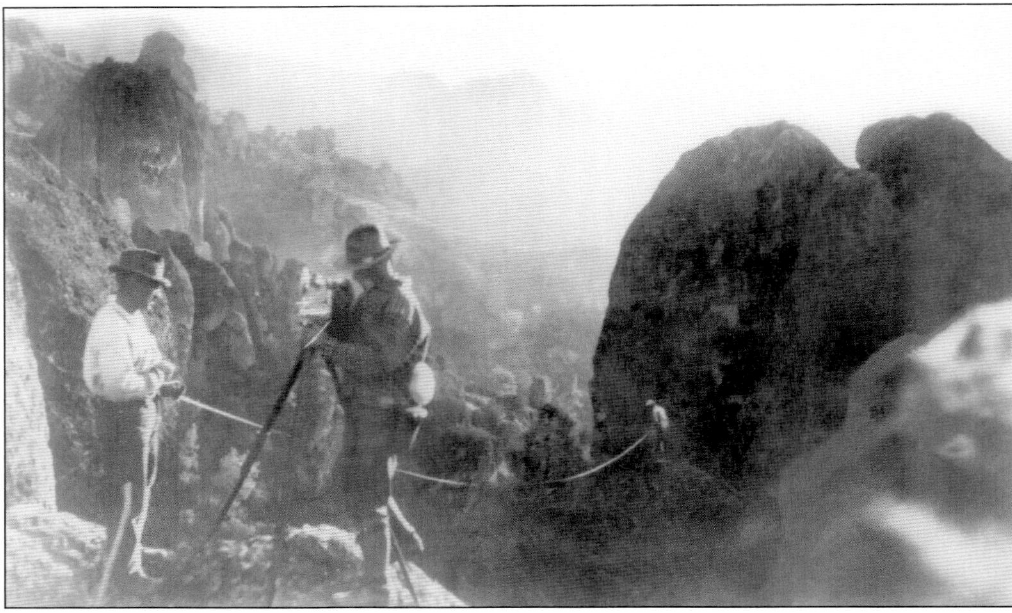

In 1879, Congress consolidated independent survey efforts into one organization, the U.S. Geological Survey, with Clarence King as first director. Surveys were conducted all across the West to map public lands, servicing the wildly growing filing of homestead claims. Ferdinand Hayden, Clarence King, John Wesley Powell, and Lt. George Wheeler conducted expeditions over the Great Plains, Great Basin, and Rocky Mountains, often under very difficult conditions. (BLM.)

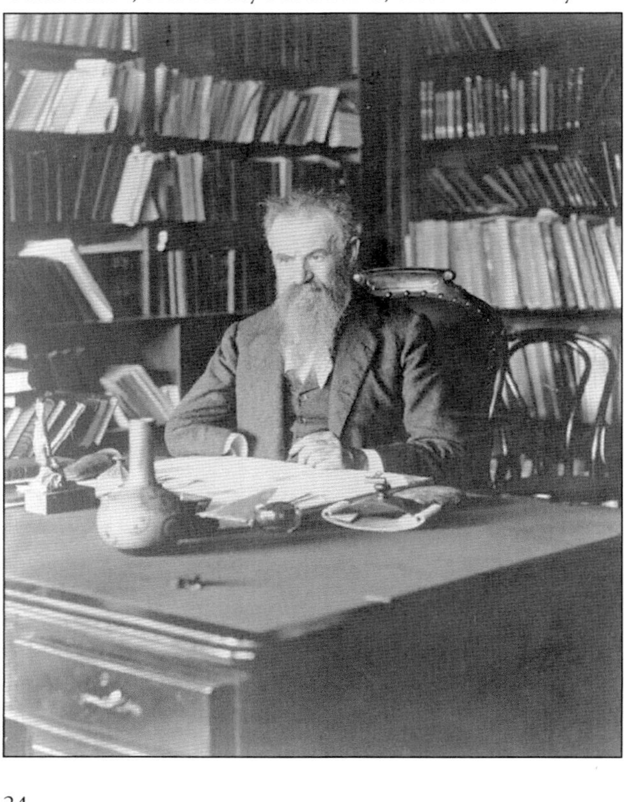

Maj. John Wesley Powell was principle surveyor of the Northern Arizona area and successor to king as director of the USGS. He was honored for his explorations, with Lake Powell being named after him. Powell stayed in the Arizona Territory and worked in his Adams Street office in Phoenix, which is shown in this 1896 photograph. (BLM.)

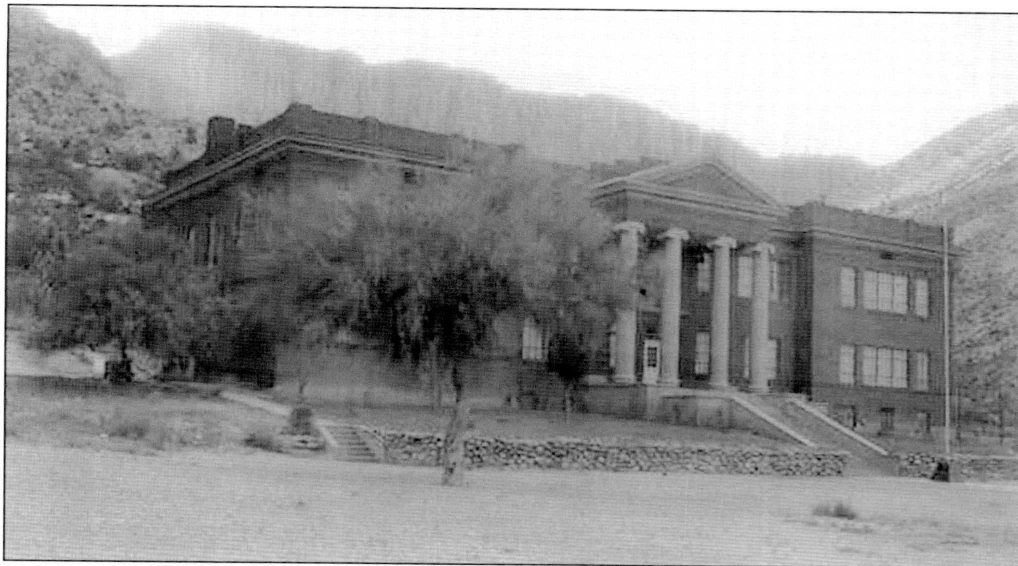

The Land Ordinance of 1785 started a tradition of reserving Section 16 in each township to finance public schools. After 1848, two sections of land were allotted and that increased to four with the admission of Utah, New Mexico, and Arizona to the United States. The 1862 Morrill Act granted states 30,000 acres of salable public land for each senator and representative to finance agricultural and mechanical colleges and prisons. (ADMMR.)

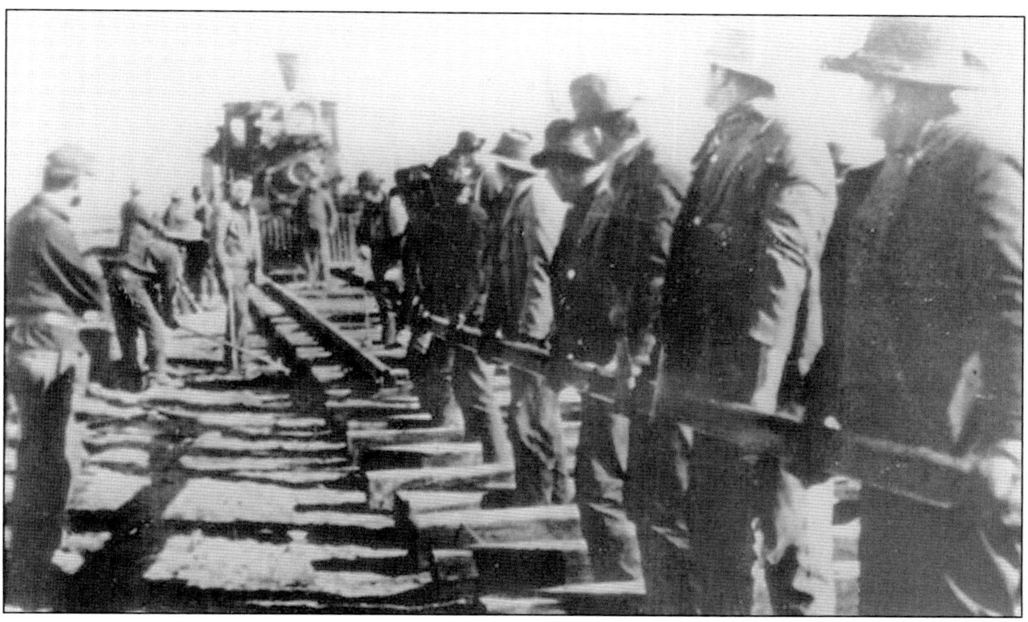

Land grants were given to railroads for construction of the first transcontinental railway in 1862. The Central Pacific and Union Pacific Railroad companies received every alternate section of land, designated by odd numbers, for five alternative sections per mile on each side of the line, within 10 miles on each side. In 1864, it became 20 sections. This policy ended in 1871 due to public criticism from Westerners. (BLM.)

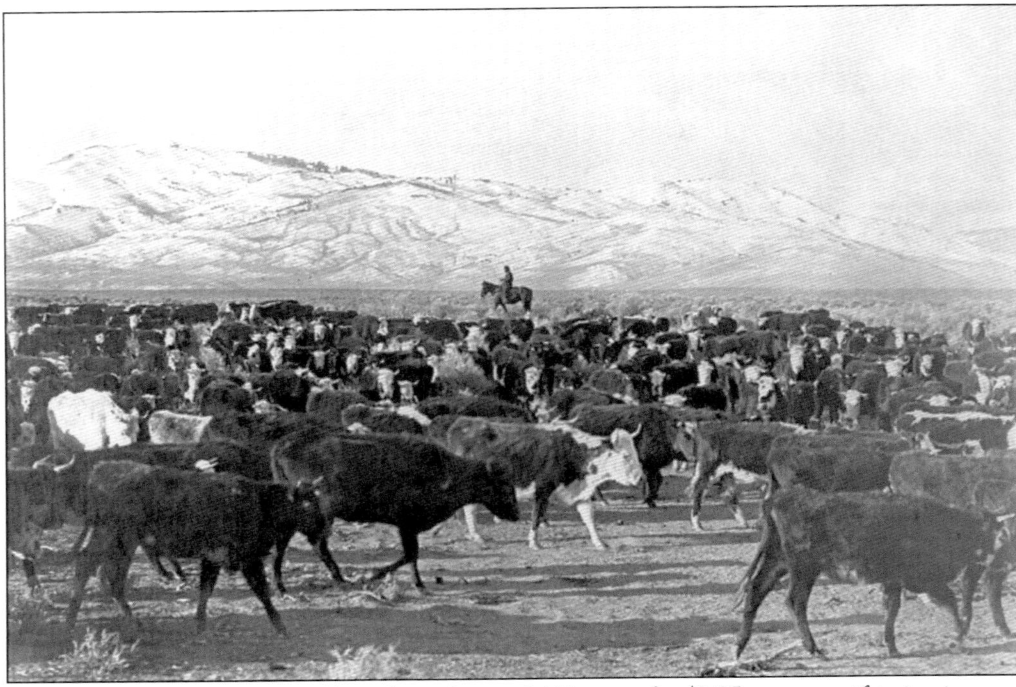

The 1877 Desert Land Act allowed purchase of 640 acres for $1.25 per acre, if irrigation was completed in three years. With no residence required, land was often used for ranching and agriculture. The increased acreage was in response to semiarid land west of the 100th meridian, causing settlers to need larger ranches to have a successful operation. Settlers in Queen Valley and Superior homesteaded under this act. (BLM.)

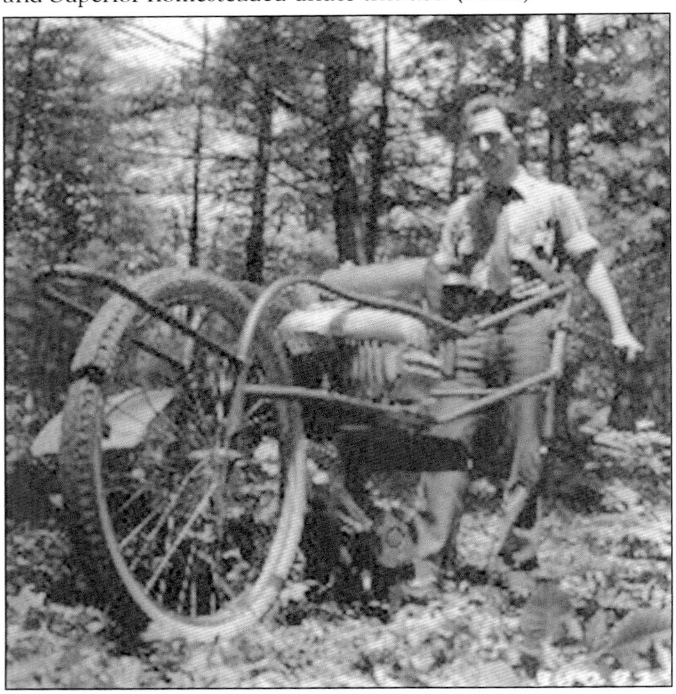

The nearby Tonto National Forest was created by the 1897 Forest Management Act, which gave the Secretary of the Interior use and occupancy authority. Non-mandatory exchanges allowed homesteaded property to be traded for land outside the reserves. This explains private land within national forests. Within the Department of Agriculture, the Forest Service was established in 1905 to administer national forests. This 1939 picture shows a ranger using a Bosworth trencher for fire lines. (BLM.)

Teddy Roosevelt, shown here, had developed his love of the land and devotion to conservation of the wonders of the West during his youthful travels. As president, he passed laws establishing federal protection and management for public lands for the people of the United States to enjoy for generations in perpetuity. (BLM.)

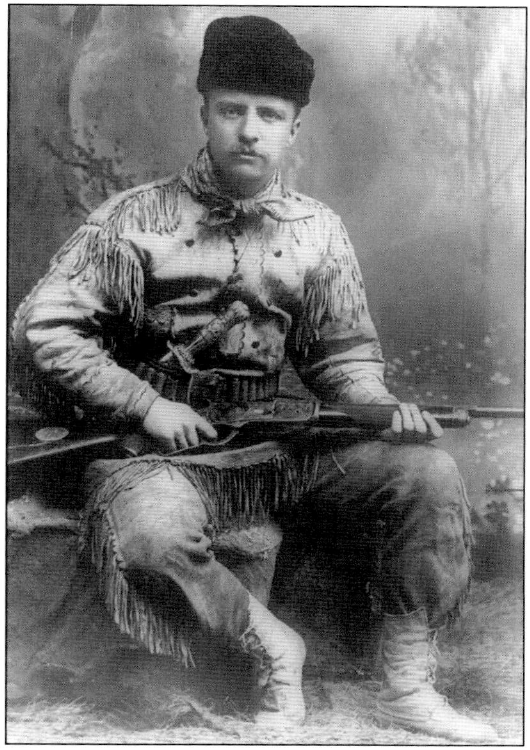

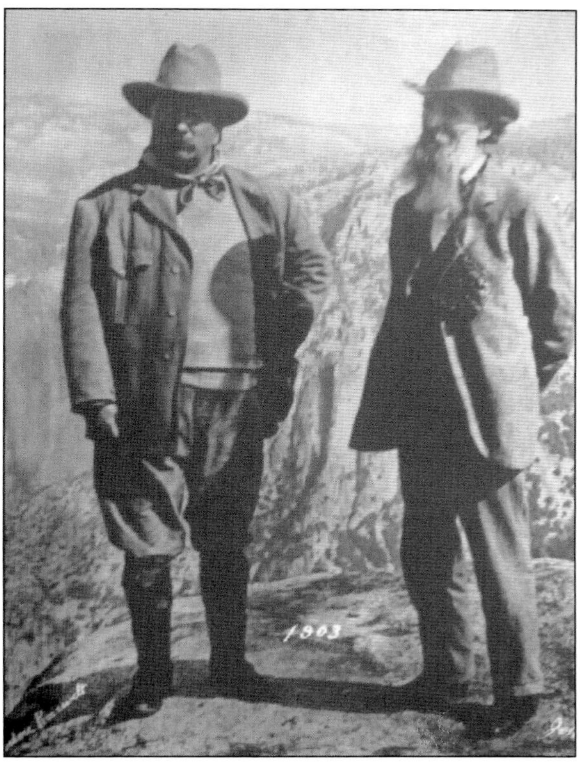

Roosevelt and Muir were avid conservationists, putting the issue high on the national agenda. Roosevelt set aside more federal land for national parks and nature preserves than all of his predecessors combined. He encouraged adoption of the Newlands Reclamation Act of 1902 to promote federal construction of dams to irrigate small farms and placed 230 million acres under federal protection. (NPS.)

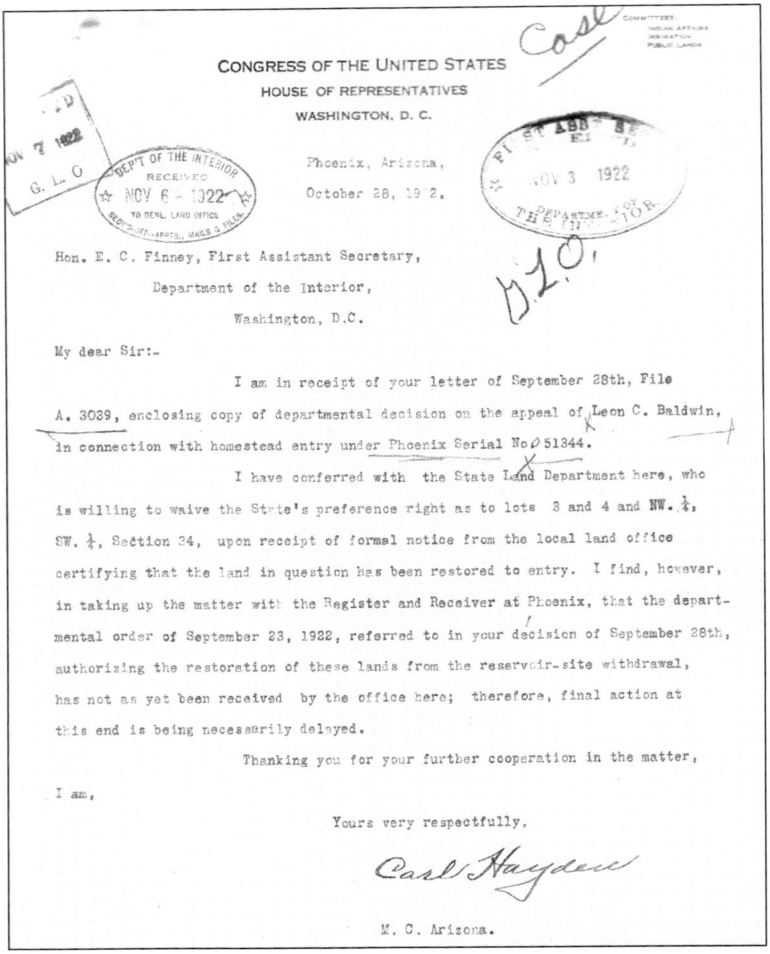

CONGRESS OF THE UNITED STATES
HOUSE OF REPRESENTATIVES
WASHINGTON, D. C.

Phoenix, Arizona,
October 28, 1922.

Hon. E. C. Finney, First Assistant Secretary,
Department of the Interior,
Washington, D.C.

My dear Sir:-

I am in receipt of your letter of September 28th, File A. 3039, enclosing copy of departmental decision on the appeal of Leon C. Baldwin, in connection with homestead entry under Phoenix Serial No 051344.

I have conferred with the State Land Department here, who is willing to waive the State's preference right as to lots 3 and 4 and NW. ¼, SW. ¼, Section 34, upon receipt of formal notice from the local land office certifying that the land in question has been restored to entry. I find, however, in taking up the matter with the Register and Receiver at Phoenix, that the departmental order of September 23, 1922, referred to in your decision of September 28th, authorizing the restoration of these lands from the reservoir-site withdrawal, has not as yet been received by the office here; therefore, final action at this end is being necessarily delayed.

Thanking you for your further cooperation in the matter,

I am,

Yours very respectfully,

Carl Hayden

M. C. Arizona.

A tract of land on the valley floor was withdrawn from town settlement for a flood control project on Queen Creek. This prompted Queen Valley homesteader Baldwin to get Arizona senator Carl Hayden involved in obtaining a release from the federal government to increase the size of his homestead claim at the base of Whitlow Dam. Hayden attended the Whitlow Dam dedication ceremonies in 1960. (NA.)

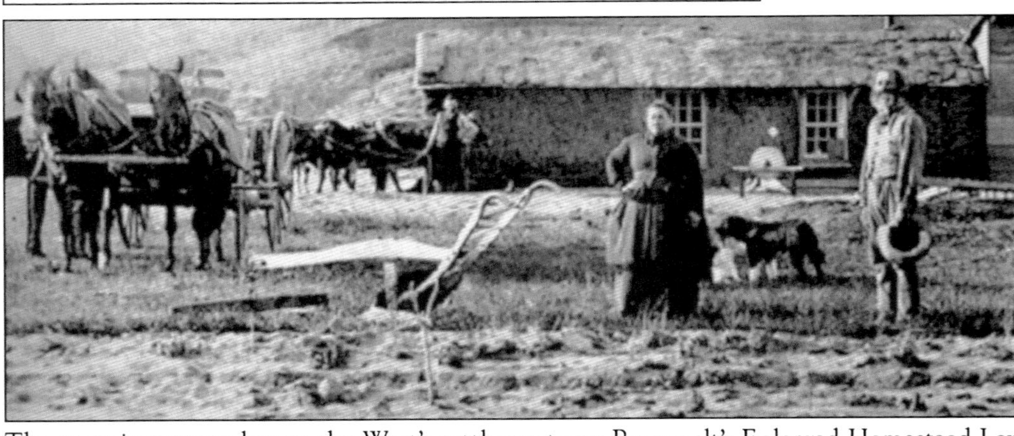

The most important law to the West's settlement was Roosevelt's Enlarged Homestead Law in 1909, giving up to 320 acres to settlers who entered public land that could not be irrigated. Conditions were residency on the land and that one-eighth of it must be planted. This law was in response to the need for dryland farming, a movement gaining momentum after the turn of the century. (BLM.)

In 1912, as Arizona became a state, Congress reduced the required five-year residency and cultivation requirement on homesteading to three years. In October 1915, Queen Valley was settled by Hart Mullins, who cultivated vegetables for Superior's miners. Warren G. Harding signed his homesteading documents on June 11, 1922. Mullins, shown on the right, is headed for the mountains. (Fran Olson Harkey.)

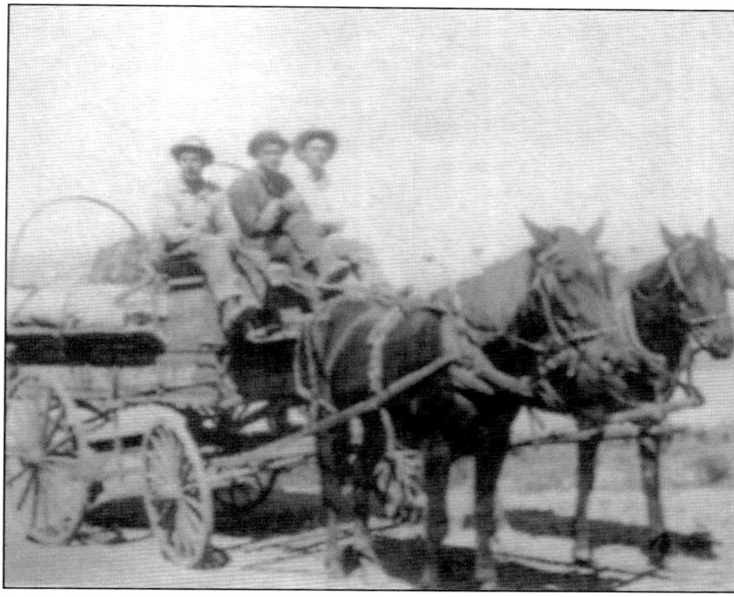

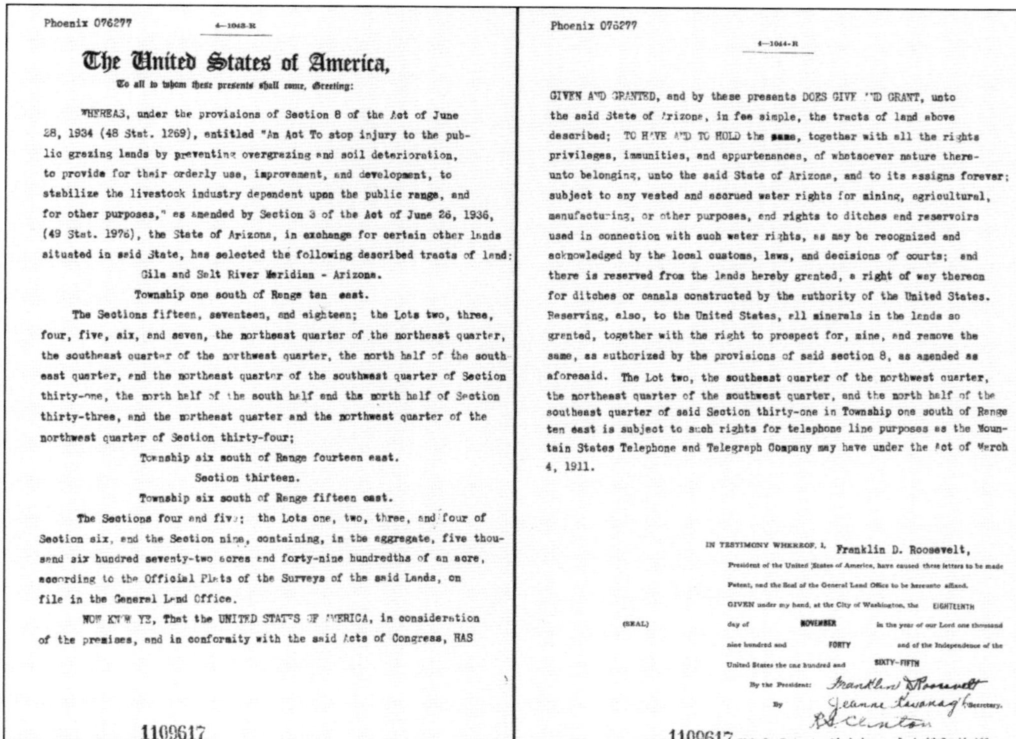

Phoenix 076277 4—1043-R

The United States of America,

To all to whom these presents shall come, Greeting:

WHEREAS, under the provisions of Section 8 of the Act of June 28, 1934 (48 Stat. 1269), entitled "An Act To stop injury to the public grazing lands by preventing overgrazing and soil deterioration, to provide for their orderly use, improvement, and development, to stabilize the livestock industry dependent upon the public range, and for other purposes," as amended by Section 3 of the Act of June 26, 1936, (49 Stat. 1976), the State of Arizona, in exchange for certain other lands situated in said State, has selected the following described tracts of land:

Gila and Salt River Meridian - Arizona.

Township one south of Range ten east.

The Sections fifteen, seventeen, and eighteen; the Lots two, three, four, five, six, and seven, the northeast quarter of the northeast quarter, the southeast quarter of the northwest quarter, the north half of the southeast quarter, and the northeast quarter of the southwest quarter of Section thirty-one, the north half of the south half and the north half of Section thirty-three, and the northeast quarter and the northwest quarter of the northwest quarter of Section thirty-four;

Township six south of Range fourteen east.

Section thirteen.

Township six south of Range fifteen east.

The Sections four and five; the Lots one, two, three, and four of Section six, and the Section nine, containing, in the aggregate, five thousand six hundred seventy-two acres and forty-nine hundredths of an acre, according to the Official Plats of the Surveys of the said Lands, on file in the General Land Office.

NOW KNOW YE, That the UNITED STATES OF AMERICA, in consideration of the premises, and in conformity with the said Acts of Congress, HAS

RECORD OF PATENTS: Patent Number 1109617

Phoenix 076277 4—1044-R

GIVEN AND GRANTED, and by these presents DOES GIVE AND GRANT, unto the said State of Arizona, in fee simple, the tracts of land above described; TO HAVE AND TO HOLD the same, together with all the rights privileges, immunities, and appurtenances, of whatsoever nature thereunto belonging, unto the said State of Arizona, and to its assigns forever; subject to any vested and accrued water rights for mining, agricultural, manufacturing, or other purposes, and rights to ditches and reservoirs used in connection with such water rights, as may be recognized and acknowledged by the local customs, laws, and decisions of courts; and there is reserved from the lands hereby granted, a right of way thereon for ditches or canals constructed by the authority of the United States. Reserving, also, to the United States, all minerals in the lands so granted, together with the right to prospect for, mine, and remove the same, as authorized by the provisions of said section 8, as amended as aforesaid. The Lot two, the southeast quarter of the northwest quarter, the northeast quarter of the southwest quarter, and the north half of the southeast quarter of said Section thirty-one in Township one south of Range ten east is subject to such rights for telephone line purposes as the Mountain States Telephone and Telegraph Company may have under the Act of March 4, 1911.

IN TESTIMONY WHEREOF, I, Franklin D. Roosevelt, President of the United States of America, have caused these letters to be made Patent, and the Seal of the General Land Office to be hereunto affixed.

(SEAL)

GIVEN under my hand, at the City of Washington, the EIGHTEENTH day of NOVEMBER in the year of our Lord one thousand nine hundred and FORTY and of the Independence of the United States the one hundred and SIXTY-FIFTH

By the President:

By Secretary.

1109617 Chief, Patents Division, General Land Office.

Homesteading declined by 1917, when America entered World War I. Over 200 million acres were vacant, un-appropriated, and unreserved land. Ranchers grazed federal land but had no homesteading rights. With the passage of the 1916 Stock Raising Homestead Act and 1934 Taylor Grazing Act, individuals could have 640 acres, if they resided and made improvements equal to \$1.25 per acre. Consequently, ranching in Queen Valley and Superior expanded. (NA.)

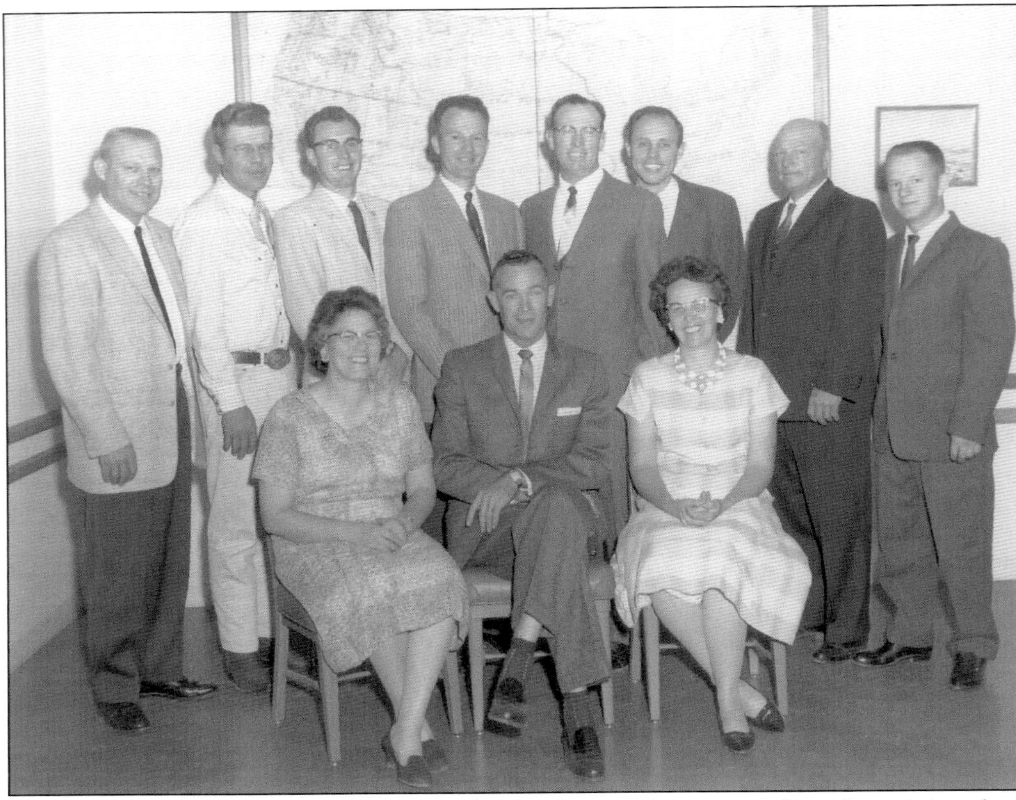

The Taylor Grazing Act of 1934, overseen by the Grazing Service, sought to "stop injury from overgrazing public lands and to stabilize the livestock industry dependent upon the public range" through the lease of public land in agreements from 1 to 10 years. Ranchers and sheepherders paid 5¢ per animal per month. Shown are the employees of the Arizona Strip Grazing District. (BLM.)

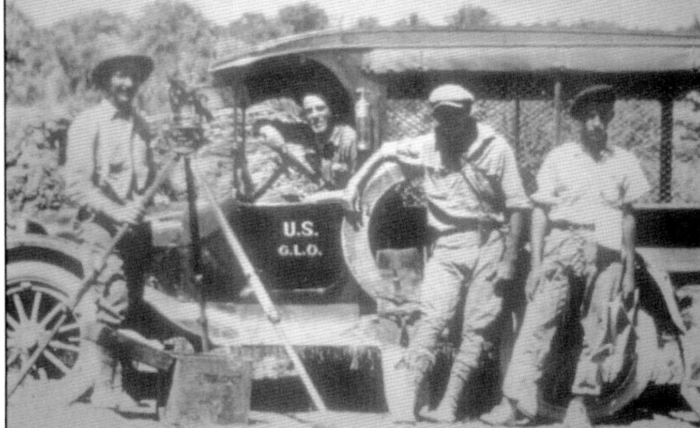

On July 16, 1946, the Government Land Office and the Grazing Service merged, forming the Bureau of Land Management. As expansion of the public lands continued, government surveyors provided the vital coordinates for the land boundaries to homesteaders, realtors, and government officials. Both Queen Valley and Superior have nearby public land managed by the BLM. (GLO vehicle courtesy BLM.)

Four

WATER AND TRANSPORTATION

Towns need two things to survive: commerce and a reliable water supply. Nowhere is this more evident than in the arid Southwest. Here deserts are full of ghost towns where one or the other has run out.

Near-continuous mining since the 1800s has helped keep Superior in existence. Water systems, developed in the 1900s by Ernest Kellner Jr., helped ensure the development of the town. Currently, Superior gets its water from Florence through pipes that run along Queen Creek. Queen Valley gets its water from town wells.

Roads through Queen Valley served as a stage route from New Mexico and the Silver King Mine to Florence and Phoenix. This same route became the major transportation route for goods being shipped from the industrial East to the developing West. With the advent of stagecoaches, travel became somewhat easier, and mail and passengers became regular deliveries to Western towns.

As time passed, the rugged and dusty trails that were used to traverse this great county were slowly converted to smoothly paved superhighways. What took wagon trains six months or more to travel, now only takes several days to traverse.

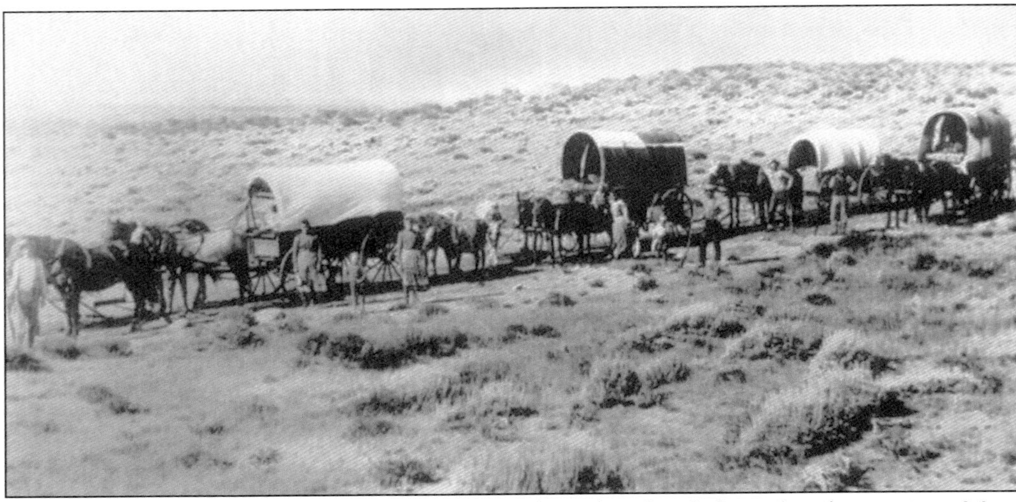

Many of the wagon trains consisted of farmers and ranchers headed to other destinations. Many of these settlers remained in the hospitable Sonoran Desert of Arizona. When word got out about the discovery of the strike that became the Silver King Mine, all available miners rushed to the area to file claims. When the news hit back East, the population in the town of Superior exploded, and the mining boom began. (BLM.)

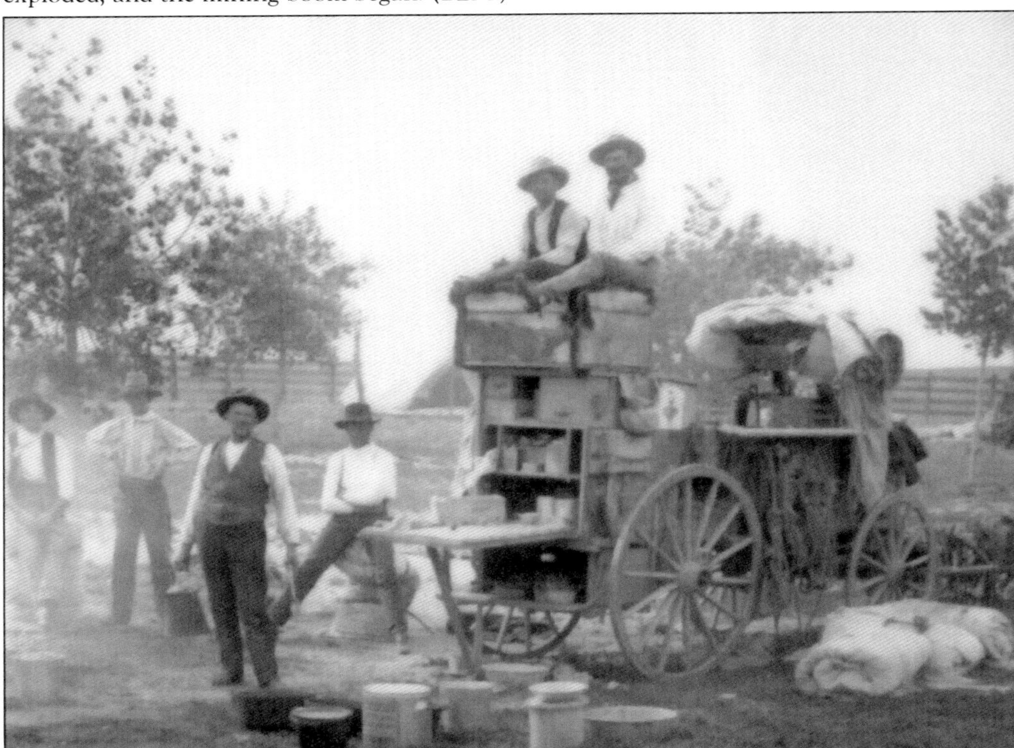

As people and cattle were moving across the country, these camp kitchen wagons kept them supplied with all they needed to prepare meals on the road. Travel was difficult. They had to follow water sources and find natural protection from the weather and Native Americans wherever possible. (NA.)

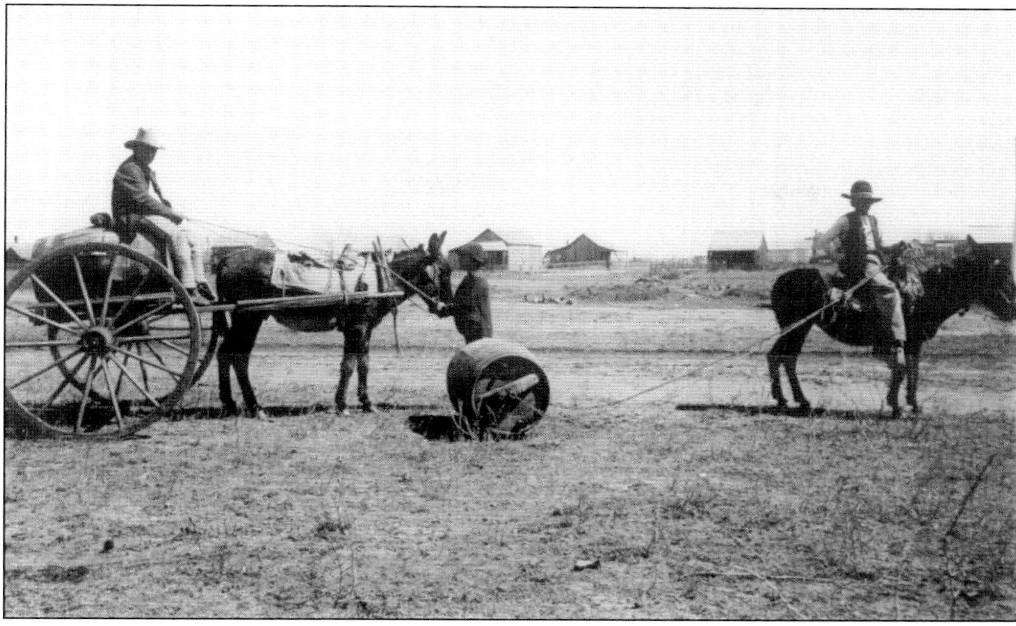

Most of the towns in the West were founded on or nearby rivers, since hauling water from one point to another was difficult to do. This lack of reliable sources of water is the reason for many of Arizona's ghost towns. Once mines played out and funding for water delivery was gone, living some places was just too difficult for settlers. (NA.)

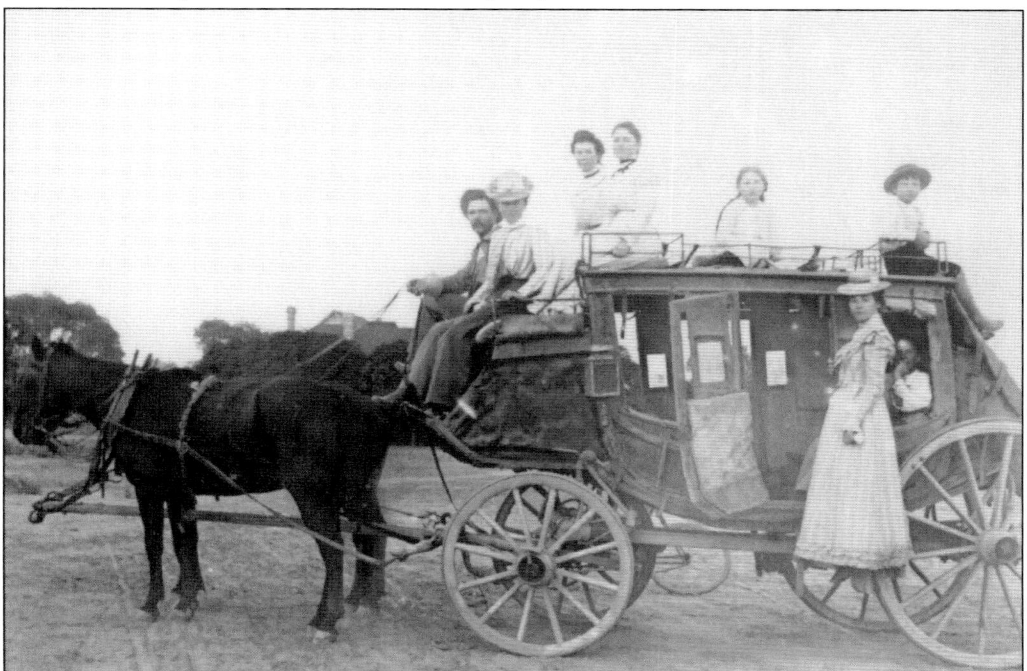

People and mail would have traveled by a coach such as this Wells Fargo stagecoach, headed for Mesa. The closest stage stops were in Superior and Hewitt Station, but they were also offered a comfort stop in Queen Valley. (Arizona Museum of Natural History.)

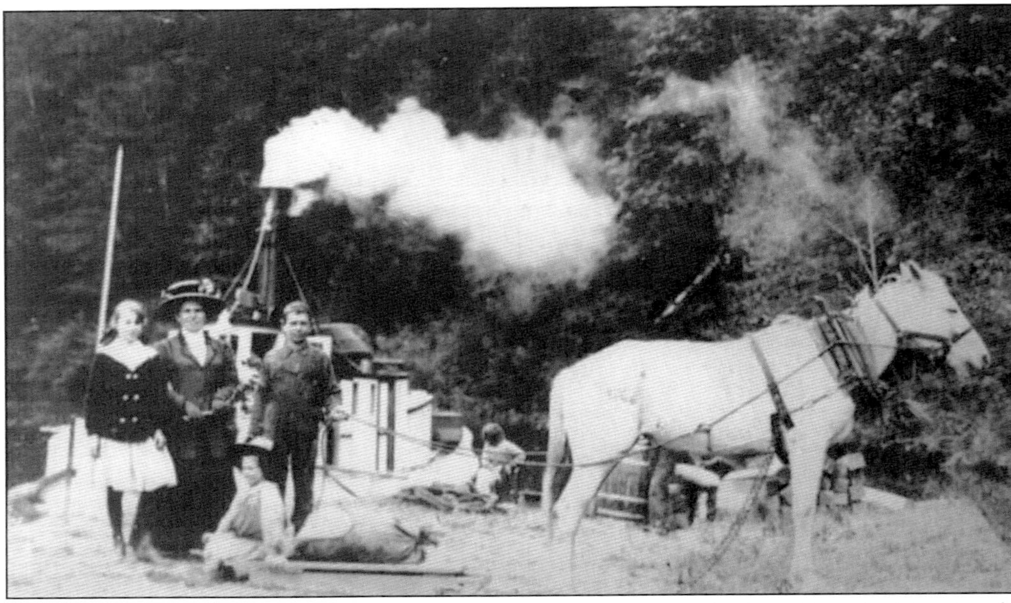

Supplies for Arizona were brought in by wagon or river steamer via the Colorado River. In the 1870s, six steamers and five barges operated without interference by Mexican authorities under the Treaty of Guadalupe Hidalgo. Families also began arriving in the West on steamships. Some began their Western adventures in the 1849 California Gold Rush and came to Arizona during the gold and silver rushes in the 1880s. (BLM.)

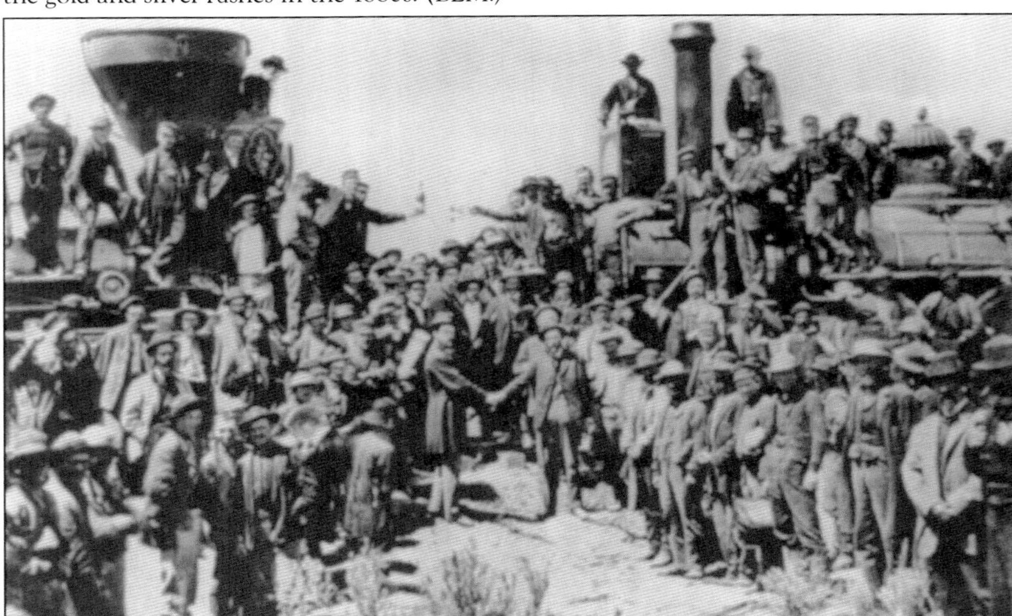

May 10, 1869, the transcontinental railroad lines of the Central Pacific and Union Pacific Railroads met at Promontory Point, Utah, where the last tie was laid. From 1880 to 1920, there was monumental activity in railroad building, bringing with it the ability to ship large amounts of goods for the people and manufactured items, such as pumps and engines, for the mines and other businesses in the West. (BLM.)

In 1877, the Southern Pacific Railroad arrived in Yuma, connecting in 1881 with the Texas Pacific, east of El Paso. Railroads allowed the shipment of heavy equipment to mines and ore for processing to California. The Globe and Northern ran from 1894 to 1898, Ray and Gila River Railroad from 1900 to 1910, and the Magma Railroad began in 1915. The tracks from Superior, along Queen Creek, to Yuma are still used today. (BLM.)

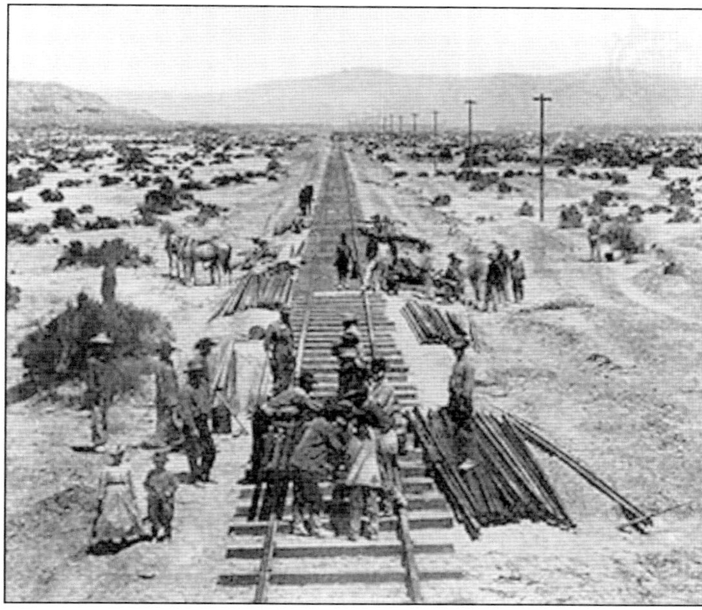

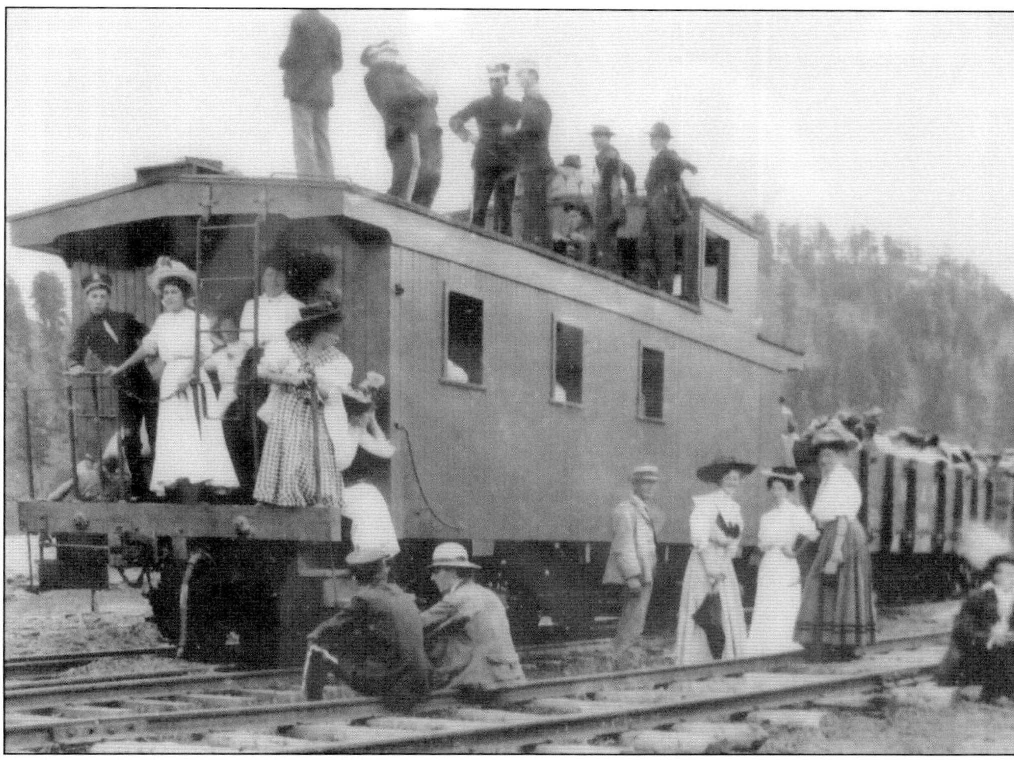

With train travel, soon wealthy people from back East began vacationing in the West. This group of travelers stops along the way to have a picnic and enjoy the scenery. It was a much shorter and a more comfortable journey than traveling by stage. Many of those travelers fell in love with the West and stayed. (NA.)

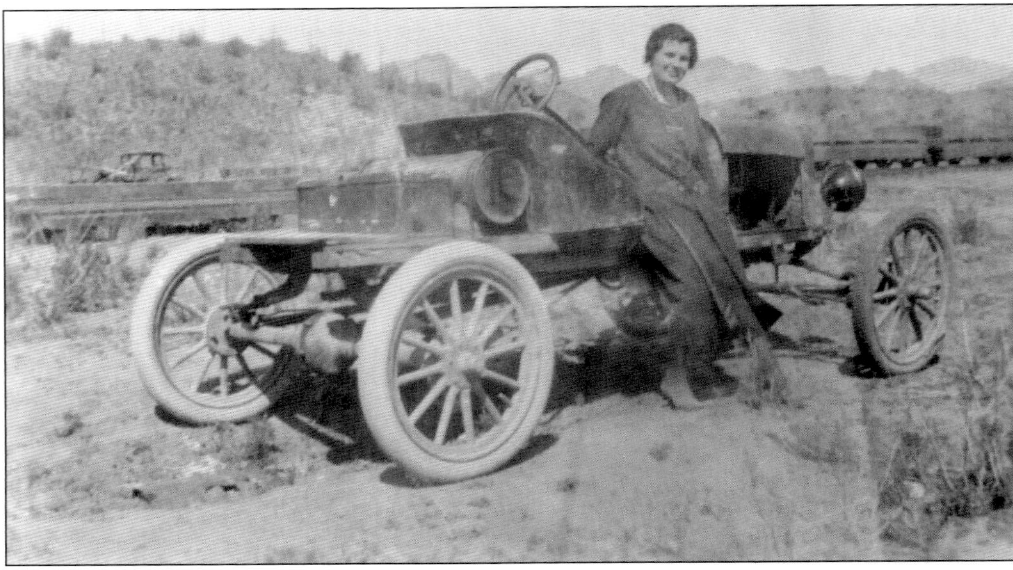

Once cars came on the scene, travel for pleasure became the reason for movement from one place to the next, even among the everyday population. People were no longer dependant on slow travel and thirsty horses to cover great distances. Shown here is a lady exploring the roads near Queen Valley, where the scenery was breathtaking and the creek refreshing. (SMM, Martin Collection.)

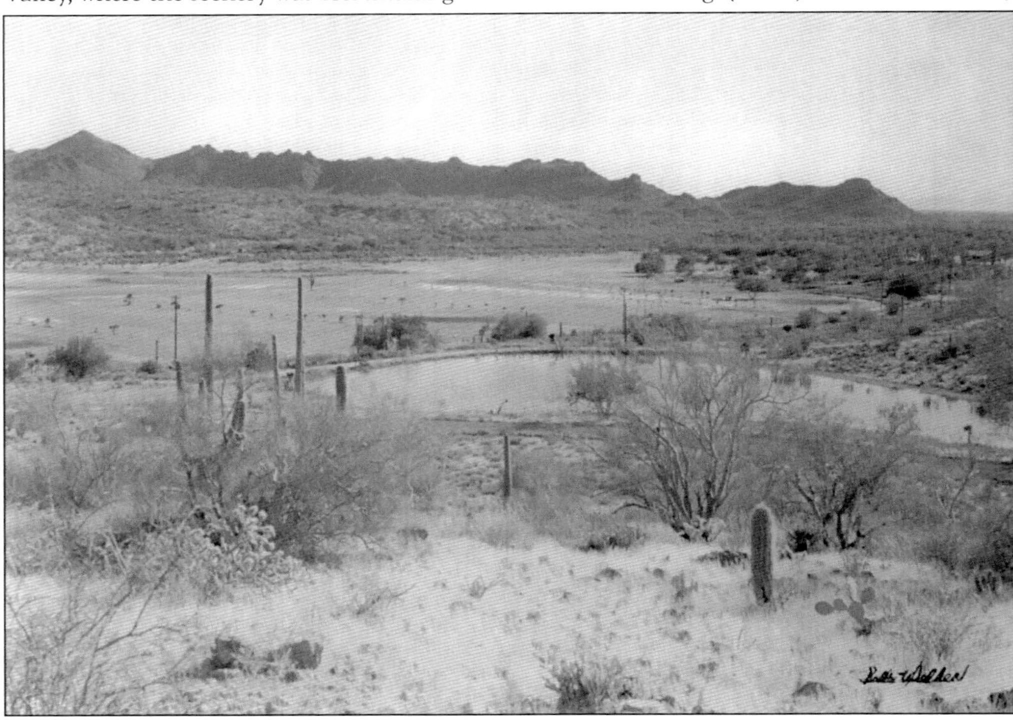

Queen Valley's settlement on Queen Creek allowed use of canals for the town. Cattle ranches and milk farms relied on this near year-round source of water. The town could not fully develop until the danger of flooding was eliminated. Appropriations for a flood control system had been set aside by the late 1800s, but a dam was not built until 1959. (QVHS.)

This canal system was dug by homesteader Hart Mullins and sparked local feuds with ranchers over the precious water supply from Queen Creek. The canal is still in use today by the Queen Valley Golf Course, which owns the water rights in order to supply the course with a constant supply of water. (ADMMR and USACE.)

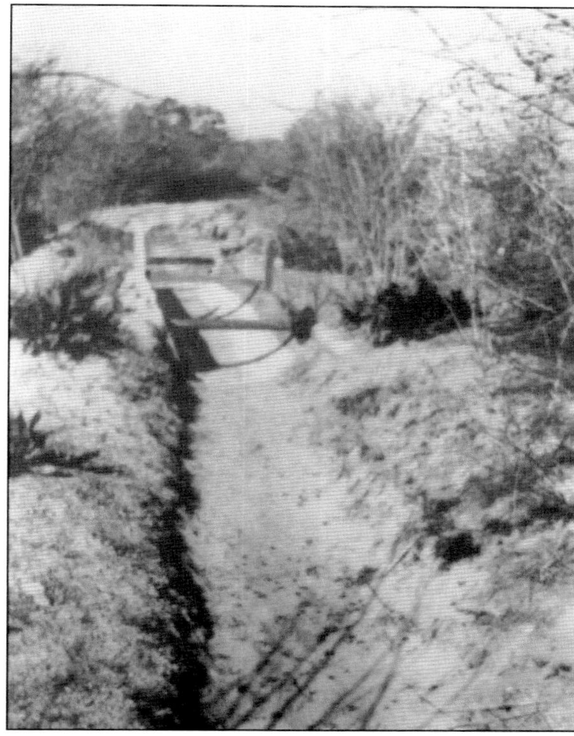

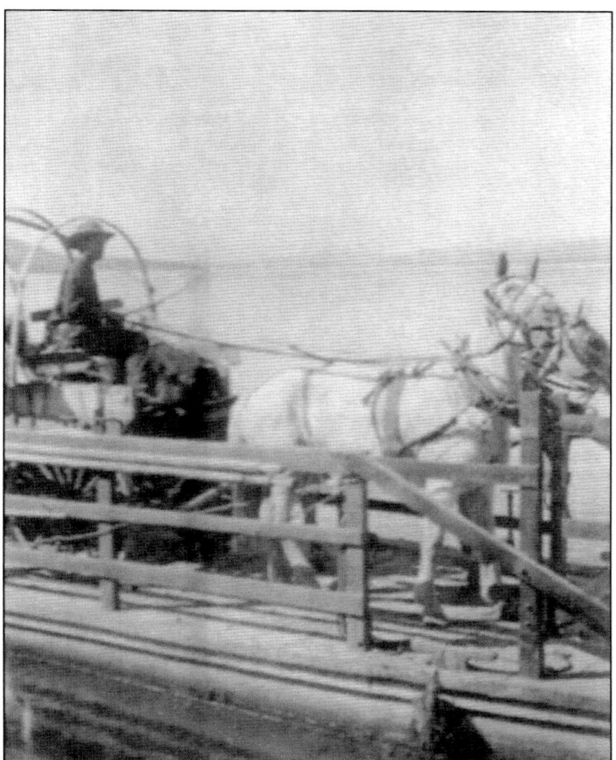

As Whitlow Dam and critical dams like Roosevelt Dam were built, year-round road travel increased, and both towns grew. Jesse Mullins (shown at left), the brother of Queen Valley homesteader Hart Mullins, drove freight wagons of lumber to Roosevelt Dam during its construction. (Fran Olson Harkey.)

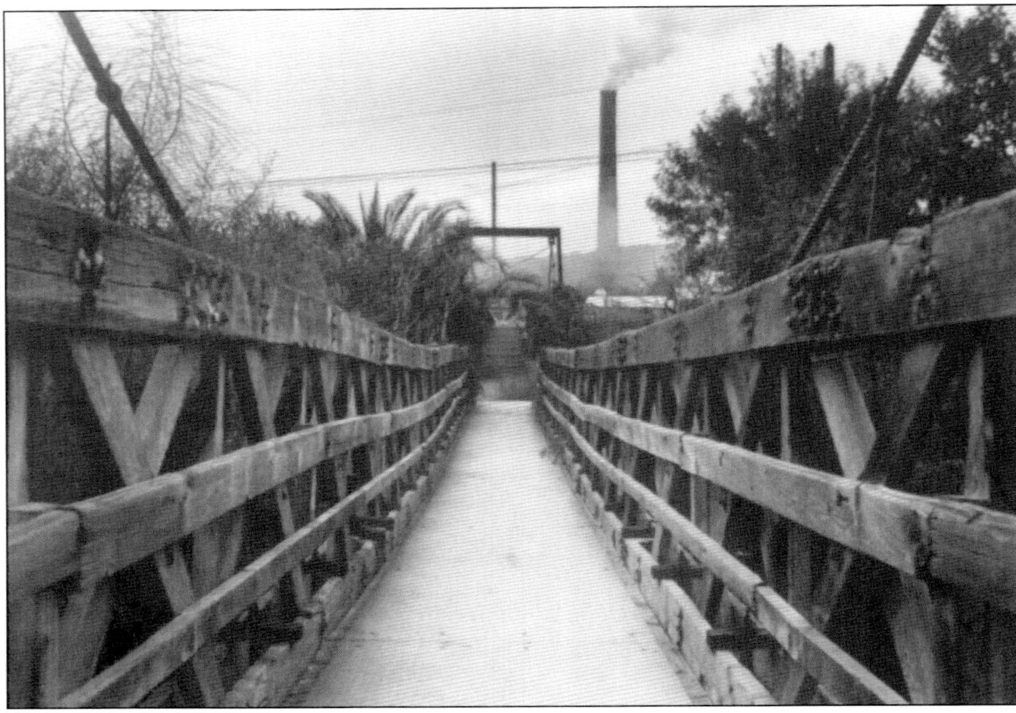

This period pedestrian suspension bridge crosses Queen Creek in the heart of Superior. Queen Creek is a seasonal creek, so there are times it is dry and crossing is easy. There are also times when, without this bridge, pedestrian crossing in Superior's early days would have been impossible. (Jack San Felice.)

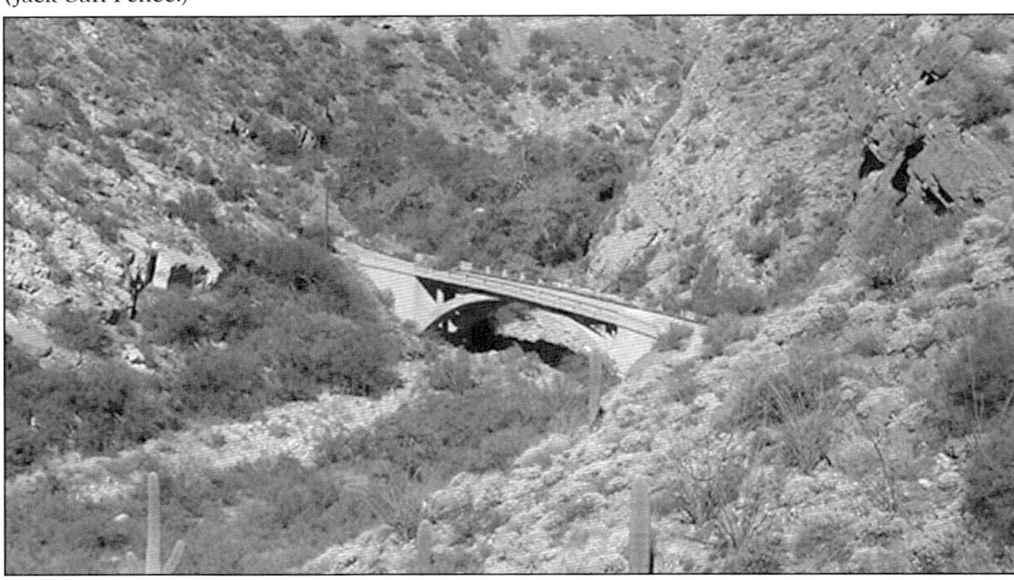

This old bridge over Queen Creek was built in the 1920s and replaced older bridges made for wagon travel from Superior, Miami, Globe, and New Mexico. A bridge over Queen Creek, on the El Camino Viejo Road to Queen Valley, was also built in the 1930s to aid river crossings for travelers from Phoenix and Florence to Superior. (AARoads.com.)

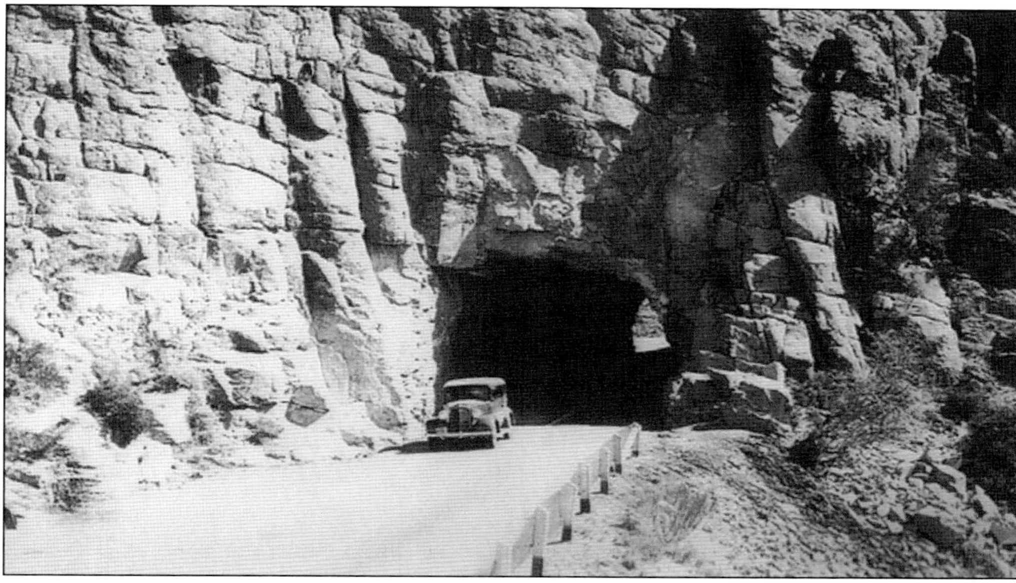

Moving travel to higher ground, the Queen Creek Tunnel was originally built in 1921 and 1922 and allowed faster and safer travel between towns in Eastern Arizona, regardless of flood seasons. The drive on the "Million Dollar Highway" from Phoenix to Superior and Globe became a popular journey for local and interstate trucks and travelers. This new road shortened the trip by 40 miles. (SF.)

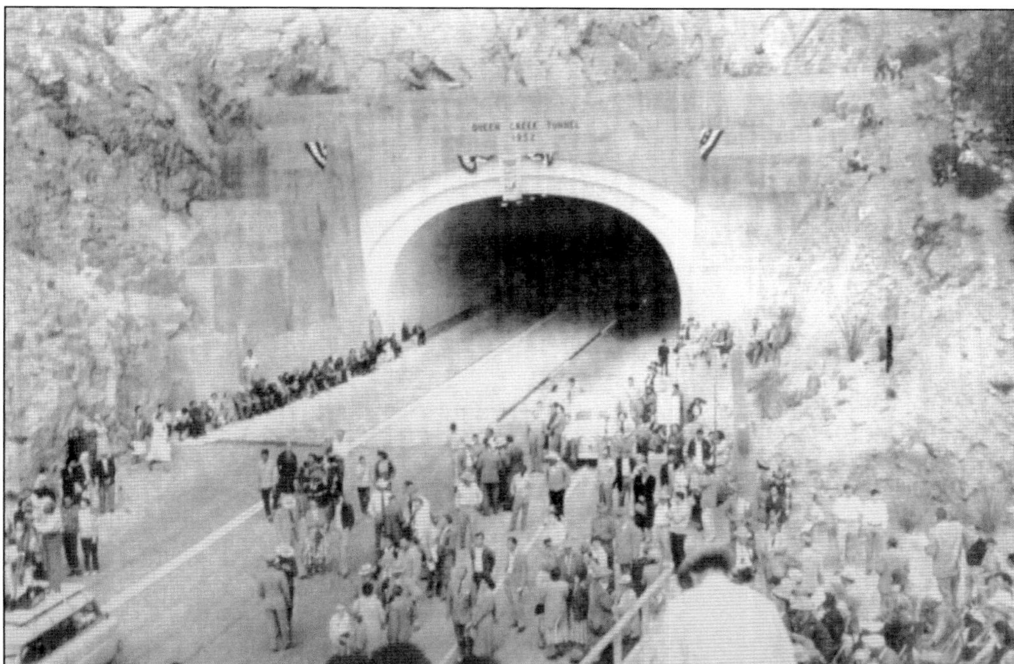

The road straightened out the severe curves and steep grades. Once completed, the new road became very popular for travel, and it remains a busy thoroughfare for interstate travel as it linked Phoenix and Safford through Superior. (Jack San Felice.)

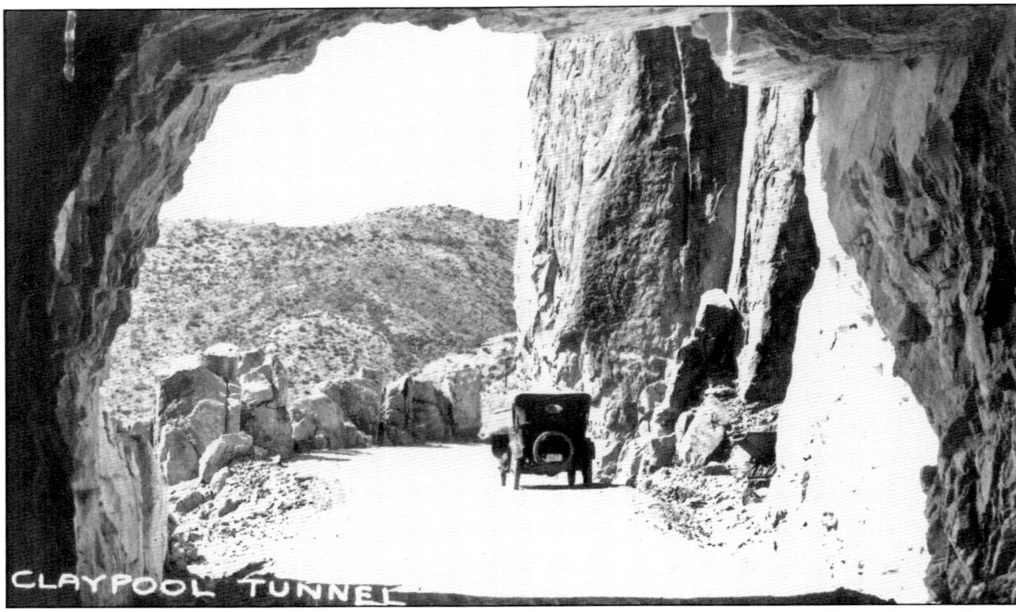

This 1920s photograph of the Claypool Tunnel demonstrates how the road has changed over the years. The tunnel was moved from the level near Queen Creek to high on the mountains between Superior and Globe, through the Queen Creek Tunnel and Devil's Canyon, to Eastern Arizona. (Edwardo's Pizzeria.)

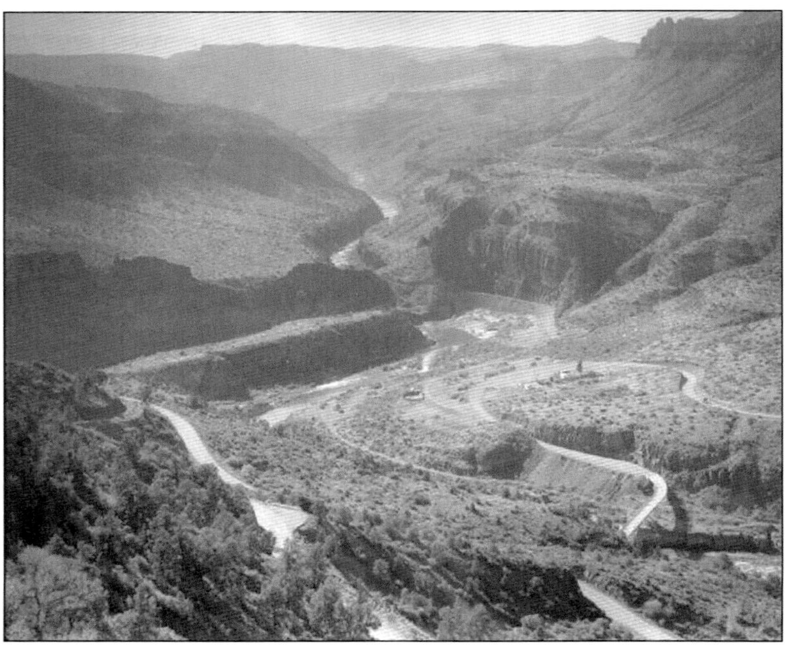

By 1945, the road to Showlow had been modernized enough to make travel for business or pleasure quicker and safer. Northbound traffic from Phoenix and Tucson, as well as southbound Interstate 40 traffic, would have used this route. (BLM.)

Five

SUPERIOR

The town of Superior has a long and fascinating history. Within a 10-mile radius, towns changed names four times. First was a military outpost called Picket Post, it was closed within a year and the area converted into a mill town called Pinal City. Once the Silver King and other mines in the area played out, Pinal was abandoned, and buildings were moved to a new location only a few miles away, near a mine discovered by a man named Hastings. The new town was named for him. Not long after that the town's name was changed from Hastings to Superior, the post office was established, and copper became the major mining effort.

The town's development and sustainability was largely due to the connection with employment from the mining industry and the products and service businesses that were established to provide for the workers and their families. Over time, these businesses evolved to serve ranchers and the townspeople in general. With this growth came community involvement and activities that bonded people to places. Clubs and associations were formed, friendships forged, and businesses built. Some predicted in the 1980s, when the town's largest mine shut down, it would mean the end of Superior and that it would become another one of Arizona's ghost towns. They were quickly proven wrong. The town is home to many resilient and self-reliant people, many of whom are descendants of the early pioneers of the West. Townspeople and others who appreciate its cultural and historic charm will remain in Superior, while it marches into its next 100 years.

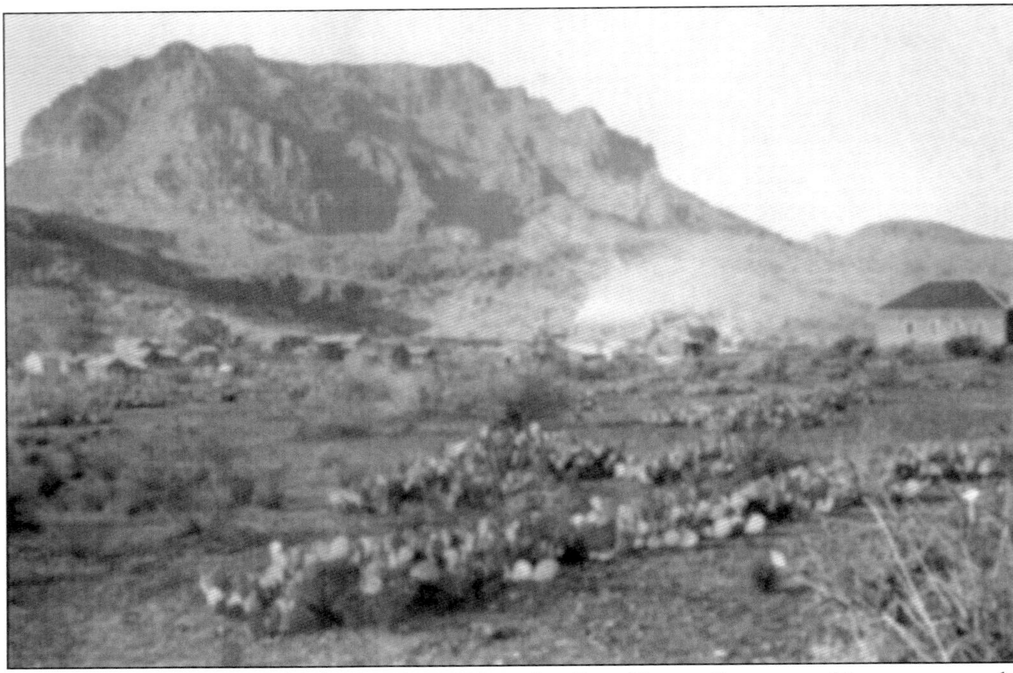

Picket Post Camp was established in the 1870s under Gen. George Stoneman. He was sent to the lands near the Gila River and Pinal Mountains of the Arizona Territory to protect the prospectors and settlers. Apache Indians were attacking the peaceful Pima Indians in the area of present-day Florence. Stoneman was replaced by General Crook, and he closed it the next year. (SF.)

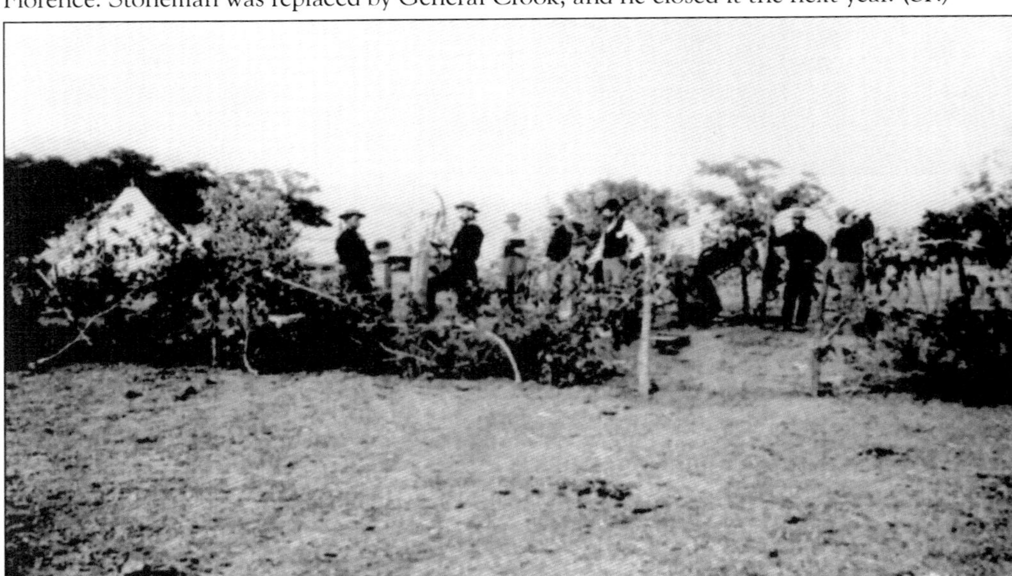

During the Apache wars, systems of heliographs were running from Fort Stanton in New Mexico to Fort Whipple in Arizona. Mirrors sent messages from peak to peak, warning troops of activity. Arizona's 14 stations were manned by 65 soldiers. Maps conflict on locations, but the nearest stations to Superior were the San Carlos and Fort McDowell; however, Pinal Mountain likely had a relay station. (NA.)

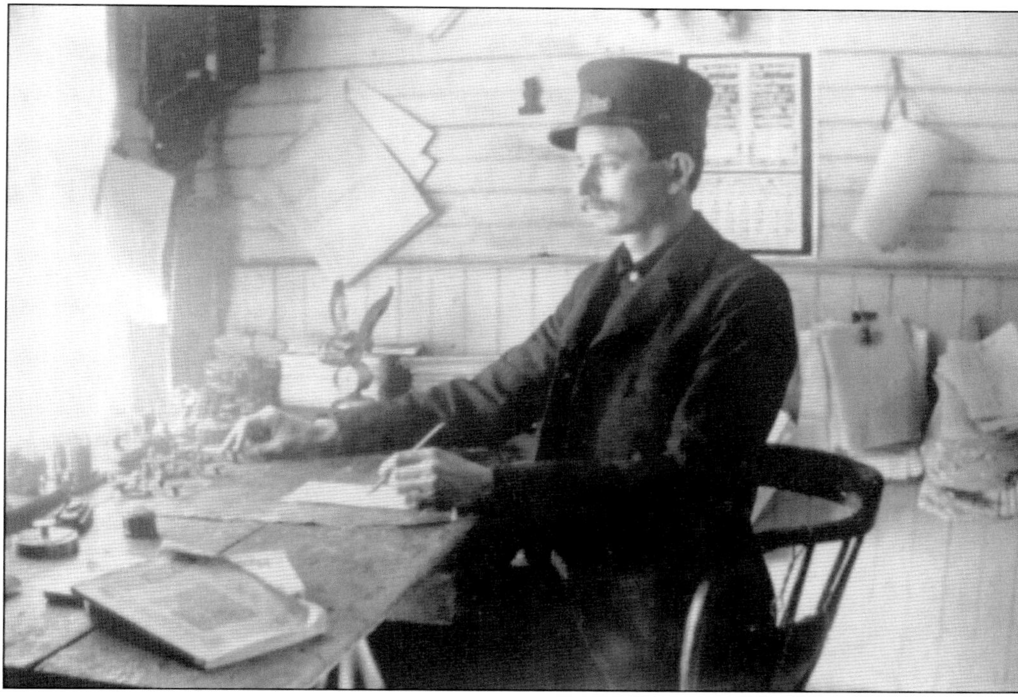

In 1871, General Crook urged telegraph line construction from California to Arizona. Congress appropriated $120,000 in 1873 for lines to Yuma, Prescott, and Tucson. Florence provided some poles free, so the line would pass through the area. Primarily used by those in the military, it was also used by civilians, and 1,000 miles of lines crossed Arizona by 1877. The military utilized telegraphs from 1873 to 1877. (Wells Fargo Museum in Phoenix.)

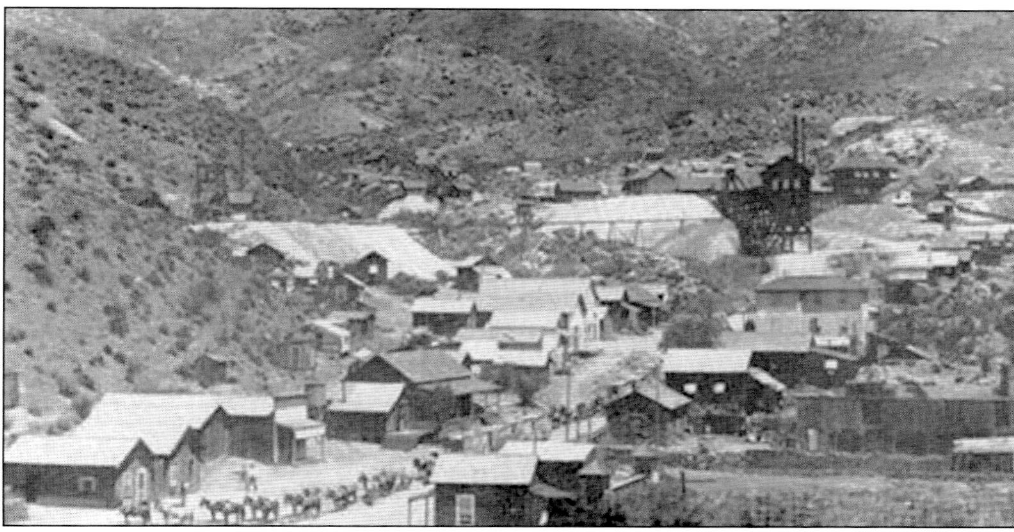

Sullivan, one of Stoneman's patrolling horse soldiers, found silver nuggets and pocketed them. He had unknowingly found the mother lode. Unsuccessful in getting others to go to the area with him, he described the location to Charles Mason for some cash and boots. Mason joined a party of five prospectors in 1875. On March 22, 1875, they filed their claim and named it the Silver King Mine. (ADMMR.)

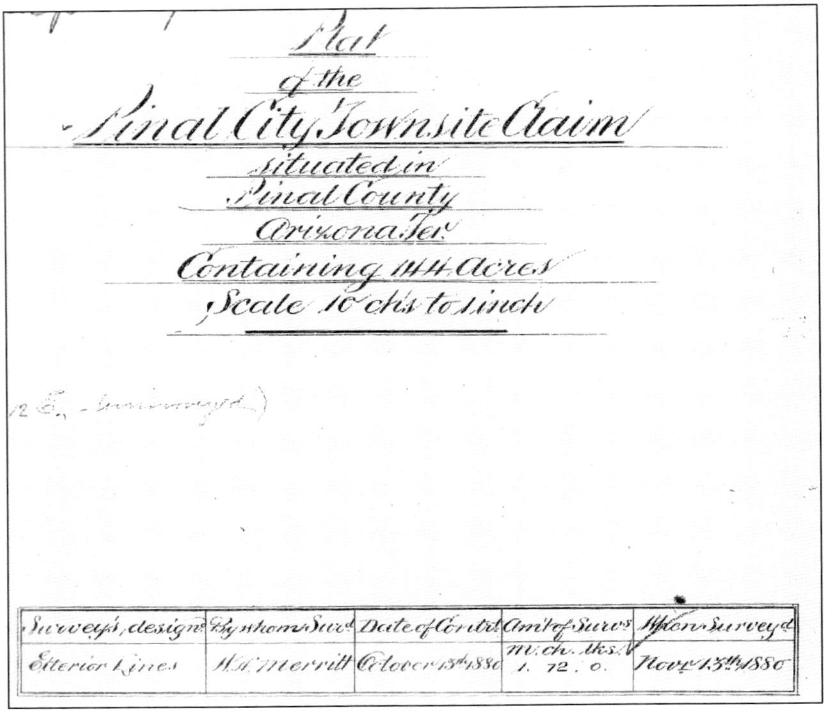

Plat
of the
Pinal City Townsite Claim
situated in
Pinal County
Arizona Ter.
Containing 1144 Acres
Scale 10 ch's to 1 inch

Surveys, design.	By whom Surv'd	Date of Contr't	Am't of Surv's	When Surveyed
Exterior Lines	W. H. Merritt	October 13th 1880	m. ch. lks. 1. 72. 0.	Nov. 13th 1880

When General Crook closed the outpost, the name of the camp was changed to Pinal City, as shown on this Plat Map cover. During its short-lived time, the town opened a post office in 1878, named Picket Post. The name was changed to Pinal in June 1879. At that time, it had 120 buildings and 2,000 people. (NA.)

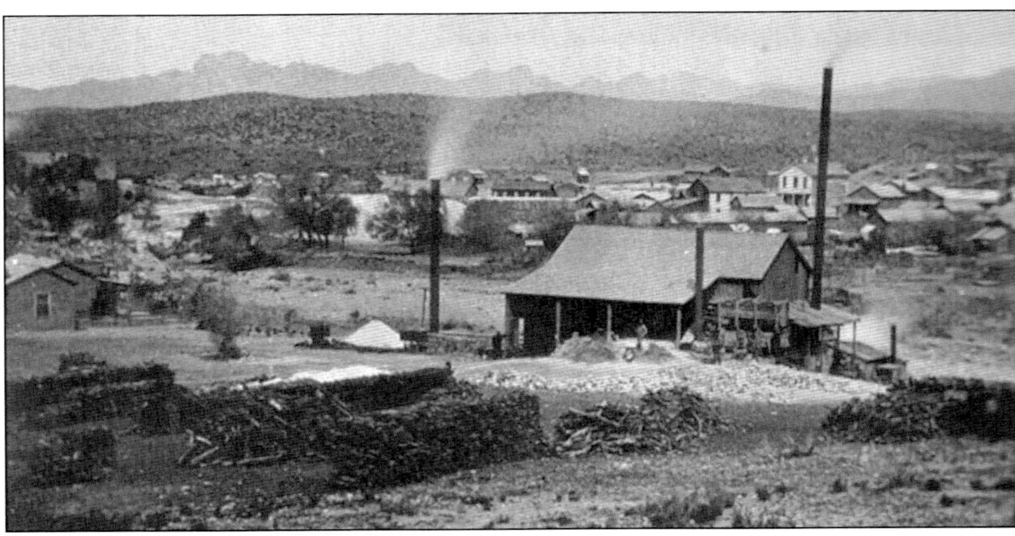

Pinal City became the headquarters for the Silver King Mine and others in the area. It had three ore mills, a mercury amalgamation plant, a 20-stamp concentrator mill, and a Bruckner Furnace, which was running in support of the mines. In 1883, the mill at Pinal City treated approximately 50 tons a day that were wagon-shipped through Queen Valley to Maricopa and on to Yuma and California by train. (SF.)

During its time as Pinal City, one of its residents was Mattie Blaylock Earp, the abandoned wife of Wyatt Earp who became famous only in our historic nostalgia. She lived and worked as a "fallen lady," until she committed suicide at the age of 38 with an overdose of laudanum. She is buried in the Pinal City Cemetery, which is located between Superior and Queen Valley. (Gladys Walker/Jack San Felice.)

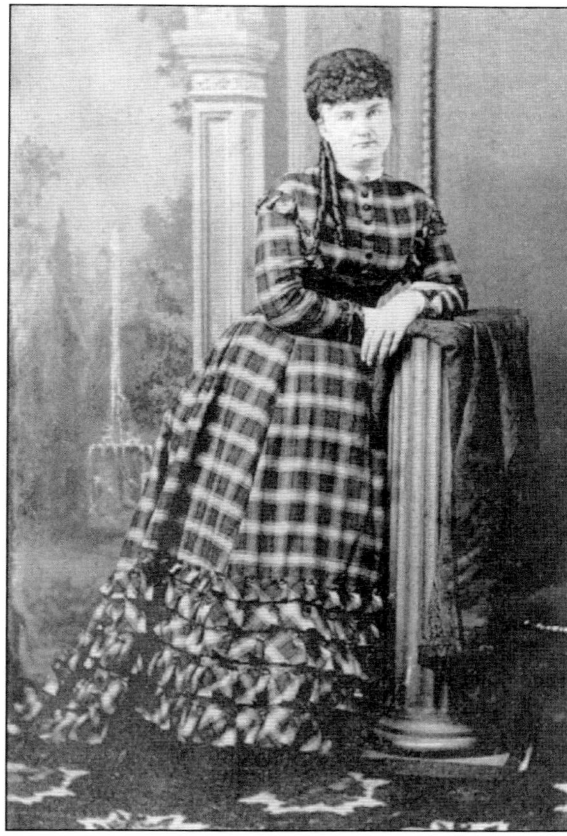

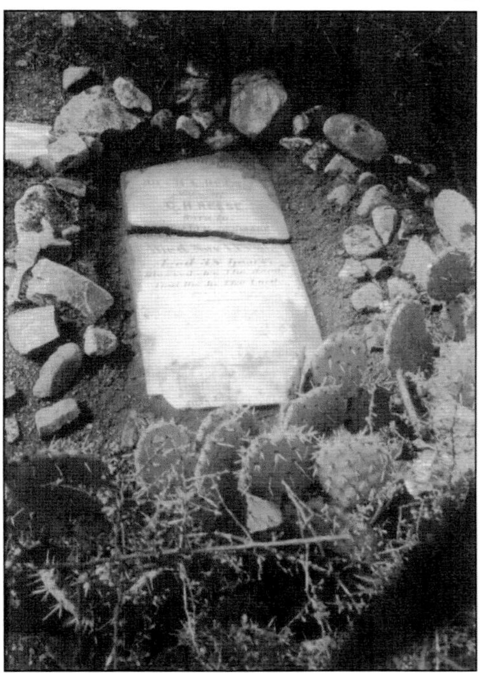

Pinal Cemetery is the last resting place for many of the pioneering men, women, and children of the early West. Life was short, with high infant mortality rates, and most women passed away before they reached the age of 40. Graves like this one from the late 1800s represented a wide variety of diverse nationalities, with people here from Denmark, China, Ireland, Mexico, and many other countries. (U.S. Forest Service.)

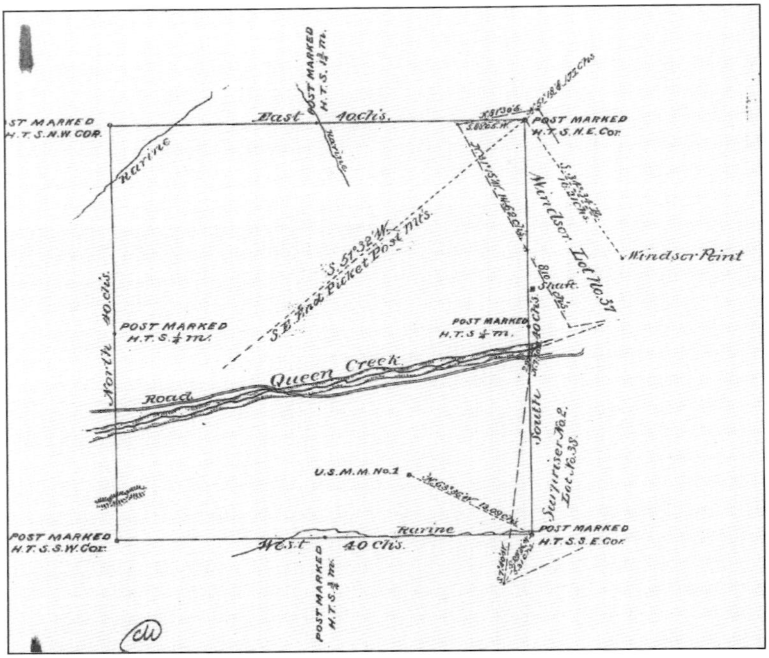

The discovery of the Silver King Mine caused the area to explode with new prospectors. When Charles Hastings filed claims near Superior on the Surpriser No. 2 mine on September 18, 1891, and the Windsor on July 31, 1882, it was processed by the U.S. Land Office in Tucson, Arizona. The town was surveyed and named Hastings in June 1882. The name was later changed to Superior. (NA.)

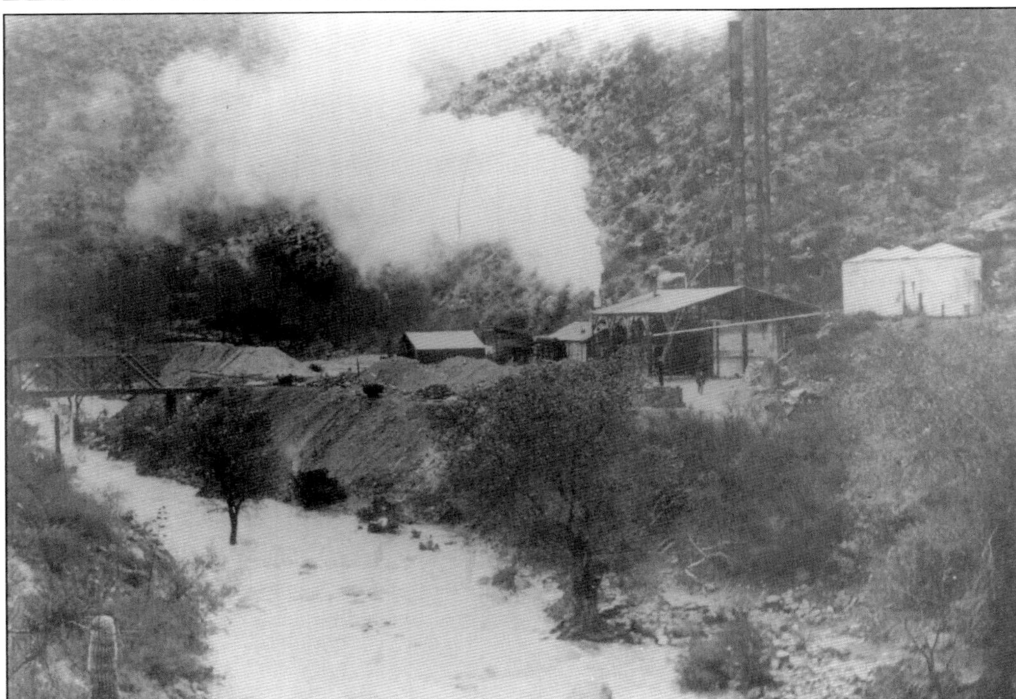

In 1888, with gold replacing silver as the U.S. monetary standard, many silver mines were eventually closed. Copper became more valuable, so mines in Superior began ramping up production. As Superior began developing, the need for managing the water supply became critical. Shown here are early water tanks on Queen Creek that were used to harness the flowing waters for mining. (Edwardo's Pizzeria.)

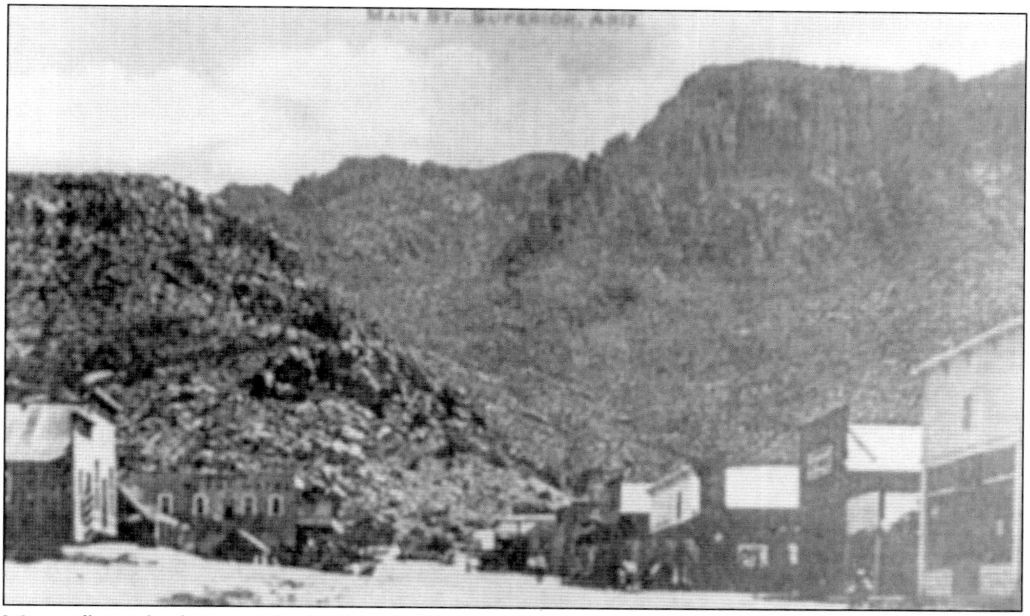

Mines flourished across the hills and all around the prosperous area east of Pinal City, and as one mine closed, another opened. The locations of the towns were sometimes changed by a few miles, as mines became more active in nearby areas. By 1891, the town of Pinal City was dismantled—building by building and board by board—and moved to nearby Hastings. By 1910, there were only 10 people left in Pinal City. (ADMMR.)

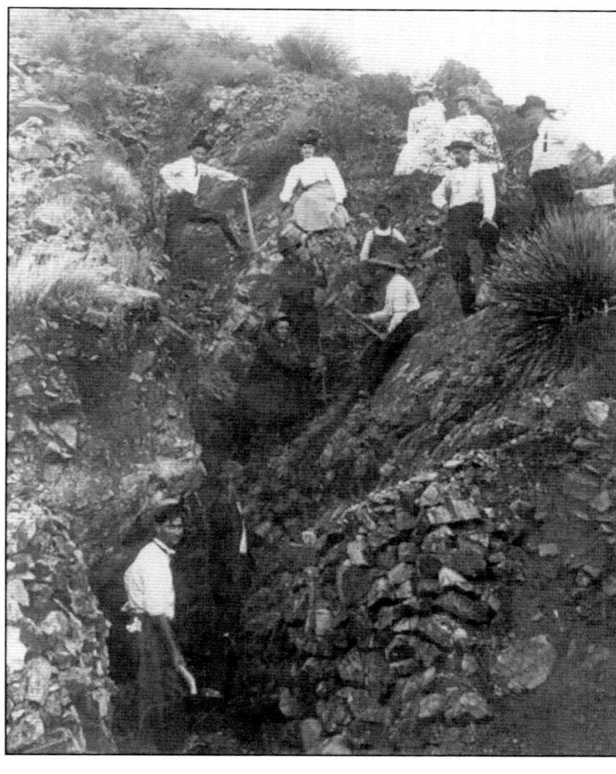

The town of Silver King served the mine and other nearby mines like the Monarch. In addition to the image on the cover of the book, this is another view of the family working the Monarch. Part of the reason the towns of Silver King and Superior developed into communities was that many of the area's miners brought their families, and by the time the mines played out, they loved the area and remained nearby. (ADMMR.)

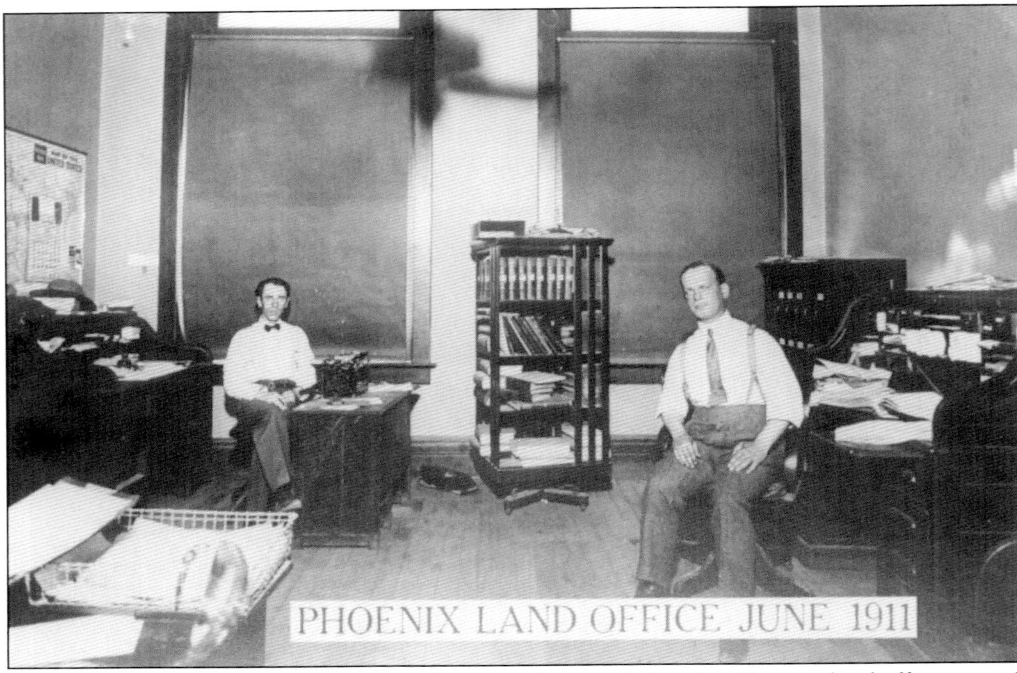

By 1912, the need for local processing had increased so much that this Phoenix land office opened. This made filing mining claims, desert entries, and homestead claims more accessible to those living in Superior and Queen Valley. (BLM.)

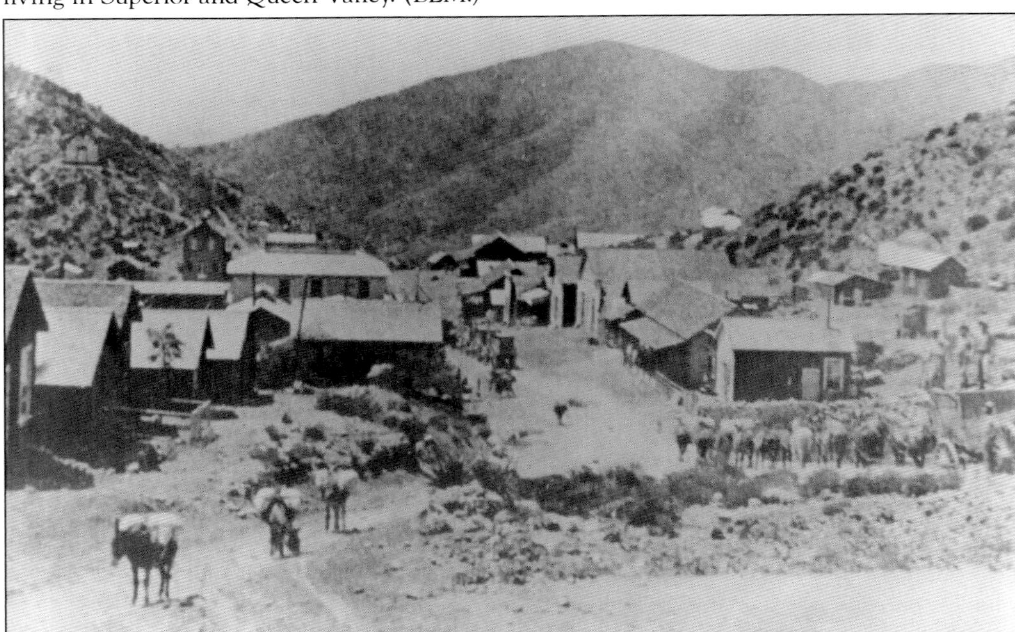

Shown here are three mules leaving the town of Silver King. By the 1920s, many of the mines were done, and the townspeople were also leaving. Many joined the miners in nearby Superior who were beginning to work the Silver Queen Mine for the Lake Superior and Arizona Mining Company. (Edwardo's Pizzeria.)

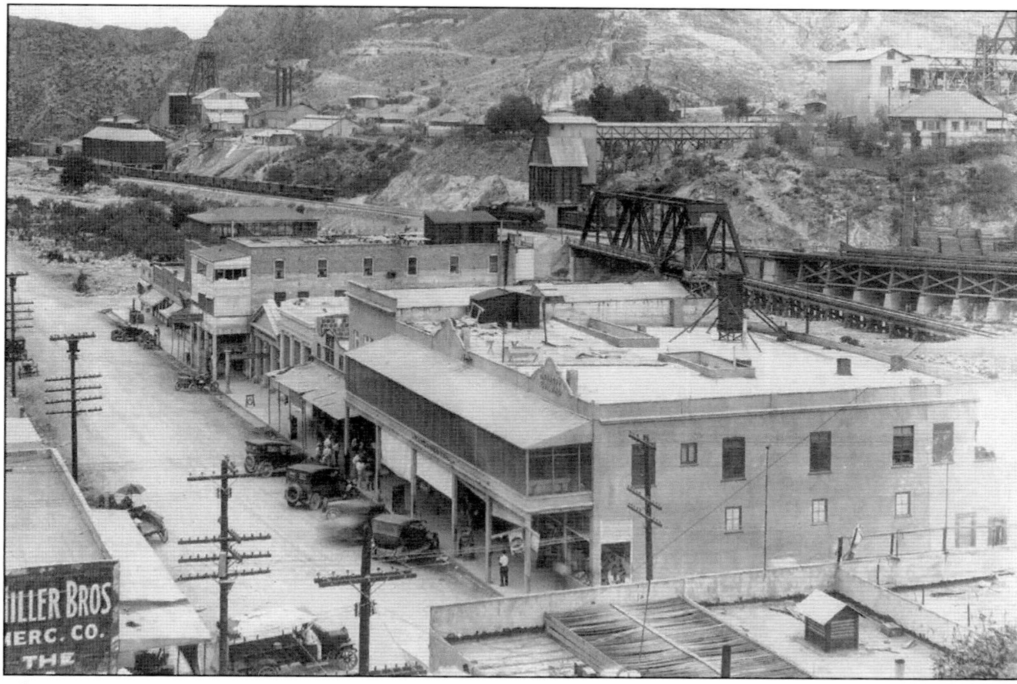

The Ray Mine was so big that a town existed to support it. The Ray and Gila Railroad began in 1900 to ship ore. Relocation of the town to Kearny and Superior began in 1958 to allow more copper extraction. Many of Ray's townspeople and descendants still live in Superior. Ray became a ghost town like many former mining towns in Arizona. (ADMMR.)

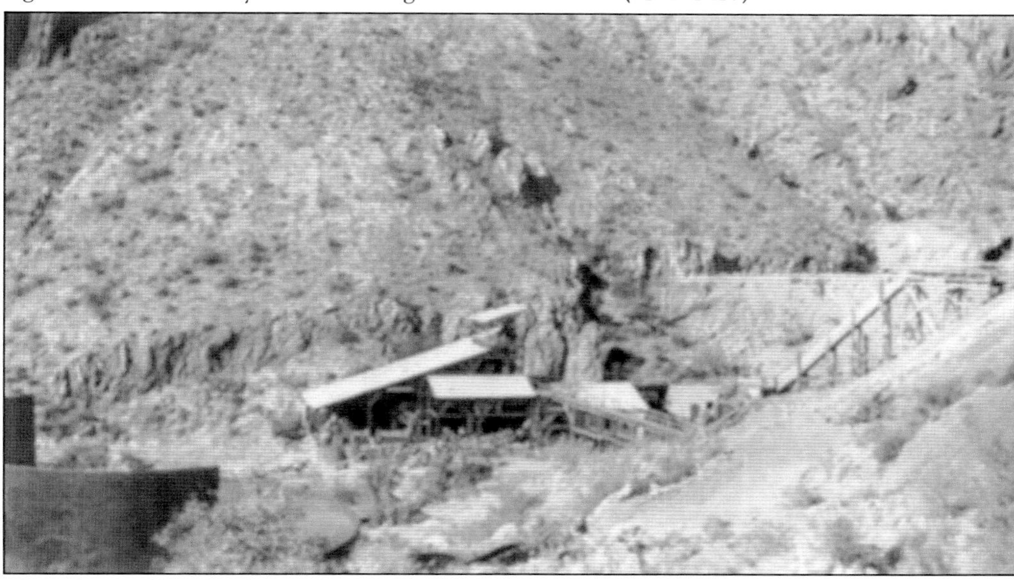

The Silver Bell-Columbia and Martinez Mines were discovered in 1880 and produced until 1971. The Silver Bell-Columbia Mine has a high silver and low lead ratio ore, while the Martinez has a high lead and low silver ratio ore. It has changed owners and operators over the years but remains in operation in the Martinez Canyon area. Currently, the Silver Bell Mining Company owns these mines. (ADMMR.)

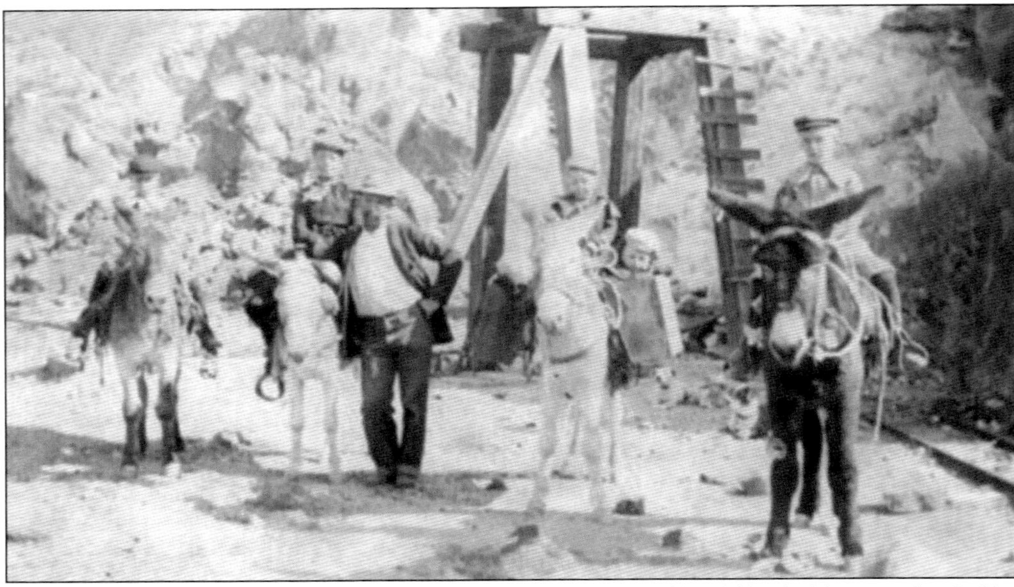

Shown above with his family, an Englishman named George Lobb sold his holdings in the Golden Eagle Silver Mine to the Lake Superior and Arizona Mining Company in 1902. He stayed in the area and platted the town site formerly called Hastings, which was named after George Hastings who owned several mines. Lobb renamed the town after the mining company, and the town got its permanent name of Superior. (SF.)

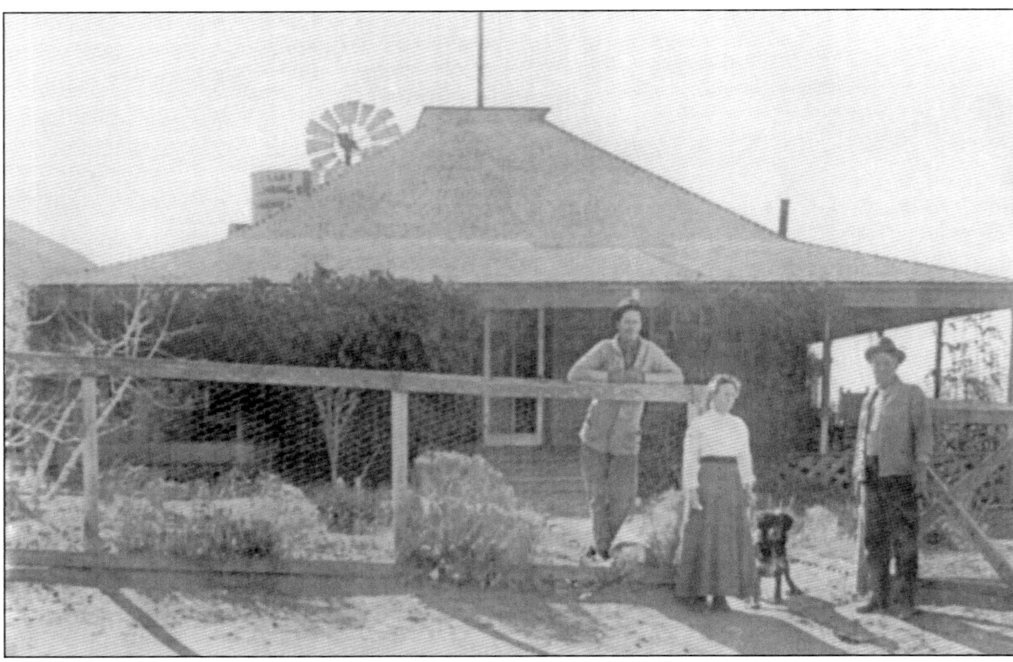

George Lobb built his home on Main Street and began serving as postmaster in 1903. By 1904, Superior had tents, primitive board homes, a store, boardinghouse, and blacksmith shop. As the town grew, businesses desired the property on Main Street for commercial use, and Lobb's house was moved to its current location. (Pamela Dalton-Rabago.)

This 1910 photograph shows the tent-style homes that many of the poorer miners and early business people called home in this new and sometimes hostile, but always scenic, area of Arizona's deserts. (SF.)

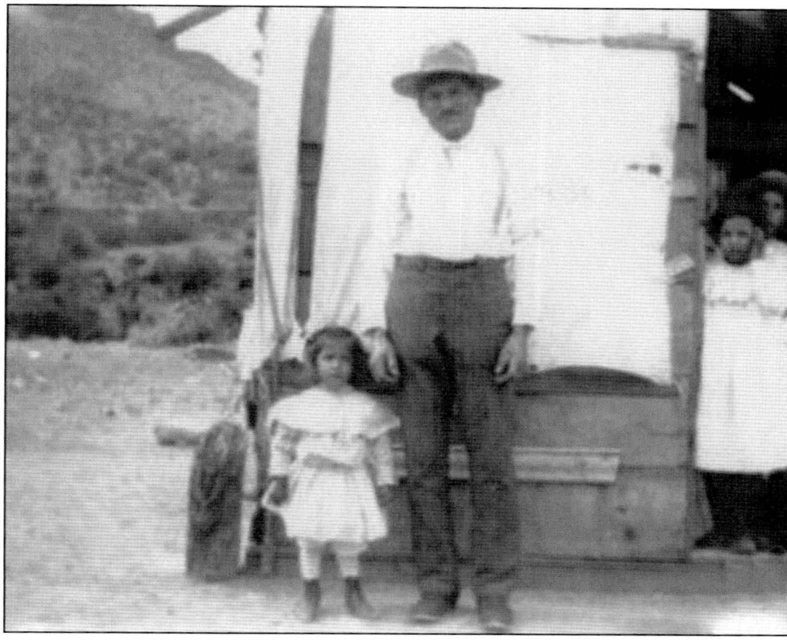

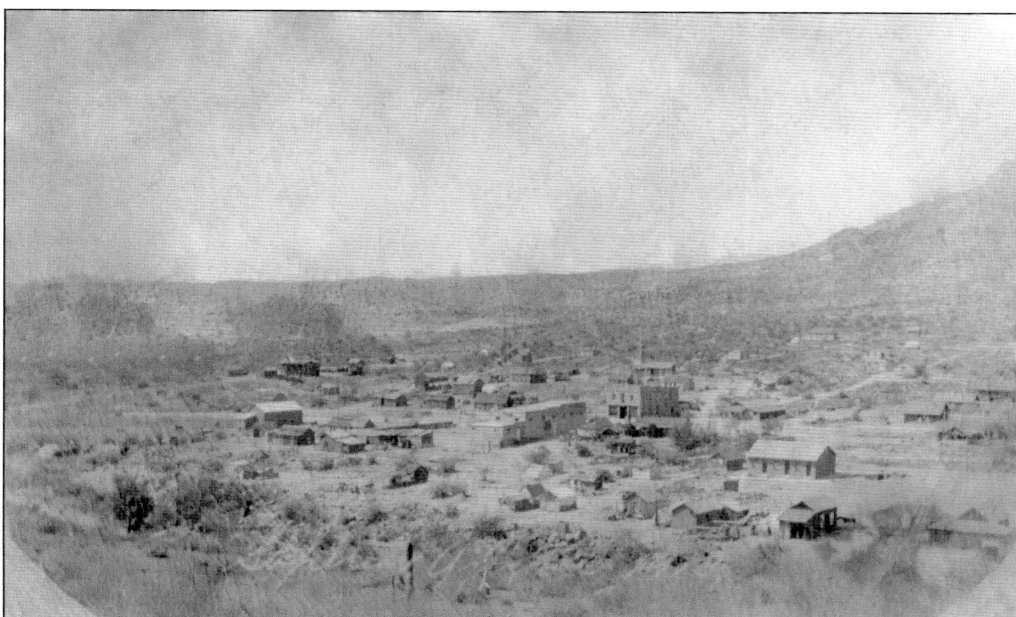

Word began spreading quickly back East about the riches to be found in the hills around Superior. Miners from California and other states nearby who had not gotten lucky came to the area hoping to strike it rich here. There is no doubt that postcards like this one were enticing to miners, families, and friends left behind back East. (Lou Oates Photography.)

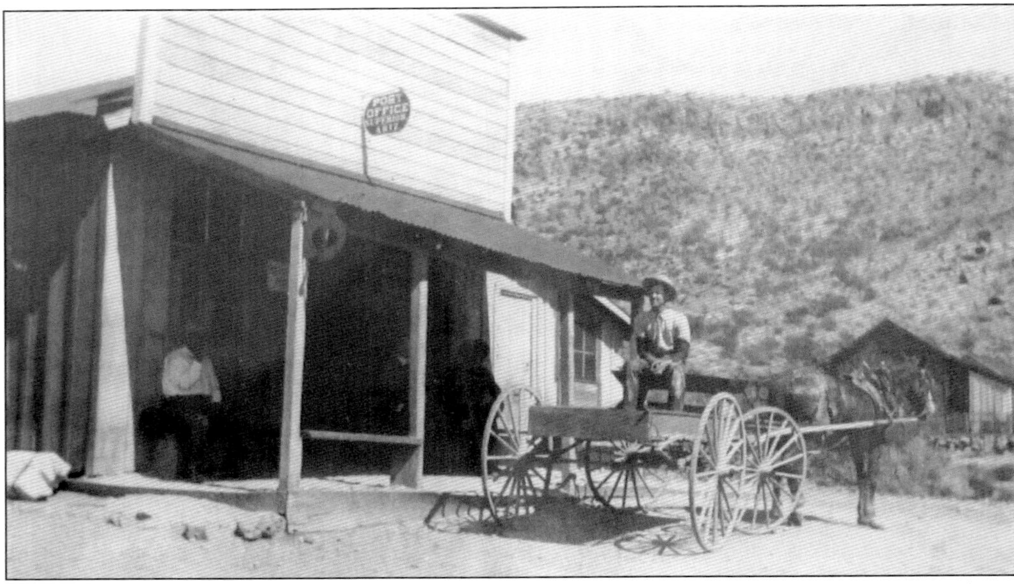

With the construction of a smelter in 1914 by the Magma Copper Company, many felt the future was secure. The town continued to grow with the discovery of more and more mines in the area. It quickly became a booming mining town with all the shops, markets, and restaurants that the miners and their families could want or need. (Gladys Walker/Jack San Felice.)

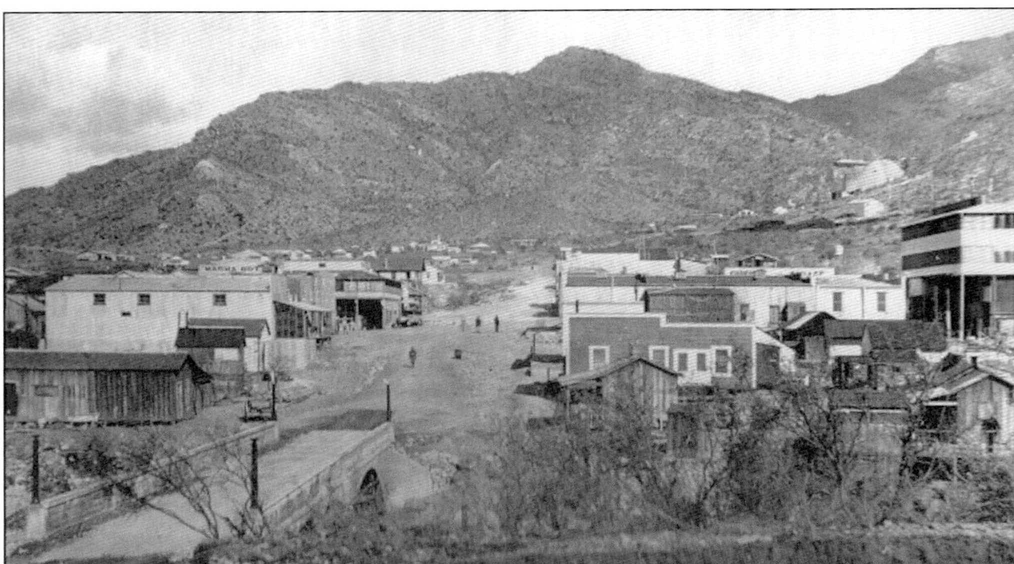

The town was continually expanding, and different areas of town were being established for specific types of people. The west area called Smelter Town was for miners, the middle of town was for families, and the east side was for mine foremen and managers. The business district and, of course, the "red light district," is shown in this photograph just across the bridge on the left. (Gladys Walker/Jack San Felice.)

William Boyce Thompson bought the Silver Queen Mine and renamed it the Magma. Originally, Thompson sent his ore by wagon to Florence and then by rail to the smelter at Hayden. In 1915, he built the Magma Arizona Railroad to carry ore and passengers, but Thompson rode in the train's private car. (Boyce Thompson Arboretum.)

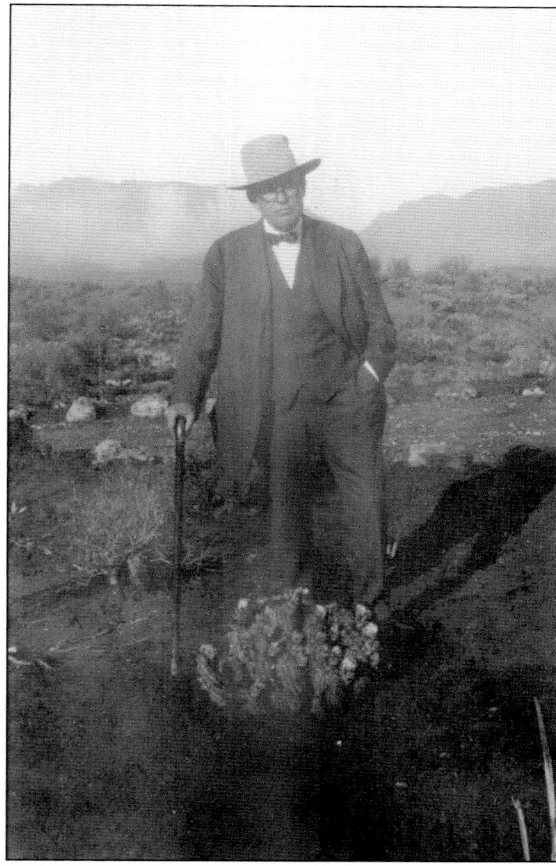

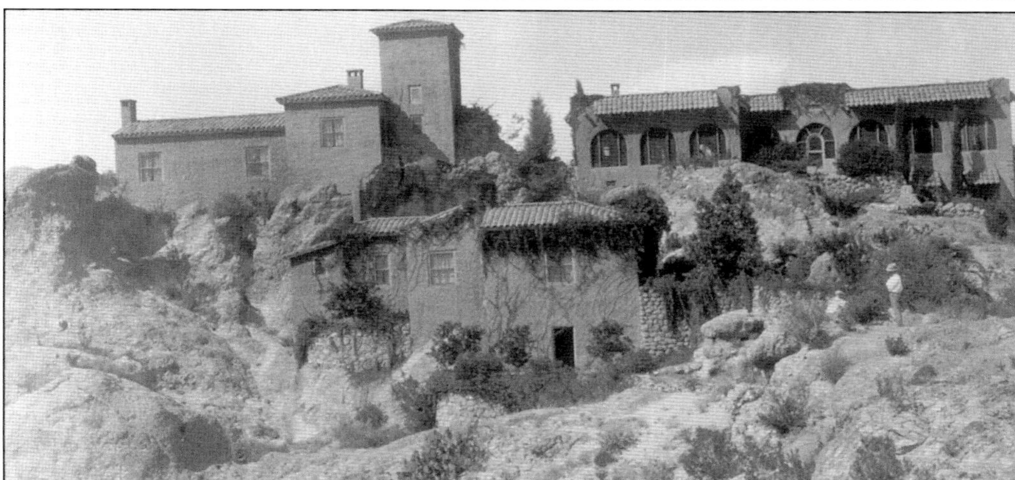

Colonel Thompson built the Picket Post House in a canyon just west of town in 1923 and 1924. He also began work on an arboretum in the canyon below, and on Friday, April 6, 1929, it was opened to the public. The Boyce Thompson Arboretum was his second public endeavor, as he already built the Boyce Thompson Institute for Plant Research at Yonkers, New York. (Boyce Thompson Arboretum.)

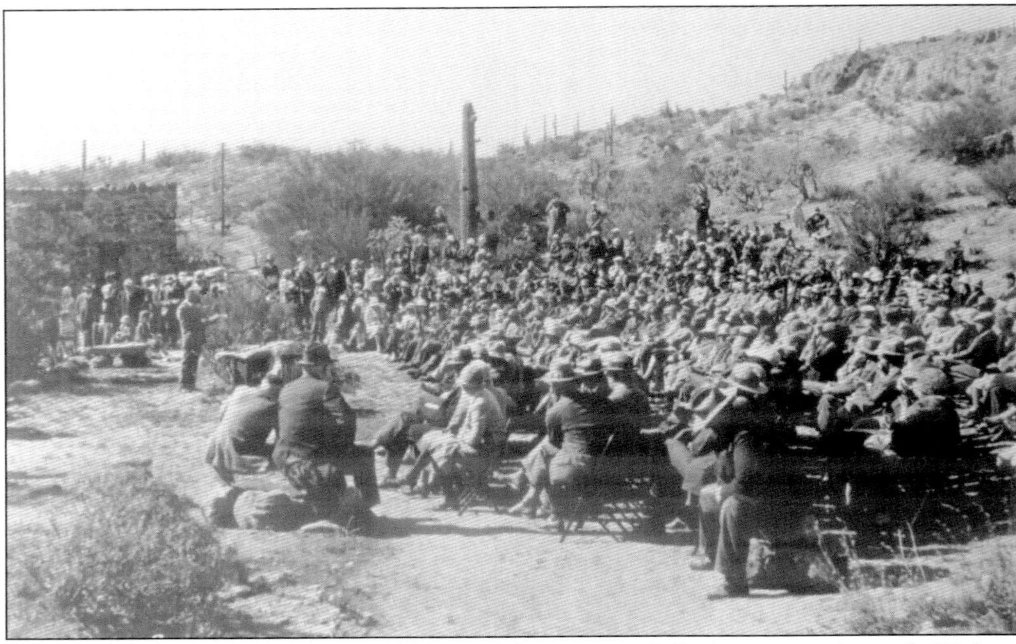

The director of the arboretum, Franklin J. Crider, presented the keynote and stated, "Colonel Thompson visualized the importance of plant study as a means of contributing to the progress, benefit, and happiness of the human race." The dedication included an inspection of buildings, grounds, and experiments; a luncheon; and a formal speaking program. It was added to the National Register of Historic Places in 1976. (Boyce Thompson Arboretum.)

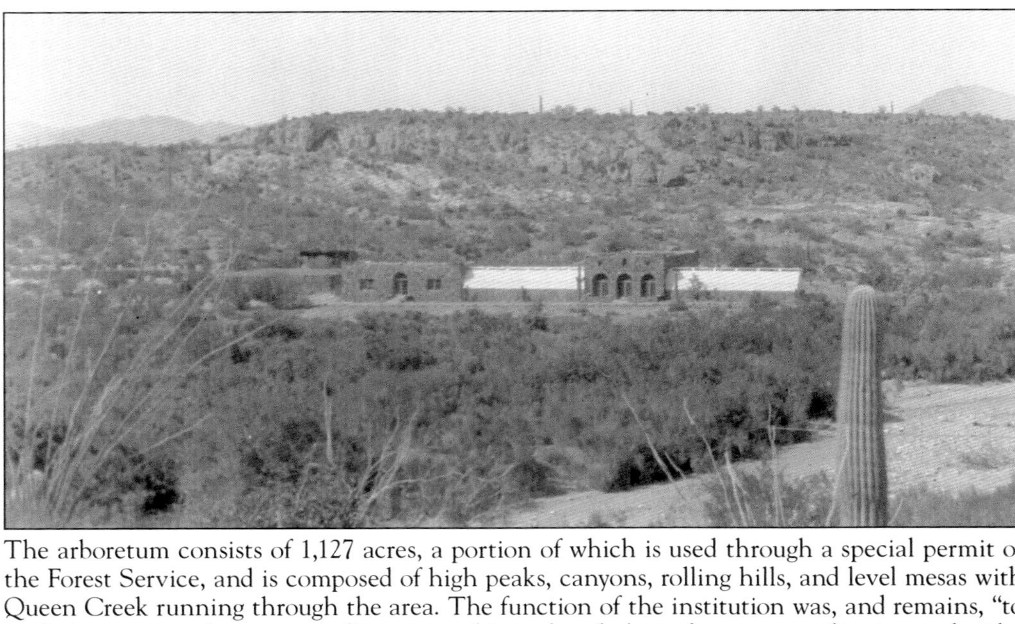

The arboretum consists of 1,127 acres, a portion of which is used through a special permit of the Forest Service, and is composed of high peaks, canyons, rolling hills, and level mesas with Queen Creek running through the area. The function of the institution was, and remains, "to study, improve, and preserve indigenous and introduced plants for greater utilization and wider economic adaptation." (Boyce Thompson Arboretum.)

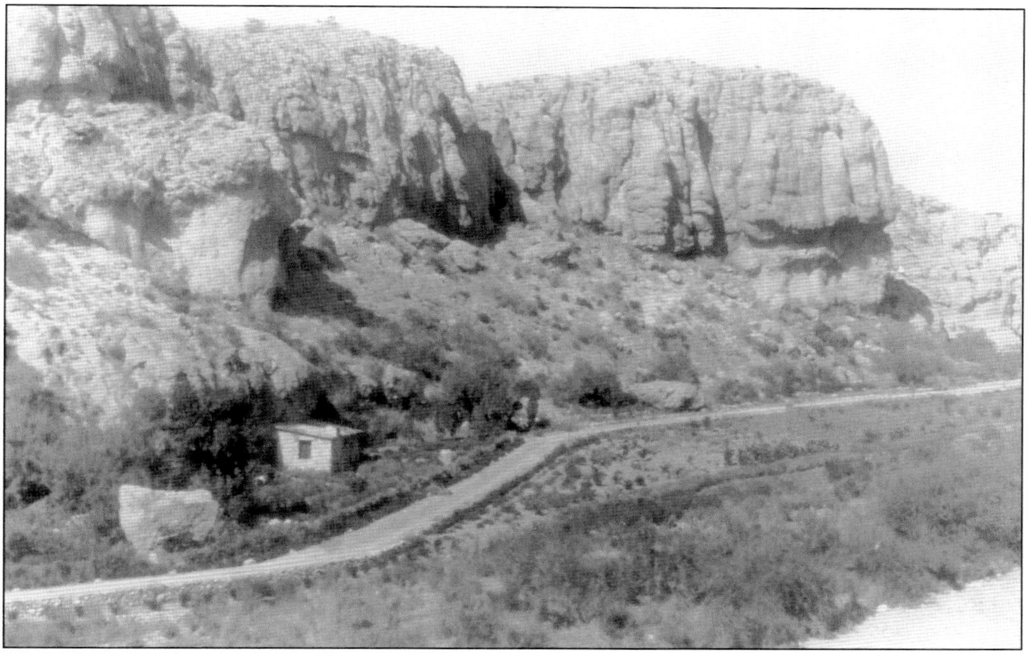

The Clevenger house shown here was part of an original homestead Patent No. 587637, signed by Pres. Woodrow Wilson on June 9, 1917. With this purchase and the development of the arboretum, Thompson brought sophistication, education, and an element of high society to the Superior area. People came from all over the country to tour the grounds and still do. (Boyce Thompson Arboretum.)

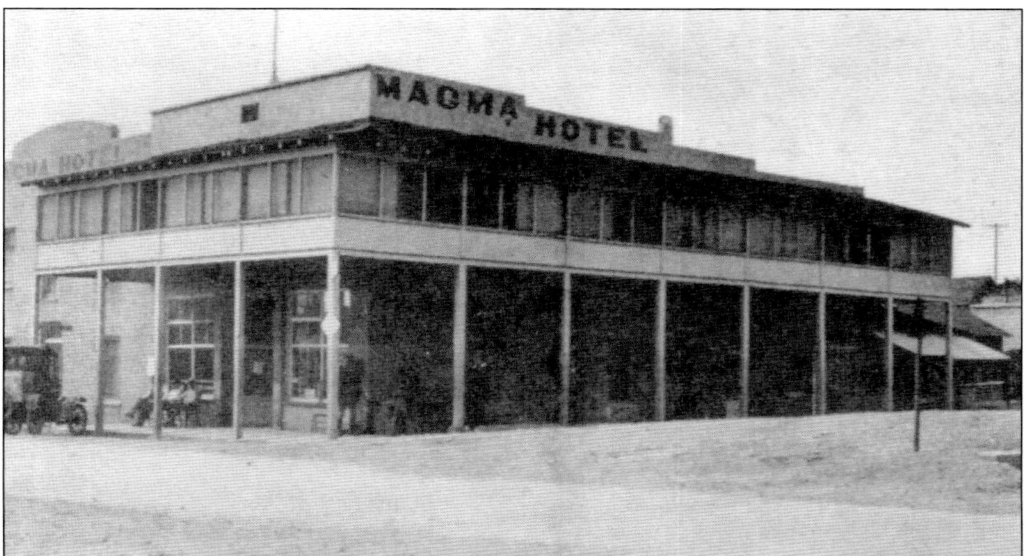

With the mining business increasing the size and sophistication of the town, the original Magma Hotel was erected in 1912. It featured screened-in upstairs sleeping rooms. The building later became the site for a drugstore and was the center of activity during the day and evening hours alike. (*Superior Sun.*)

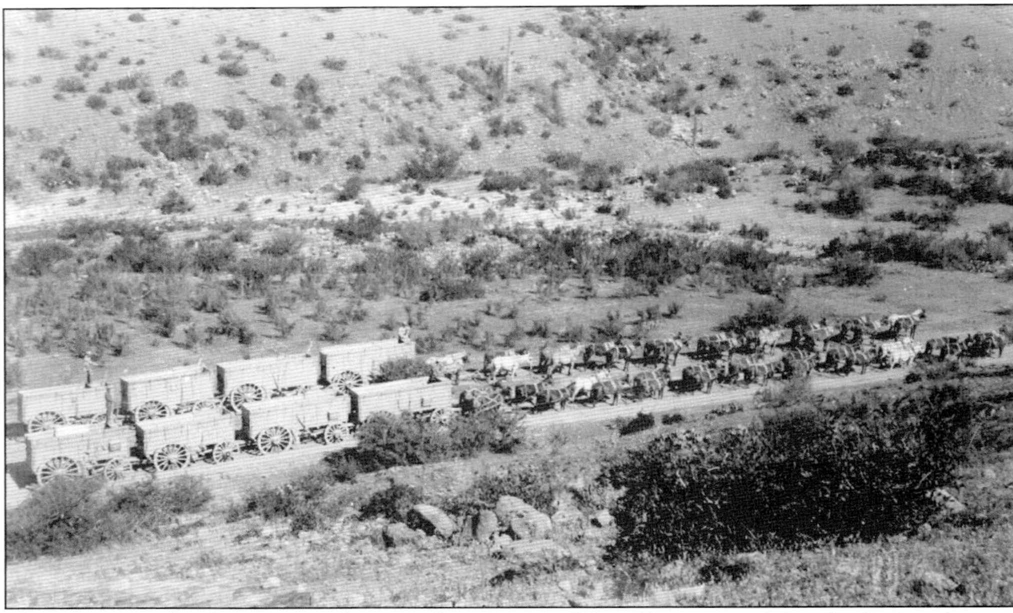

This photograph of ore wagons leaving the mines in Silver King exemplifies the high volume of money that could be spent in and around Superior. With that came the need for more businesses to serve the needs of the town. Families, shops, hotels, and banks joined miners, and the town secured its staying power through the community that was developing. (Bowen family/Jack San Felice.)

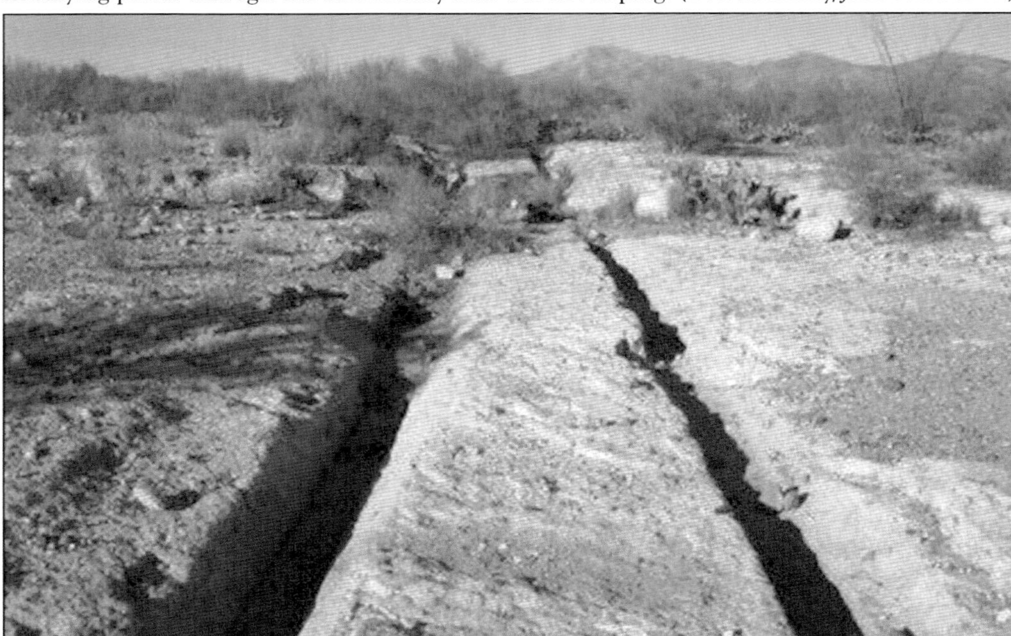

Mule and wagon tracks just outside Superior are evidence of the many ore wagons traveling to and from the mines. The grooves were dug into the rock by the mule's hooves and steel wheels on wagons loaded with tons of ore leaving the mines. The ruts are a popular tourist attraction for those that romanticize about old West mining towns.

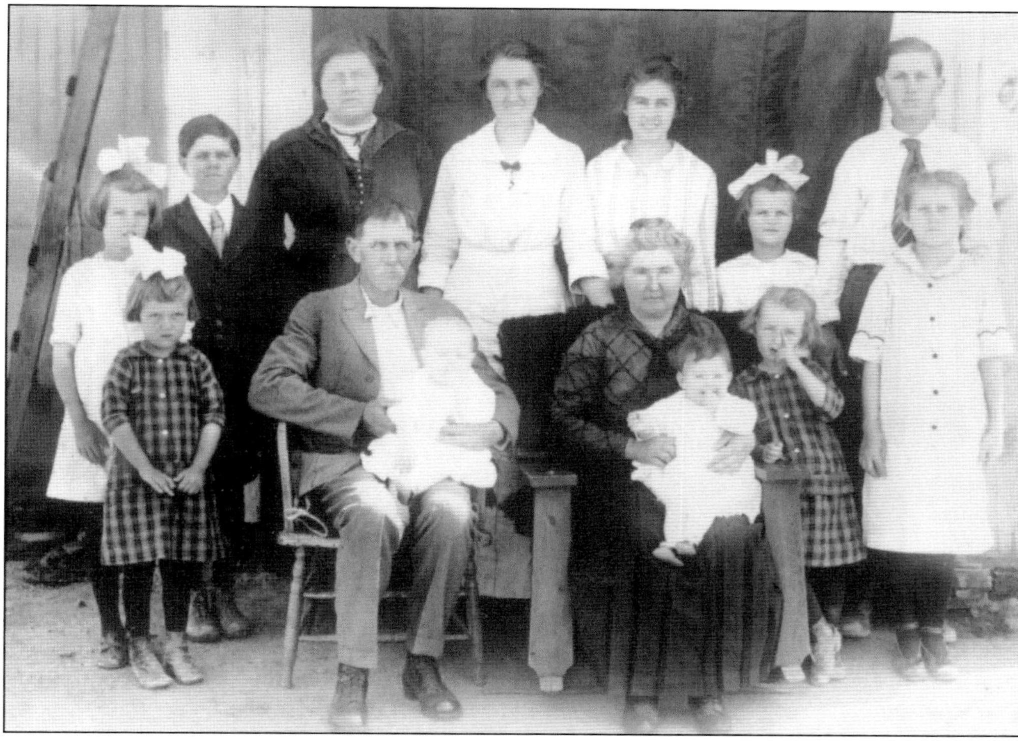

This 1910 photograph shows Clayton Obediah Brown with his wife, Cora Elizabeth, and family. Grandson Dennis Brown said, "No one now knows who all those kids are. My father, Forrest Eugene Brown, is on the left in the back row. Aunt Pearl (described in the 2002 Superior Historical Society Calendar as the daughter of Superior cofounder Clayton Obediah Brown) is on the far right." (Dennis Brown.)

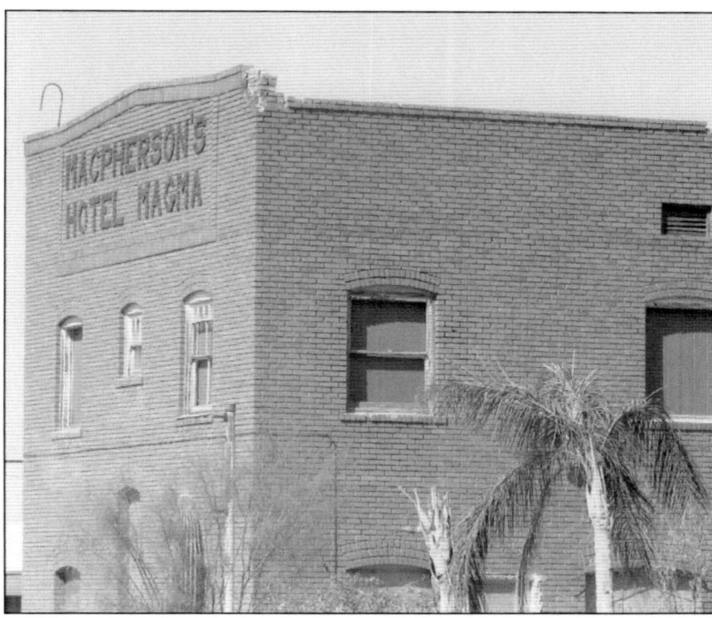

The Spanish Revival–style Hotel Magma, which is on the National Register of Historic Places, was built in 1910 by Jack Davey for J. M. MacPherson. It hosted the *Superior Sun* beginning in 1916, and in 1917, Mountain States Telephone and Telegraph Company installed a booth for the guests and residents of the town. In 1918, O. C. Hing leased and managed the hotel's restaurant. Over the years many businesses utilized the beautiful building.

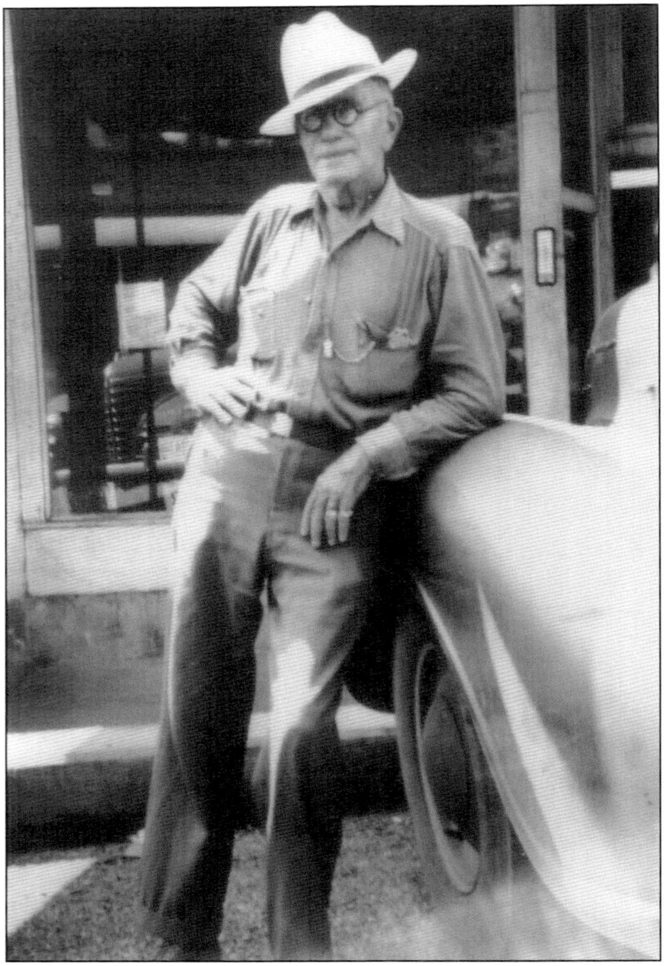

Pat Gorham was sheriff from around 1915 through the 1930s. Since murders and theft were rare, he was brought in to protect miners and prostitutes so that they could reliably go to work. In 1929, Phoenix gangsters tried to move in but were loaded up at midnight and left barefoot with hands tied on Gonzales Pass to return to Phoenix. They never returned to Superior. (Jack Gorham.)

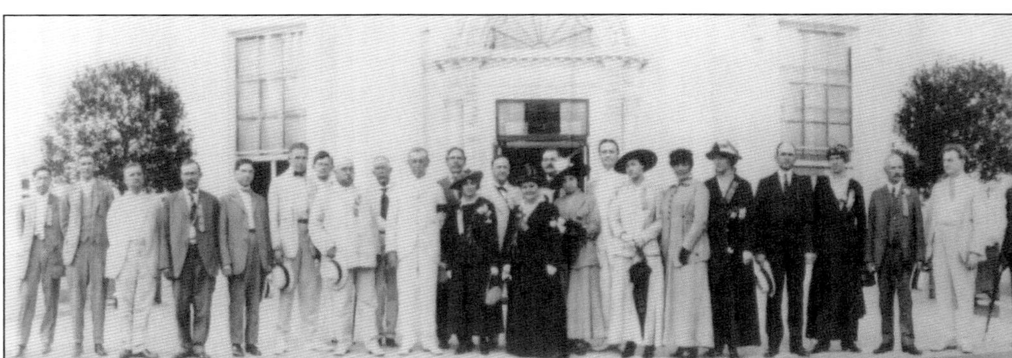

Sheriff Gorham also served as an occasional bodyguard to Governor Hunt and went with him, serving as a delegate to the White House commissioning of the USS *Arizona* in 1916. Gorham is fourth from the left, Hunt is eighth, and Pres. Woodrow Wilson is tenth (with the arm band). In June 1915 in the Brooklyn Navy Yard, it was christened with the first water that had crossed Roosevelt Dam. (Jack Gorham.)

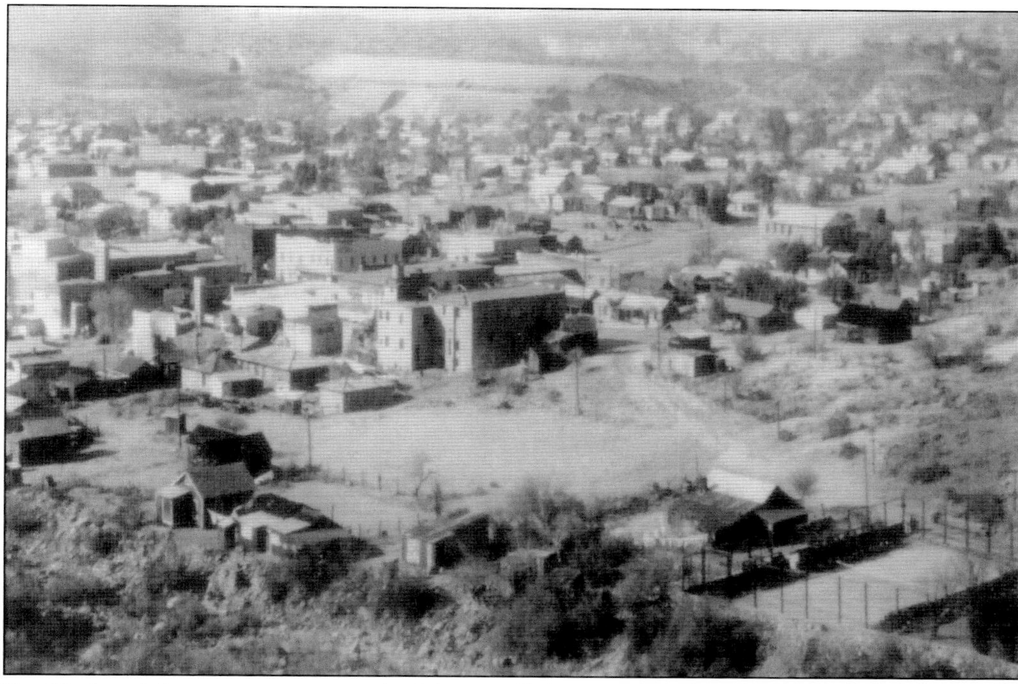

Pat Gorham's house was next to the Magma Club tennis courts. He and his wife had eight children. His descendents still live in the area, including Superior native Mike McKee. Because of his grandfather's influence, McKee and many others grew up respecting Superior's richly diverse townspeople. McKee says Superiorites fought each other occasionally growing up but stood together against trouble from outsiders. (Jack Gorham.)

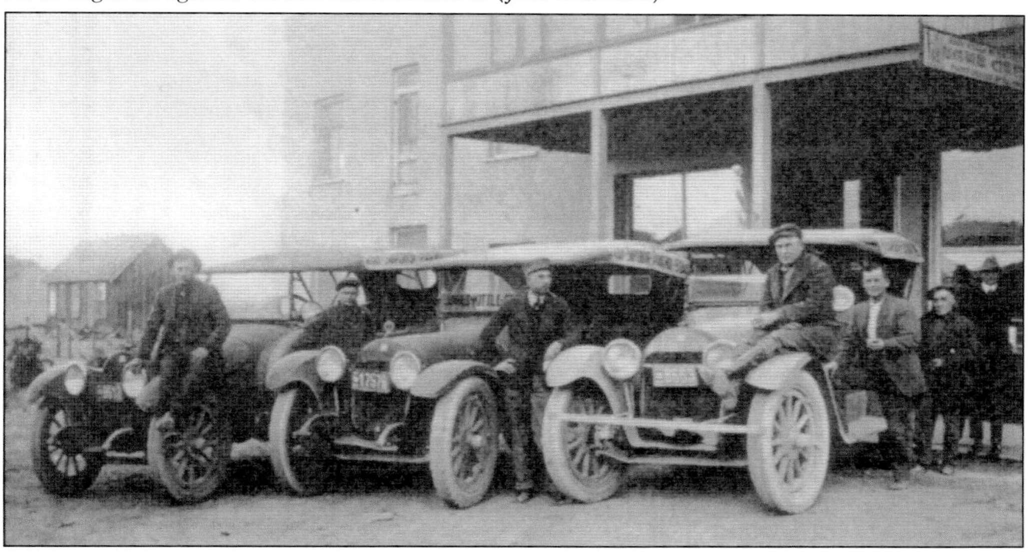

The Jones-Kettle Stage Lines, shown here in front of the Magma Hotel and Café in Superior, operated between Ray, Superior, and Phoenix. Sitting on the fender of the car at right is Marion Hickock, an electrician for Magma Copper Company; Tom Gray Sr. stands next to him, and Herman Flanders is to the right. Others in this photograph, taken in June 1917, are unidentified. (*Superior Sun*.)

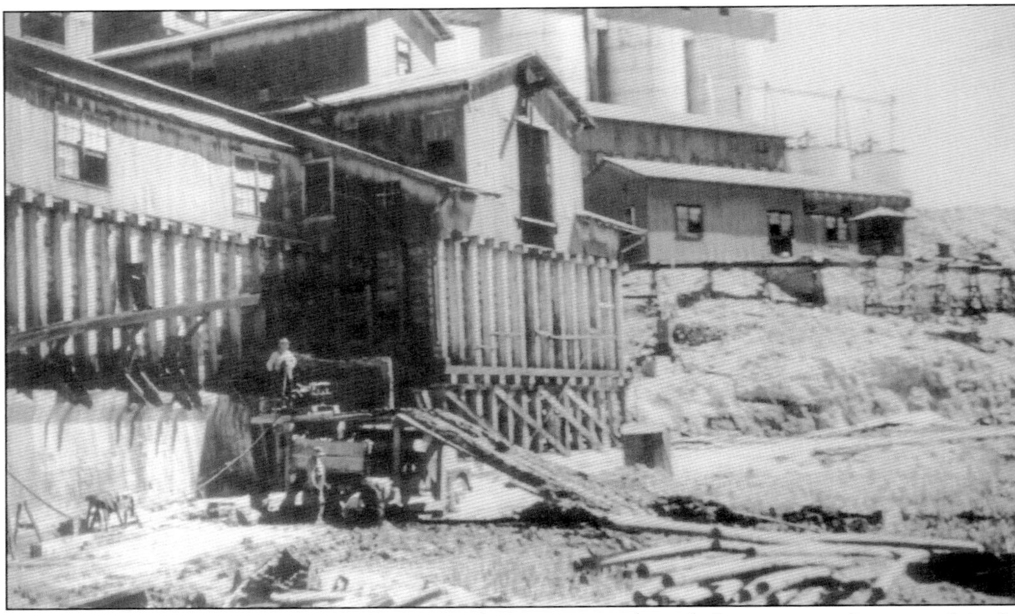

Previously the Silver Queen Mine, Boyce Thompson purchased this mine and renamed it the Magma. In 1910, under Magma, the no. 3 shaft was at 3,000 feet, and the mine had 8 miles of underground workings. Over 600 men were employed under a triple shift. Shown is the Magma Mill in the 1950s. (Richard C.)

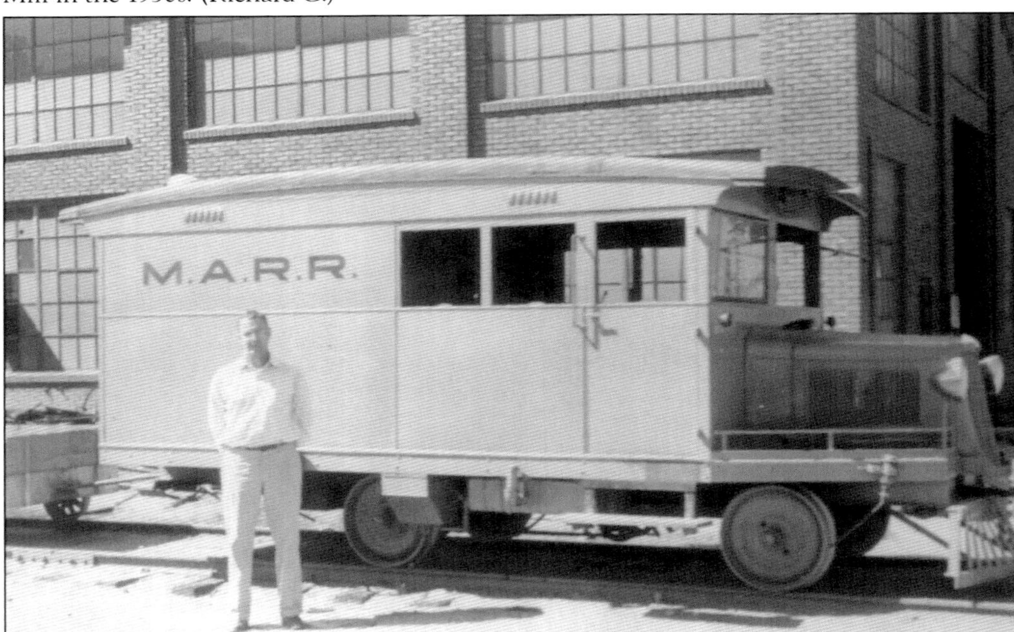

Richard Botkins of Queen Valley is shown here with the payroll/mail car for the Magma Mine. It was a popular sight to see on payday after a long, hard week of working in the mines. Much of the money made likely went back into the community's businesses as there were several hotels, 23 bars, dozens of restaurants, and a bordello operating until 1952. The mine closed in 1982 and reopened in 1990. (Richard C.)

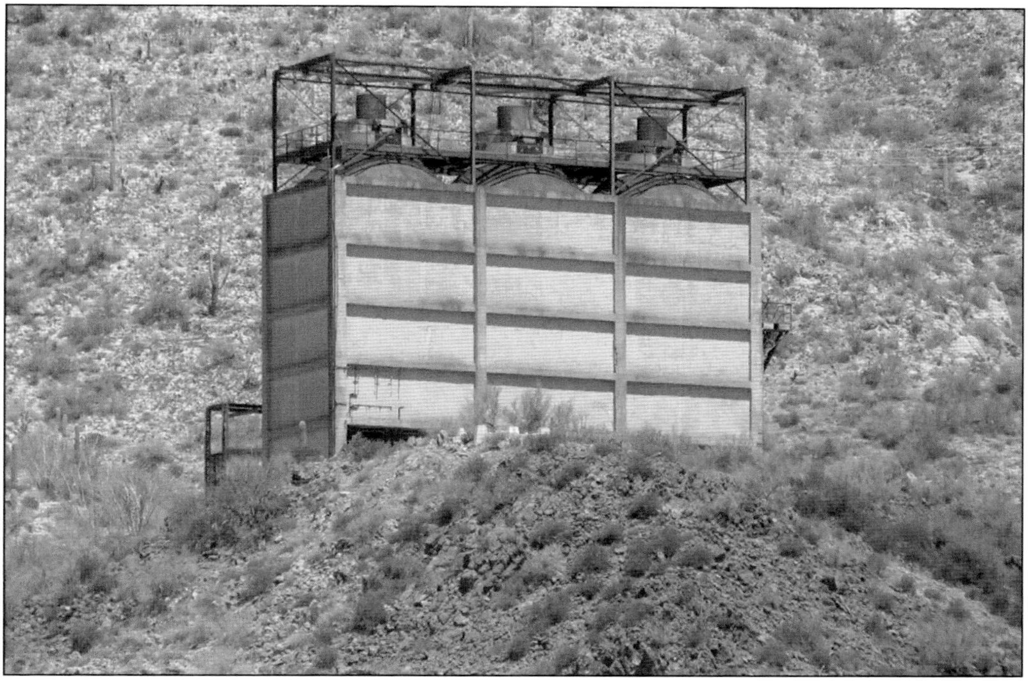

Having been dug deeper into the earth, the original 200-foot shaft began experiencing underground temperatures averaging 158 degrees. In 1936, an underground ventilation process was developed to cool mining levels with a vast refrigeration system. Even with this powerful system, some areas were shut down for safety reasons during the summer months. (Resolution CC Tour.)

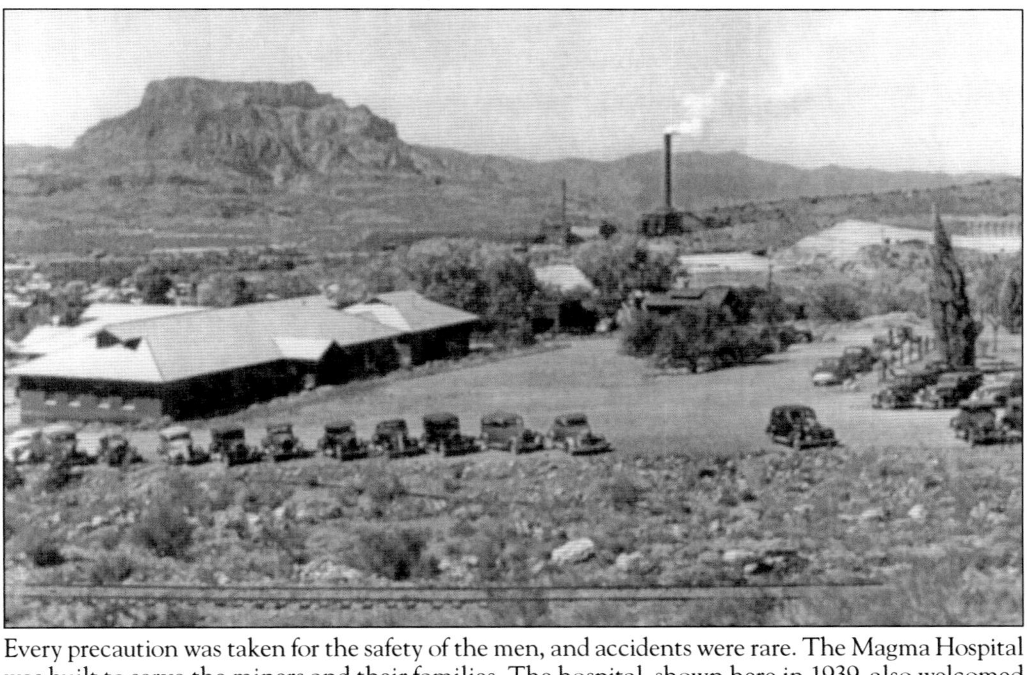

Every precaution was taken for the safety of the men, and accidents were rare. The Magma Hospital was built to serve the miners and their families. The hospital, shown here in 1939, also welcomed the entire community, regardless of mine affiliation. (K. Deffenbaugh and Richard C.)

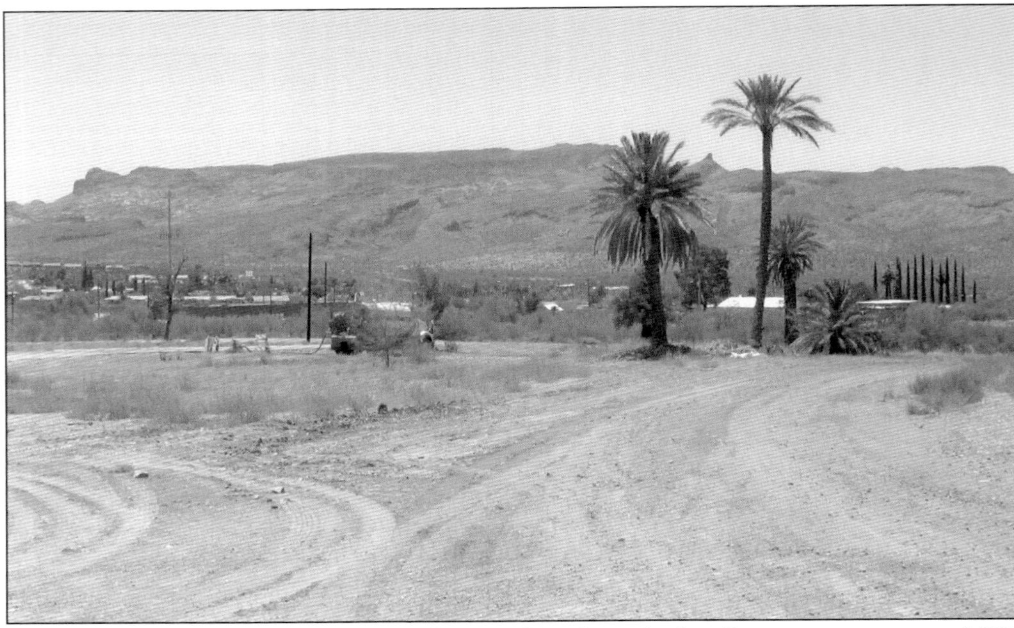

This area is all that is left of the original town of Smelter, which still appears on maps and GPS systems. Smelter was a close-knit community, located southwest of the Magma Mine. Many workers and their families lived here, which is where the roots of Superior started. (Copper Company Tour.)

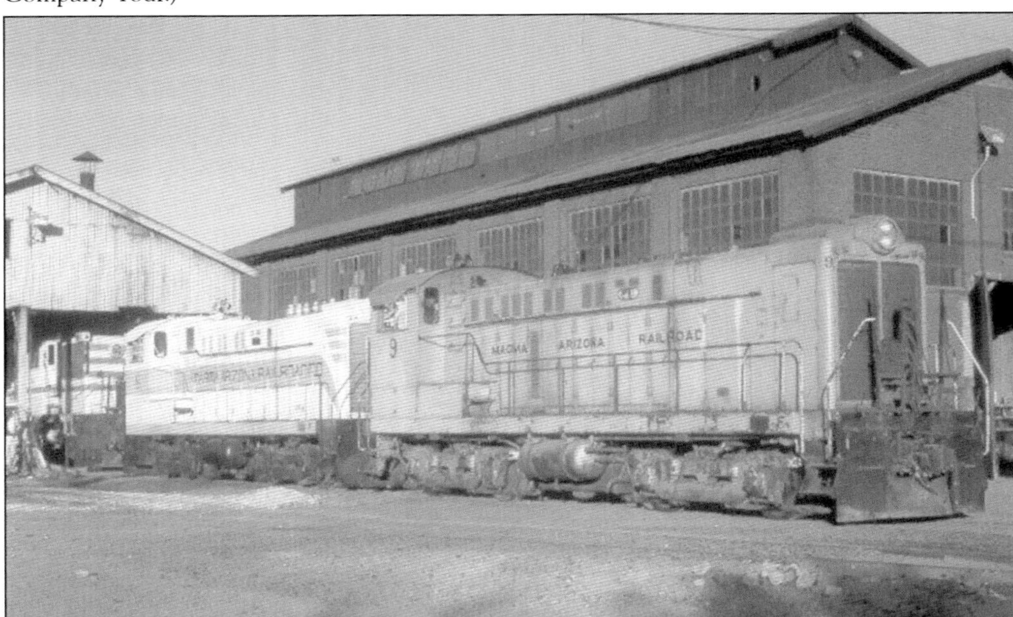

Prior to the Magma Arizona Railroad, ore was hauled 32 miles to Florence, keeping 20 to 30 teams of horses on the road all the time. Beginning in 1915, Arizona Eastern Railroad began and both served the mines. The cost of developing the 30-mile route was $300,000 and offered a mixed train service that handled mail and freight. Queen Valley resident Bruce Wittig worked for the railroad. (Wittig family collection.)

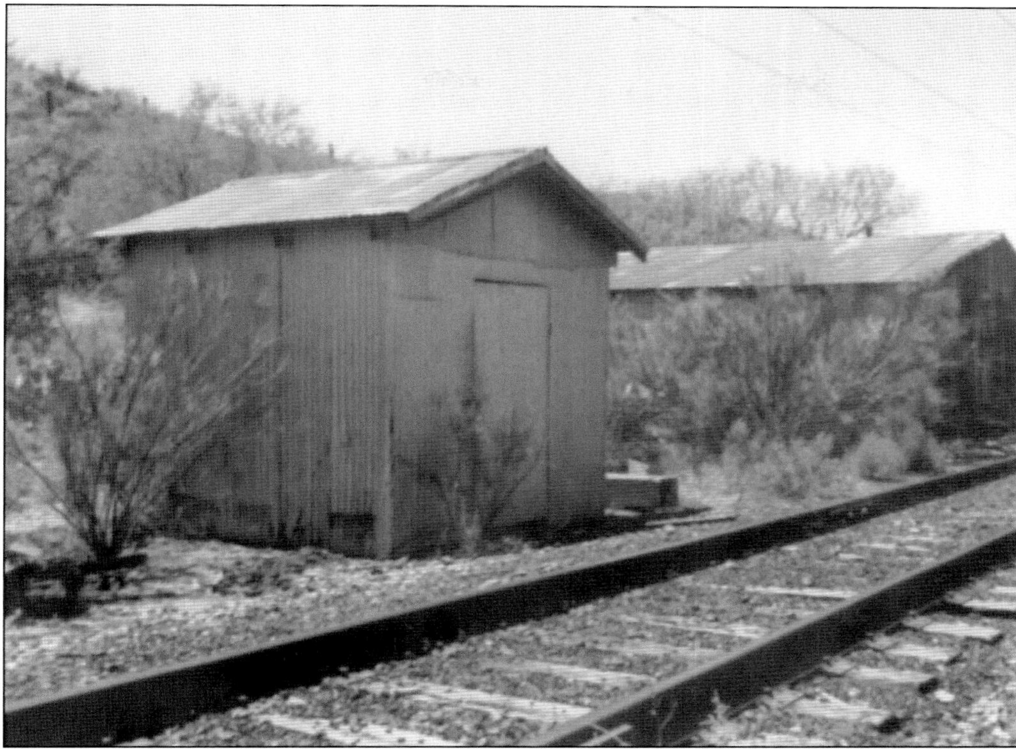

This was the Queen Station Railway building, located along the Hewitt Station Road, connecting the two towns. The Magma train ran from the mines in Superior to other railroad connections near Florence Junction. From there, the ore was transported to Yuma and California for processing. Returning trains carried lumber for building and supplies for the town's residents and businesses. Only the tracks remain today. (Wittig family collection.)

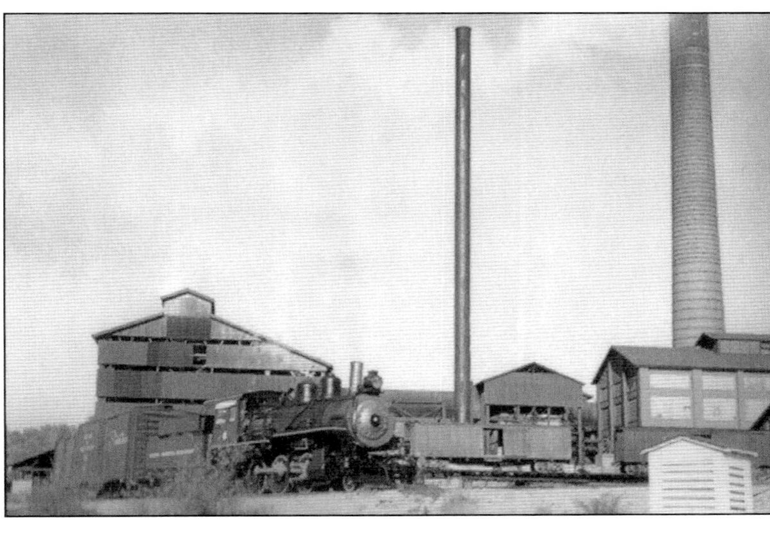

The Magma smelter was constructed in 1914. In 1970, Magma announced it had reserves of 9.5 million tons of ore, averaging 6 percent copper. Plans were also announced for the sinking of a new 4,800-foot shaft to extend the life of the mine. (Wittig family collection.)

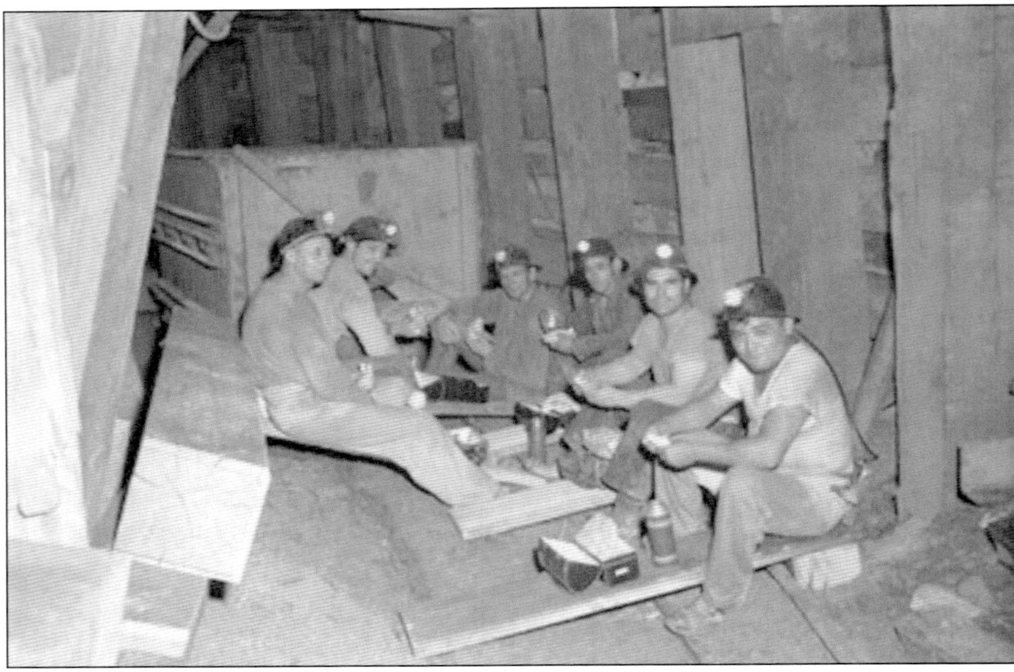

Old-timers still tell stories about how, during lunch breaks, much trading from lunch boxes took place. Each miner would bring his own culture's traditional foods, and, enticed by the allure of trying different things, bologna and fry bread were traded for egg rolls and burros. Indian, Chinese, Mexican, and caucasian workers of various decent learned to boil eggs and heat up cans of soup in the hot water deep underground. (SF.)

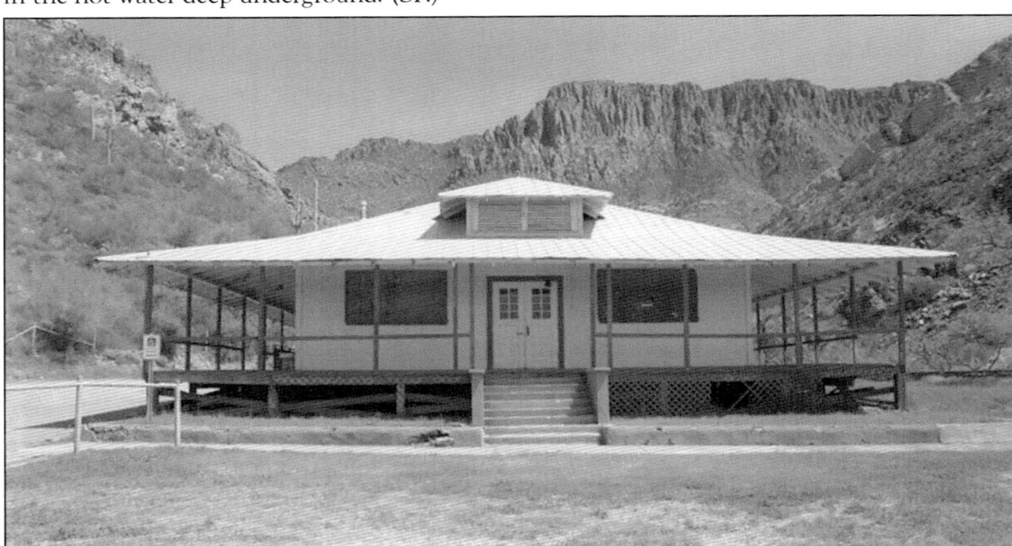

The Magma Club, completed in 1920, provided a social club for Magma employees. It was the center of Superior's social life and featured a swimming pool, tennis court, and horseshoe pit. They held movies, dances, and prizefights, entertaining the townspeople for over 60 years. The mine closed in 1982, and the Magma Club in 1985. The Magma Club was donated to Superior. (Eddie Gomez.)

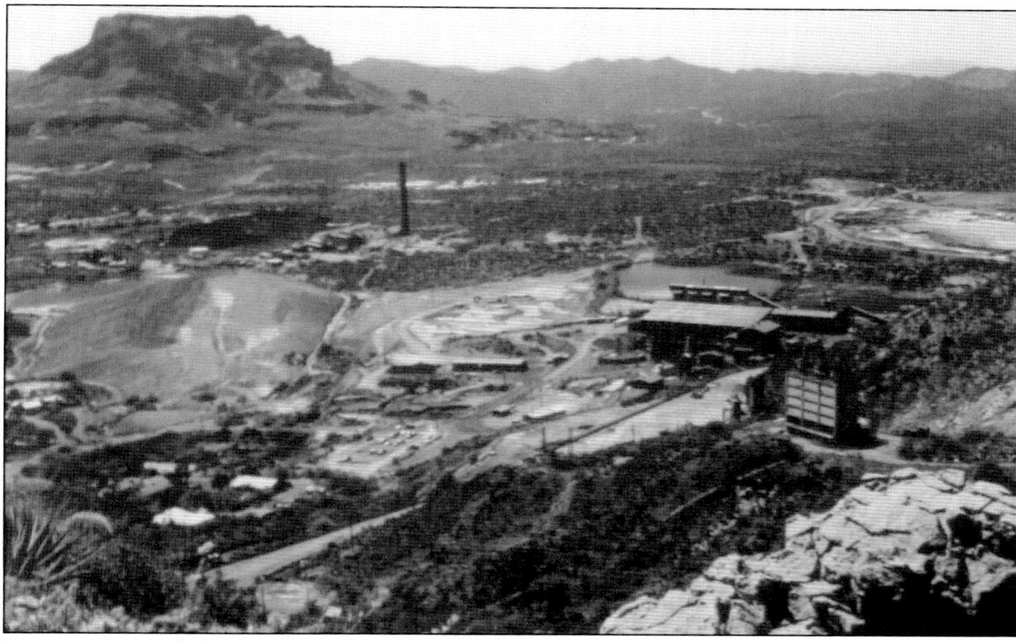

Magma was in full production by the 1930s and was a vital part of Superior's and the state's economies. In a U.S. Census of Mines and Quarries done in the 1930s, Arizona was reported as employing 17,566 people in the mining industry. This was followed by Montana at 14,139, Utah at 9,238, Colorado at 8,433, Idaho at 6,514, Nevada at 6,059, and New Mexico at 3,817. In the picture above, notice the road that cuts in front of the Picket Post Mountain and runs through the Gonzales Pass, connecting Superior with Queen Valley and Phoenix beyond. (Above, Jack San Felice; below, Richard C.)

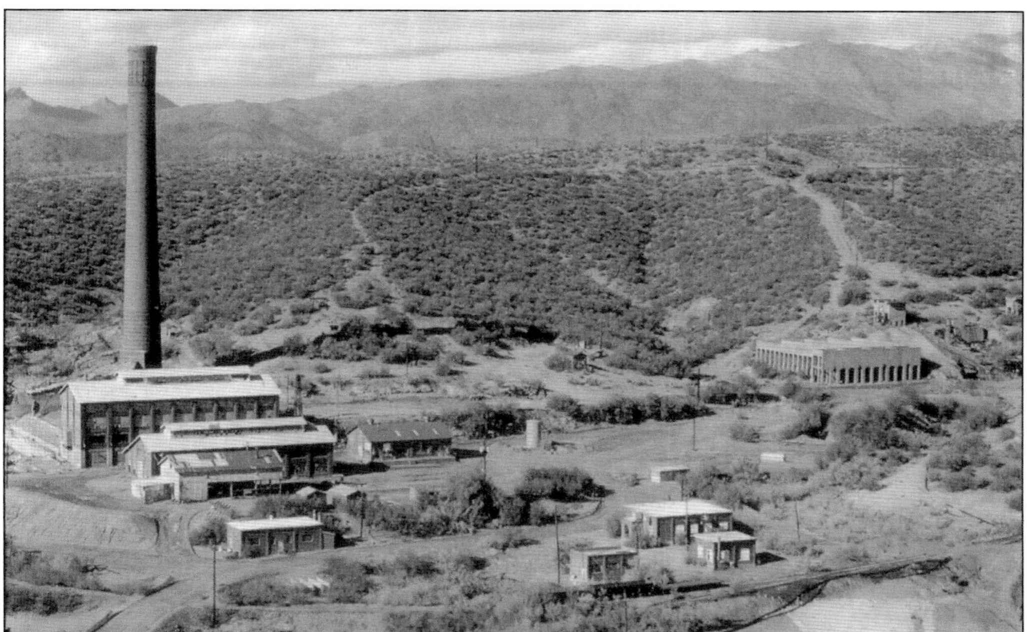

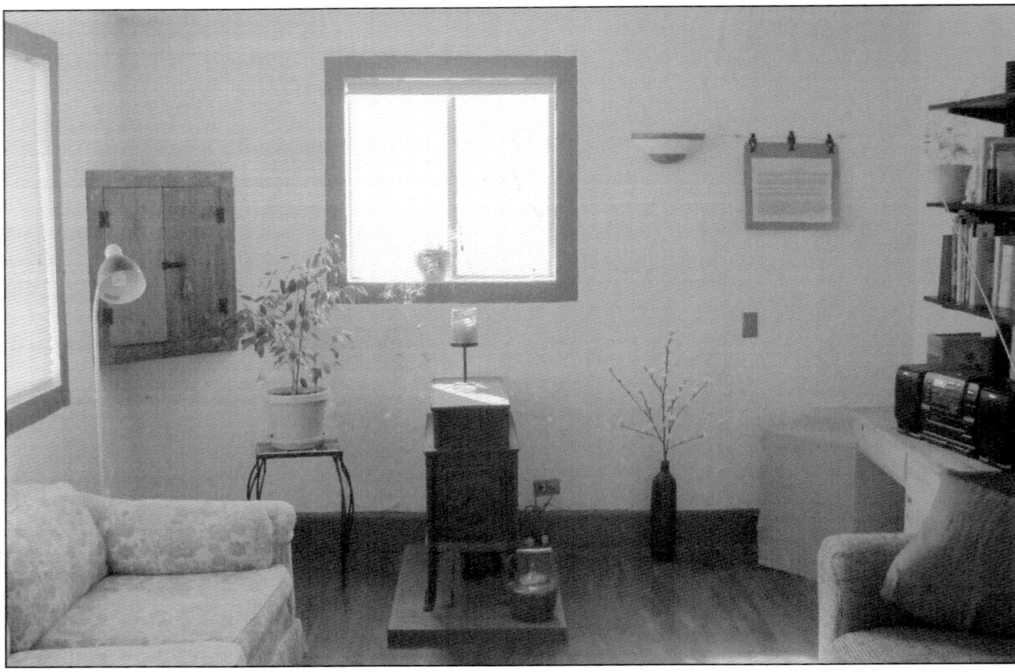

This miner's home at 56/58 Rainbow Street housed a family of 10. Well designed and compact for heating and cooling purposes, it would have been cozy and comfortable. When visiting from Chicago, the mine owner's wife rode with the car window blinds pulled down, shielding her eyes from the "rough conditions." (Margaret Pemberton.)

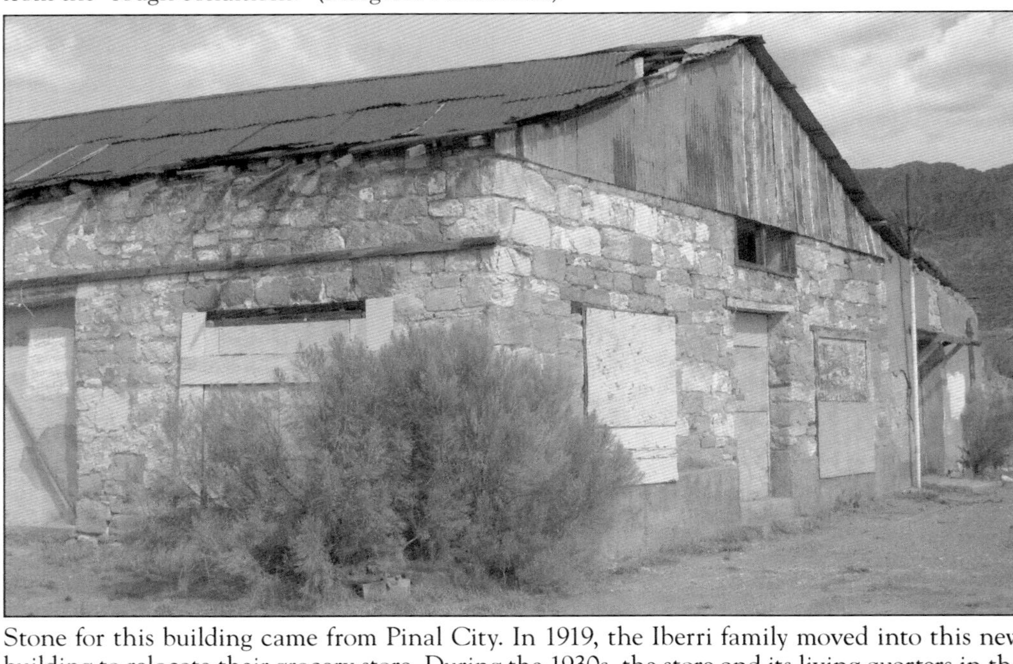

Stone for this building came from Pinal City. In 1919, the Iberri family moved into this new building to relocate their grocery store. During the 1930s, the store and its living quarters in the back were rented to the Sawaia family who ran a grocery store from the building. Son Carlos Iberri ran the store until the mid-1980s, when the building was purchased by Glen Wilt.

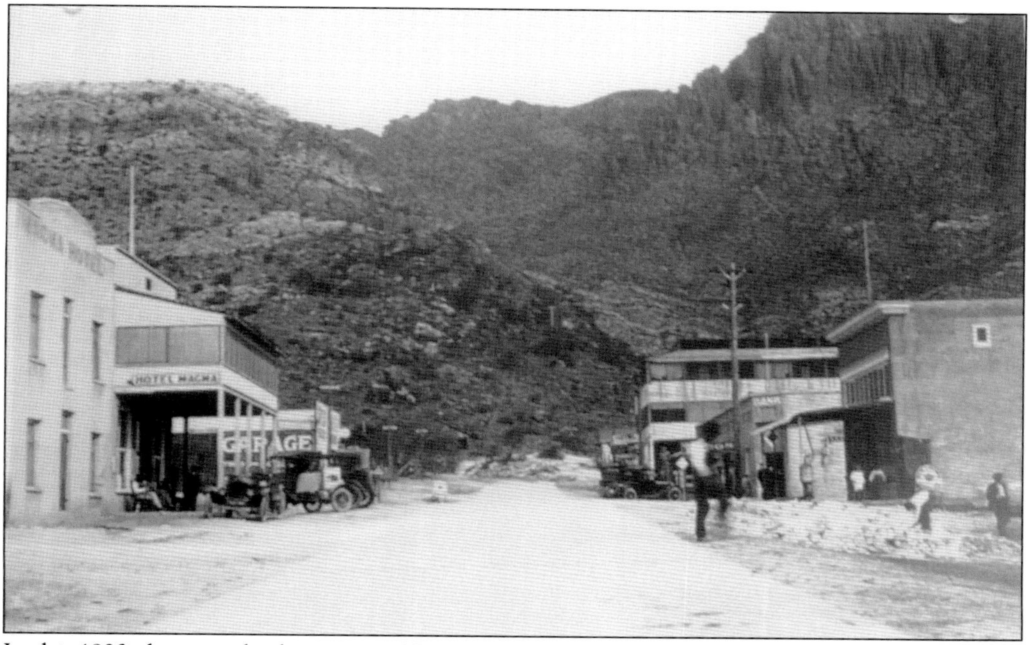

In this 1923 photograph, the streets of Superior are paved, but sidewalks are not yet in place. The Magma Hotel is still in its original shape, and the redbrick addition had not yet been built. The restaurant at the right was owned by O. C. Hing. (*Superior Sun*.).

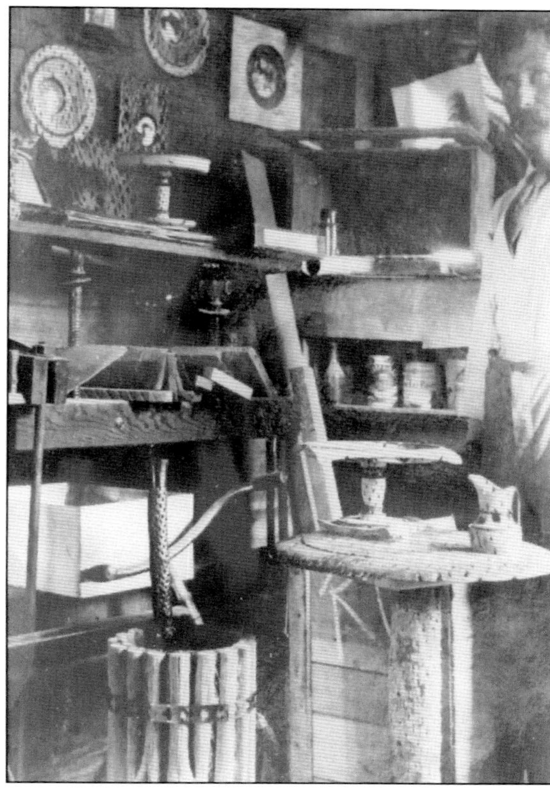

Many people like this Superior butcher chose to set up shops and services for the miners, ranchers, and their families. These shopkeepers, laundresses, inn keepers, cooks, and other service providers made their living by making life easier for others in these rugged pioneer towns. They helped establish the communities that are still in existence today. (Martin Collection.)

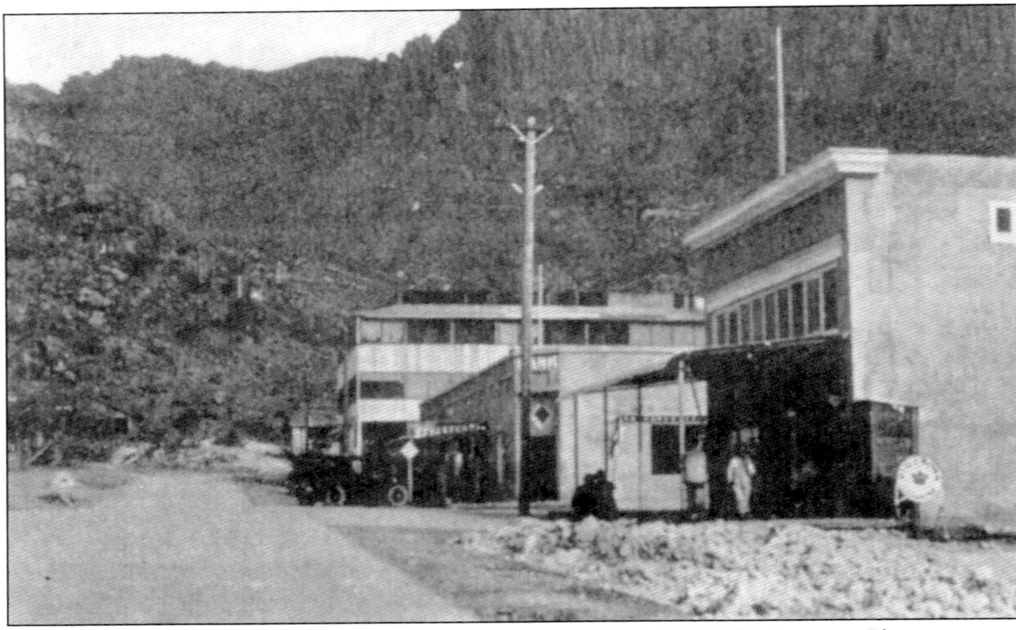

In 1923, this building was the Kellner's Mercantile. In 1970, it was the Superior Pharmacy, and across the street is the Union Bank. While the businesses occupying Superior's historic buildings change over the years, the character and charm of the town remains intact, waiting patiently for its revival. (*Superior Sun.*)

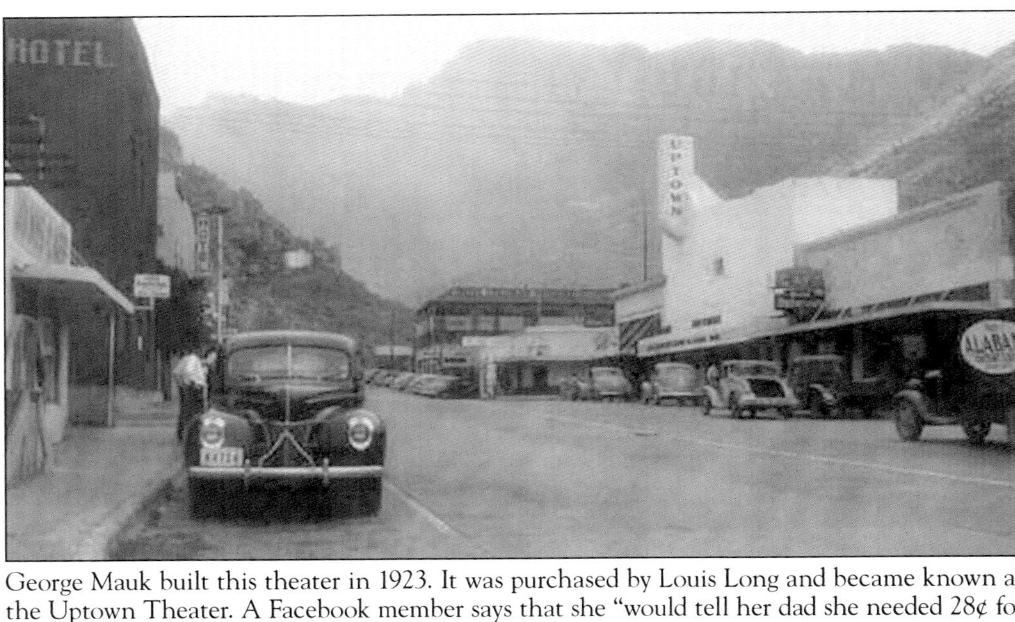

George Mauk built this theater in 1923. It was purchased by Louis Long and became known as the Uptown Theater. A Facebook member says that she "would tell her dad she needed 28¢ for the movie, which covered the movie, popcorn, soda, candy, and tax." Long also opened a drive-in theater in 1952, west of Superior. Both have been closed for over 20 years. (ADMMR.)

Originally a grocery store owned by Junior Assyd, this building was repainted for the movie *U-Turn* that was filmed in Superior. Because the town has kept is western mining charm and the chamber welcomes productions, the film industry has made a large number of movies here including the epic *How the West Was Won*. There is even a set building company on Main Street today. Pictured is Tim Fitzgerald, a mountain man reenactor.

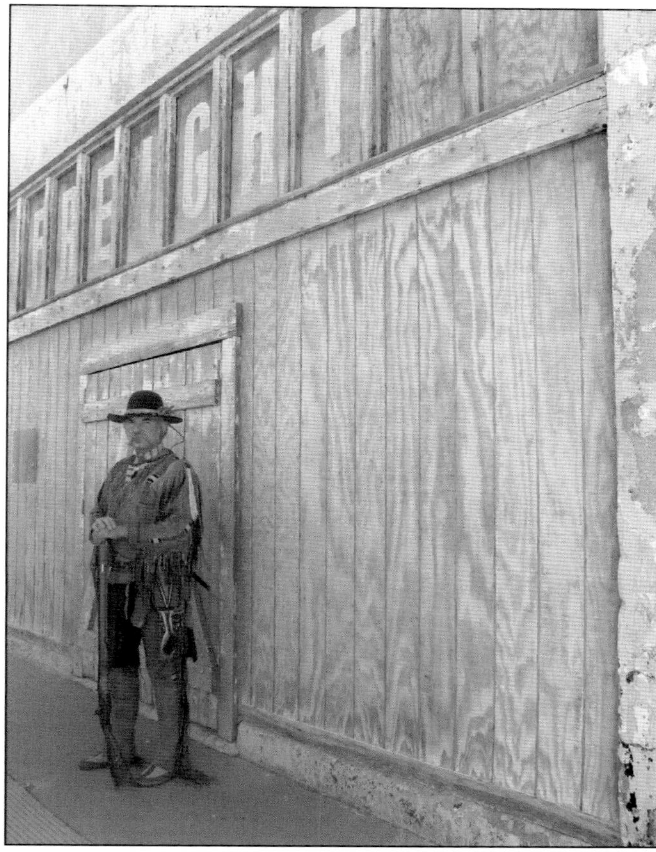

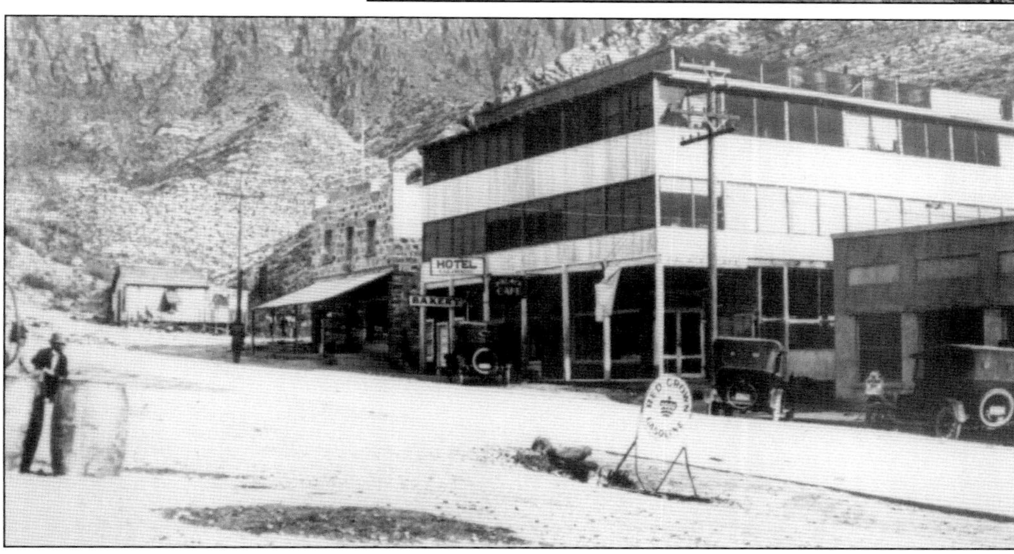

The Coleman Hotel, owned by Mary Coleman, offered rooms for single men upstairs. The street floor housed the Palace Cafe where many of the Magma Mine workers ate. It had a well-stocked bakery that was popular with the townsfolk. The stone building at the end is the grocery store that was owned for many years by Mr. and Mrs. Tom Dowling. (*Superior Sun*.)

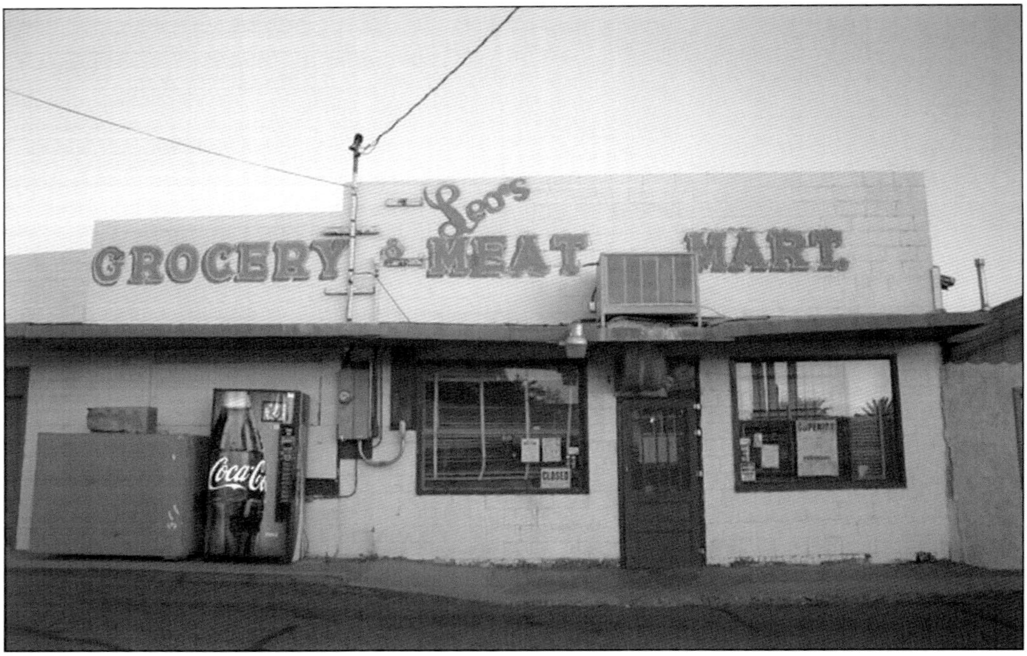

In 1928, the Sawaia family opened their first grocery store in Superior and sold it to Charlie Haynes in the 1930s, when they moved to the building that is now identified as Iberri's Grocery. Haynes ran a store here until 1948, when Ramon Lopez purchased the building. He and a friend Edward Garcia and brother-in-law Leo Gonzales opened the market in 1948. A 1982 addition to the north side of the building doubled the space. (SF.)

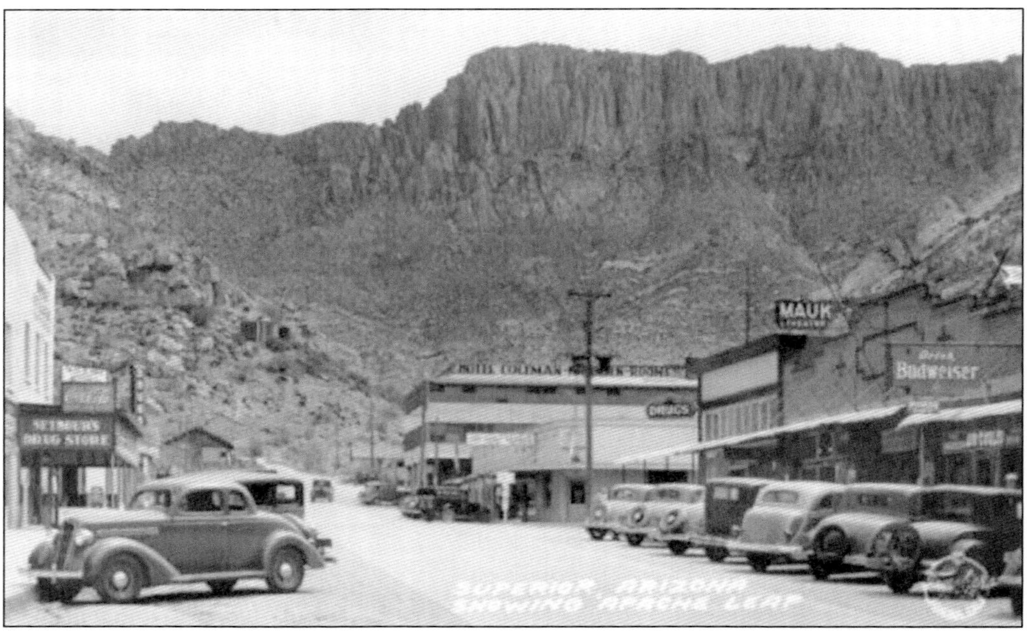

This 1930s-era photograph shows a busy day on Main Street. This was the time of heavy mining by the Magma Copper Company; so many people came to town on business and for pleasure. (SF.)

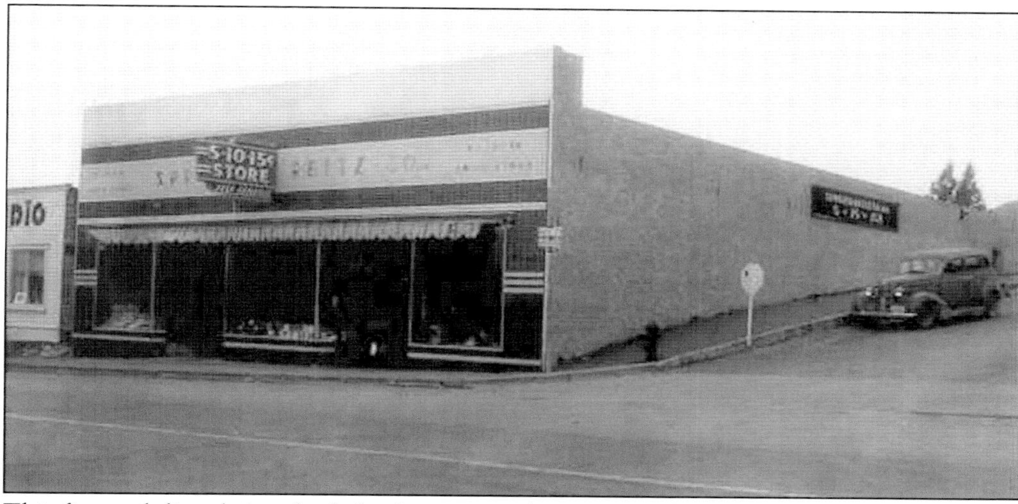

This five-and-dime brings back fond memories for many as the place to go after school. One Superior Facebook member says, "We would go there every day at lunch to buy candies. When I was nine or ten, two guys got in a fight on Main Street, and one of them came flying through the glass door in front of us." (ADMMR.)

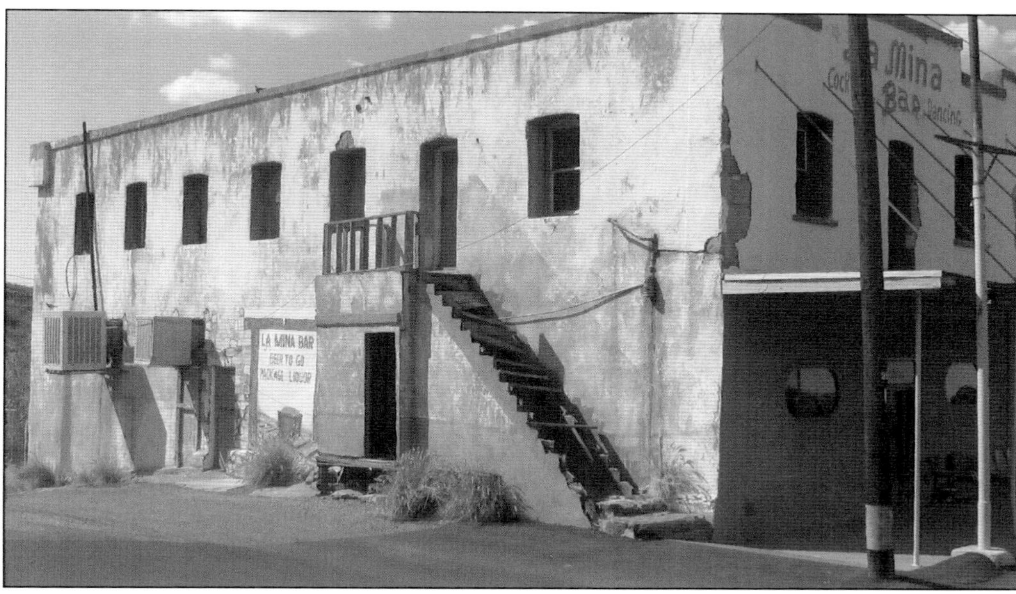

Built from salvaged Pinal City stone and first opened as Dahling's Grocery Store, this building had several upstairs rooms for club meetings. Interestingly, the upstairs was only accessible by the outside staircase. For a time, the Griffee family operated Griffee's Market here. Later the building became the Town Tavern Lounge, owned by Mary Coleman. In 1946, the Haddad family purchased and created the La Mina Lounge. Manny Chaidez has owned it for 31 years.

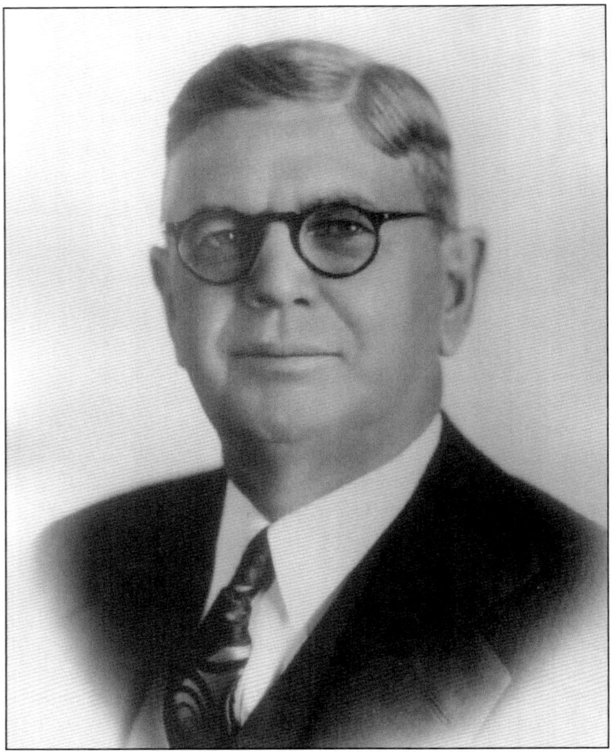

Robert Taylor Jones came to the Arizona Territory in 1909 as a railroad surveyor. He worked on the Globe and Gila Valley Railroad. In 1911, he married Elon Armstrong, settled in Superior, and had two children. He worked for Ray Consolidated Mines and the Southern Pacific Railroad prior to opening a drugstore in Superior. He became a state senator and served as the sixth governor of Arizona from 1938 to 1939. (PCHS.)

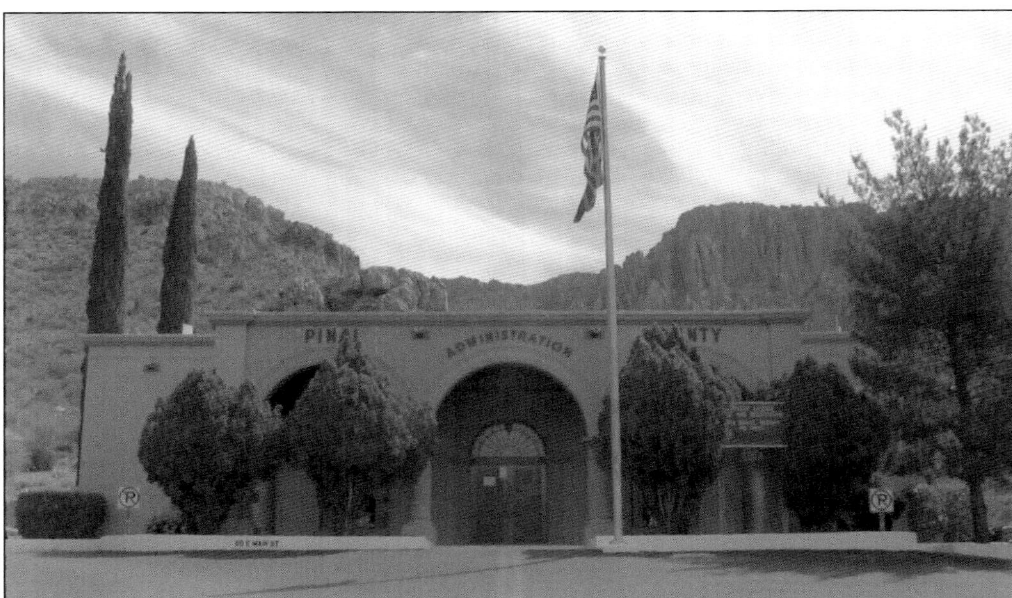

The Superior Municipal Court was built in the 1970s. The court handles criminal misdemeanors, traffic citations, and city code violations. For more serious issues, townspeople travel to the Pinal County Courthouse in Florence, which was completed in 1891. In June 1899, Pearl Hart was jailed and hung there for robbing a stagecoach near Queen Valley; she remains the only woman in Arizona to be executed.

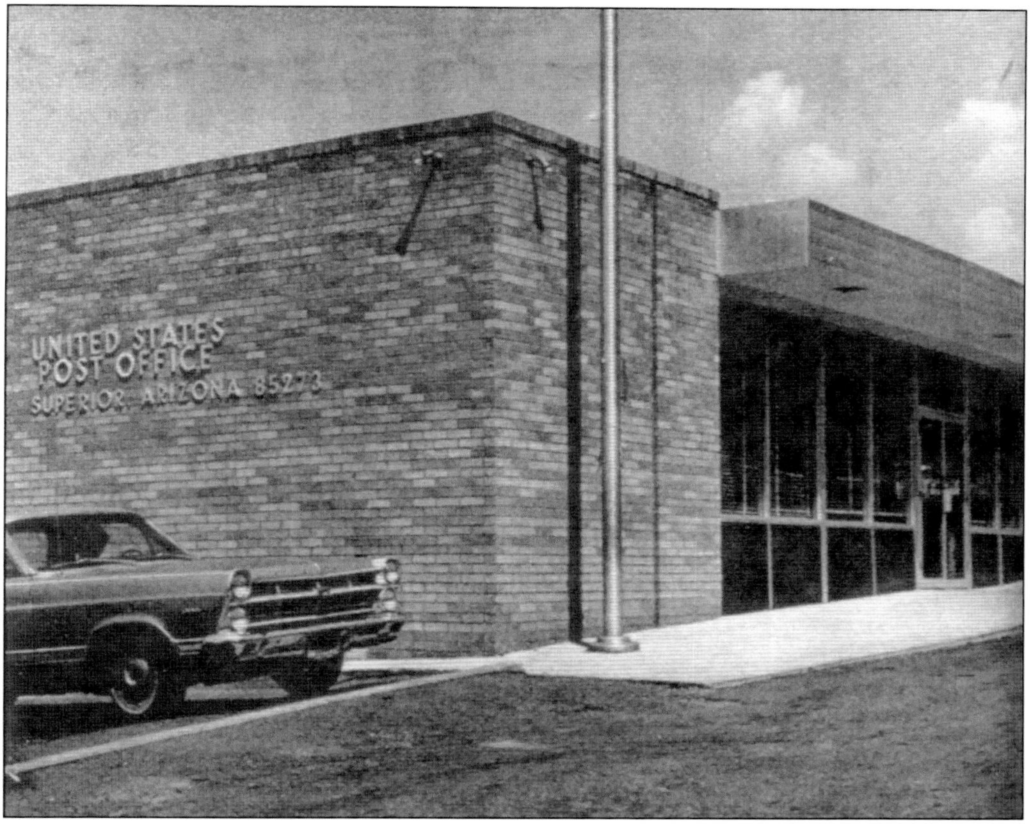

The post office in Superior opened in 1965 at a cost of $56,000. Prior to this new building, the post office was a small office that changed locations periodically. Dorothy Ybarra was the assistant to the postmaster and supervised route delivery. Paula Tapia was a distribution clerk, Florence Aldrete and Lucy Sinteral sorted, and Frances Tomerlin delivered mail. (*Superior Sun*.)

Postmaster Gladys Jeffries Walker, a former editor for the *Superior Sun* newspaper, developed a precise schedule for processing and delivering the mail to the town. The Superior Post Office is a vital part of the U.S. Postal Service and a welcome employer to the people living in Superior. Gladys was born in Superior and raised in Hewitt Station. (*Superior Sun*.)

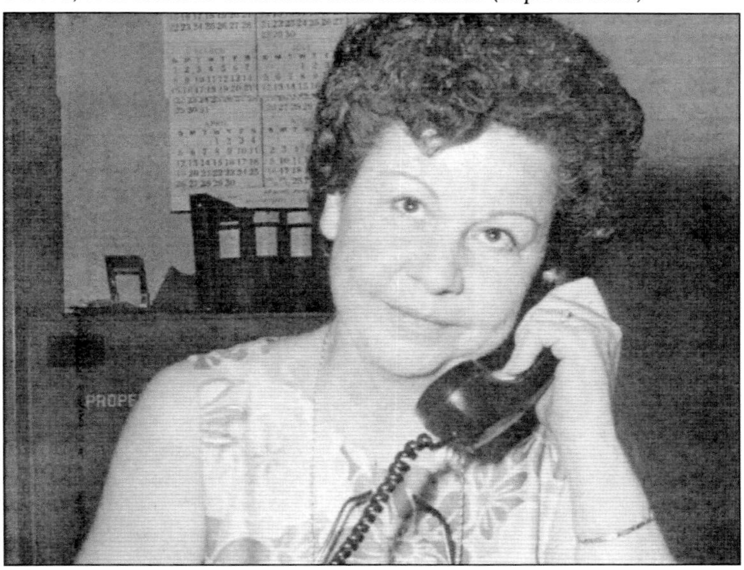

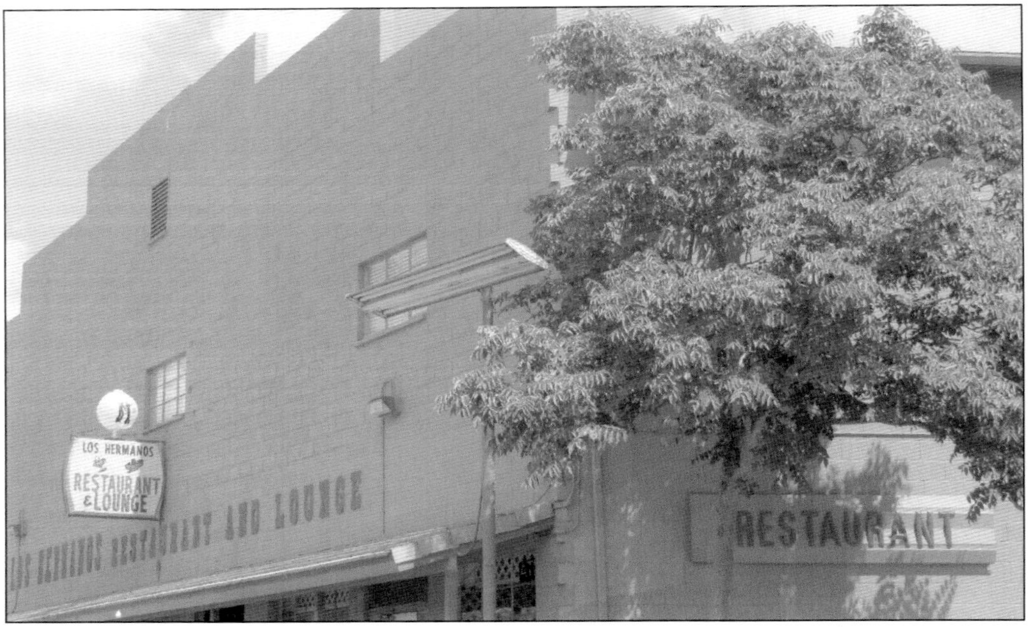

Originally the Copper Valley Tavern that was run by Josie Pino in the 1950s, the Los Hermanos was established by Mary Tameron in 1976. Over the years, it has been run by her sons Tony Donlin and Eddie, Joe, Richard (manager), John, and Rudy Tameron. Having a location next to the Route 60 rest stop makes it convenient for visitors and residents to keep the restaurant busy constantly.

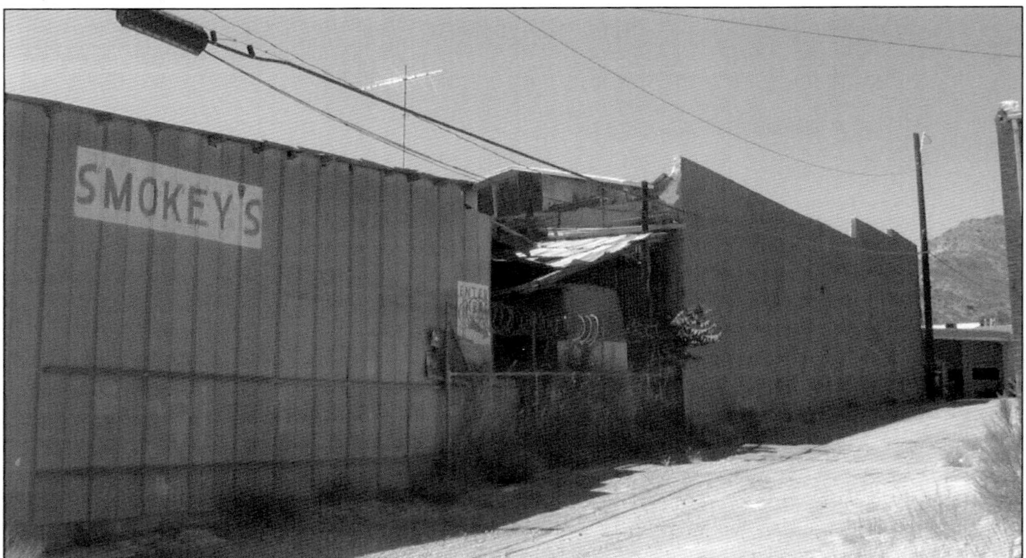

Hartwell "Smokey" Deffenbaugh, a full-time employee of Magma, was the owner of Smokey's. His wife, Florence, ran the appliance store while he repaired appliances on his days off. In 1963, their son Landis started a lumber and hardware business at the same location. In the early 1970s, a fire gutted the building. They moved across the street, continuing to run the business for many years.

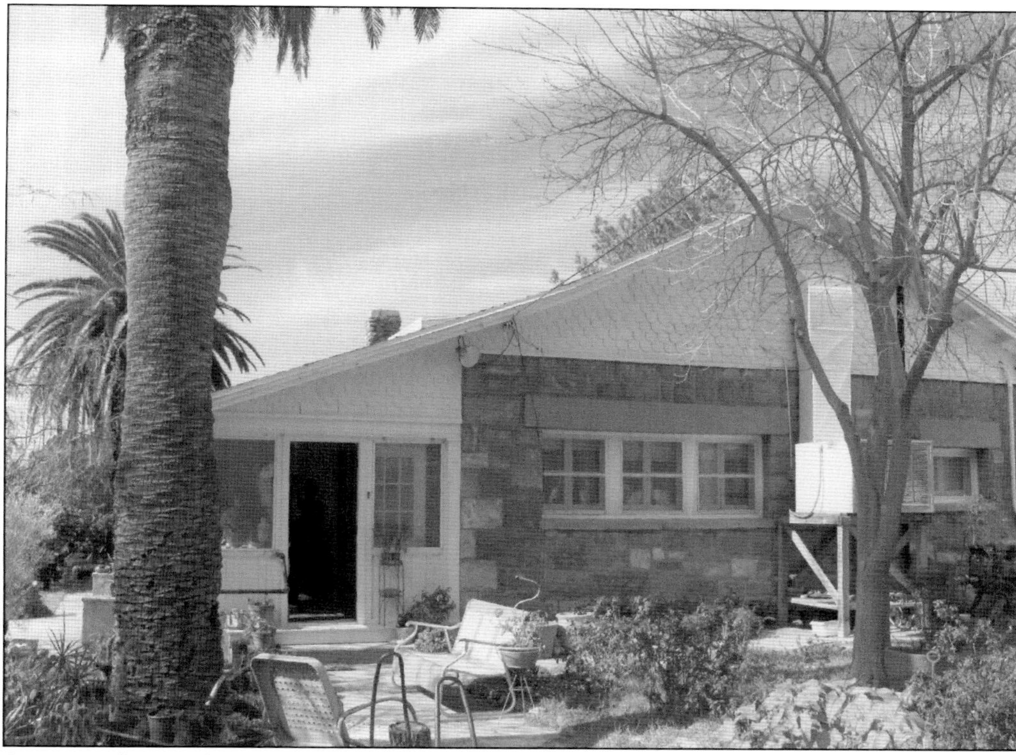

Sara M. Kellner, wife of Ernest Kellner Jr., purchased this lot from the U.S. government in 1916. The home was built with rocks from abandoned buildings in Pinal City. Ernest, a prominent businessman, brought a water system to Superior. An apartment on the lot was rented to single teachers. Hardware store owner O. C. Banks later occupied this home until the 1980s. (Polly Drachovich.)

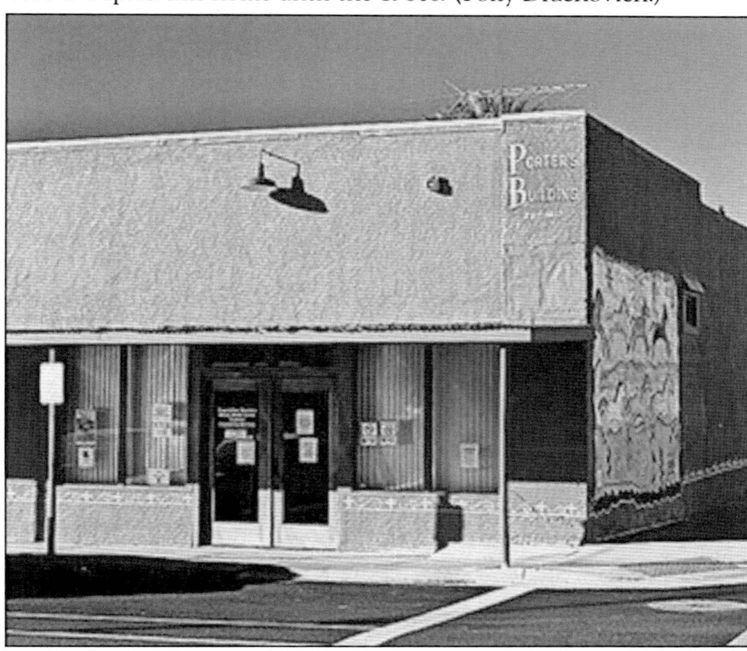

Mrs. Porter had a furniture store on Main Street, where Manny Ruiz's wife, Aurora, worked for a number of years. Mr. Porter had a gas station nearby. The building retains the Porter name and currently houses the Resolution Copper Company and Lyn Heglie's Porters Bar and Grill.

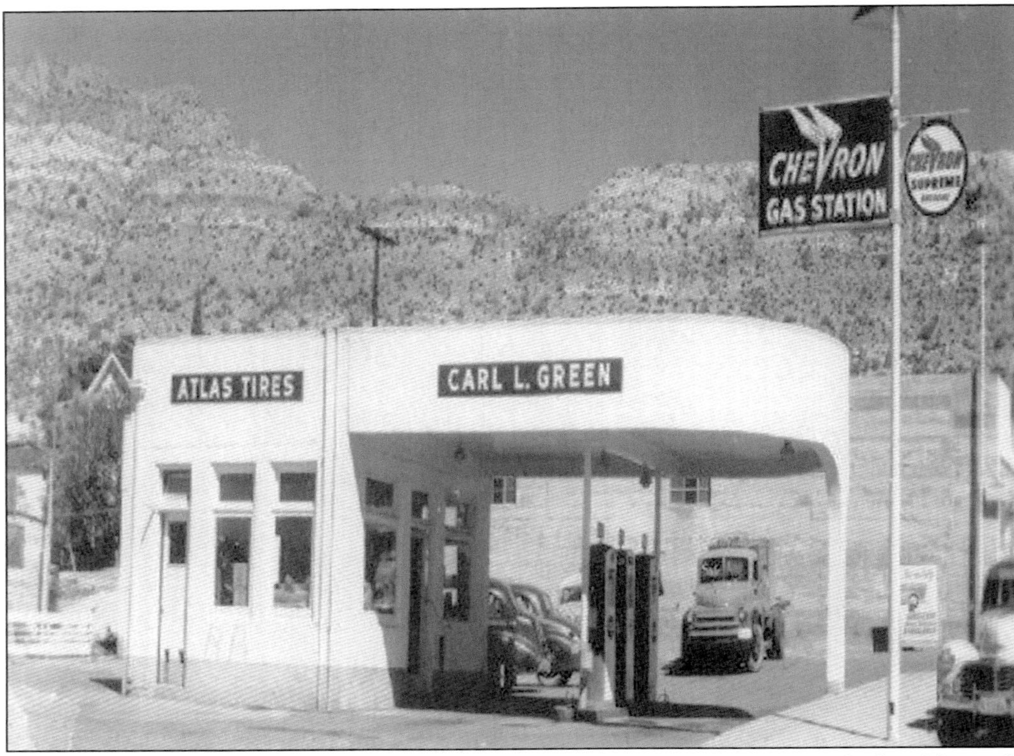

Carl Leeman Green was born January 6, 1918, in Thatcher, Arizona. In 1942, Carl and his wife, Ruby Phillips Green, moved to Superior, which was where Carl worked at a Standard service station until they returned to Thatcher in June 1949. This property is now Besich Park. The last owners, the Besich family, donated it to the town. (Wittig family collection.)

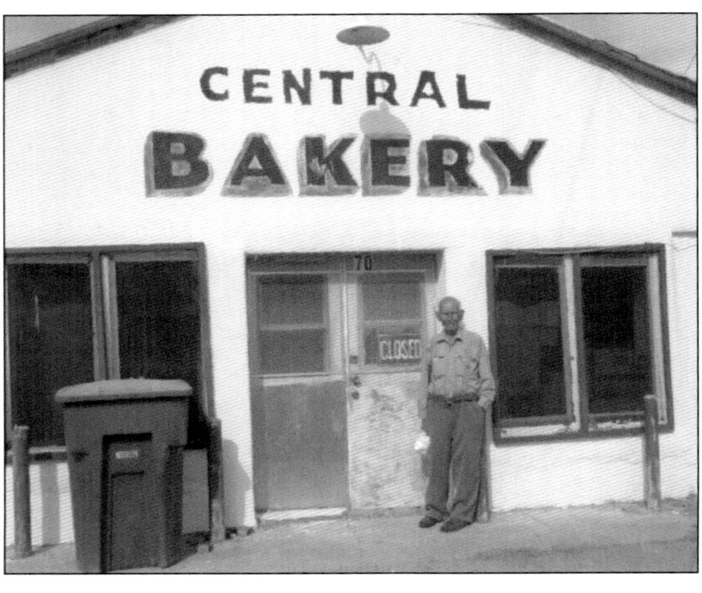

Juan Cardenas, according to many, was a hard worker and deserved the utmost respect. Some can remember fondly the aroma of the Central Bakery that wafted throughout the neighborhood. Maria Hjelle says memories of her grandfather's bakery, him in his little white hat, are fond ones. She believes that her grandfather loved "his" town and "his" friends, and everyone knew it. Even folks from Queen Valley traveled there for the cream puffs every Friday.

This building served as the Pass Time Bar and Hotel. Its brothel upstairs did not close until the 1950s. Stories are told that on Mondays the women were escorted down the street to the bank and were very careful not to publicly recognize any of the townspeople who were their customers. Schoolchildren watched with whispered giggles as they walked by. It now serves as the town hall.

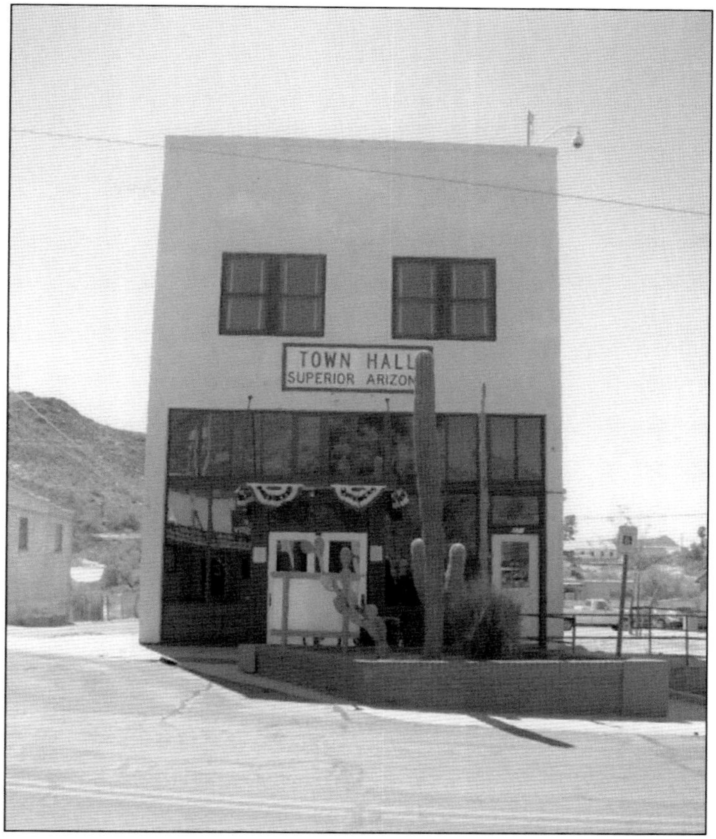

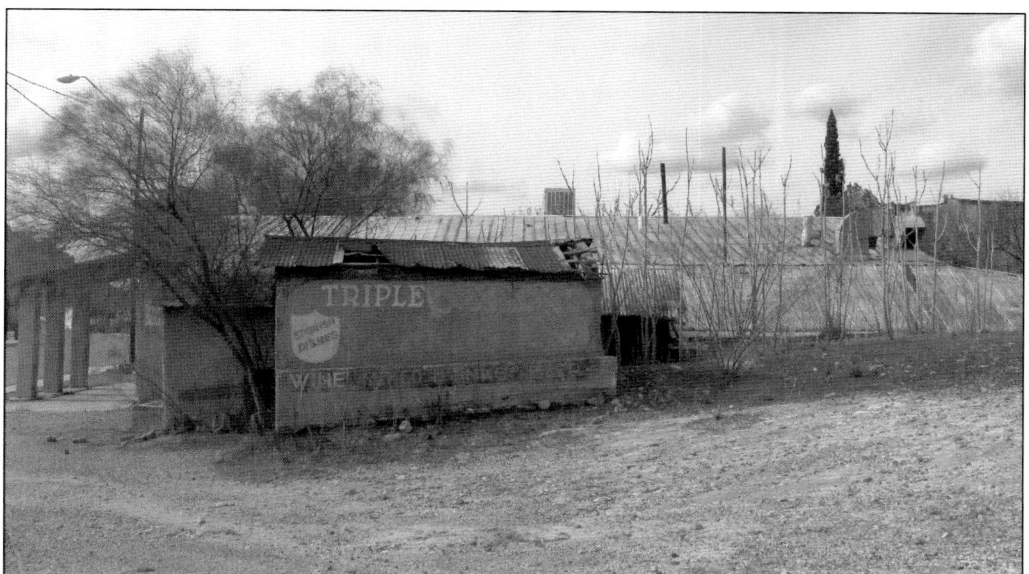

During the 1980s, when owners Olivia and Nana Rosie Nuñez were at the Triple X bar, they had a contract to make the children's lunches at the bar for the school cafeteria. The bar was a very popular place to congregate for locals and visitors from Phoenix, alike.

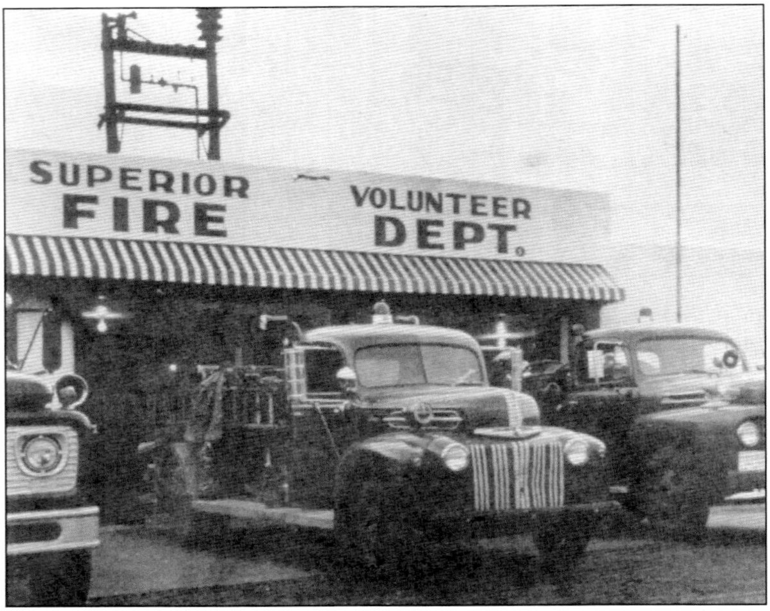

In the 1970s, about 20 volunteers answered the sound of the fire alarm. Truck No. 1, located in the center, was purchased in 1942 for $4,800, and a newer truck was purchased in the 1970s for $20,000. The Superior Fire Department was started in 1915, and the Superior Fire District was started in 1941. They now employ around six full-time and four part-time firefighters. (*Superior Sun.*)

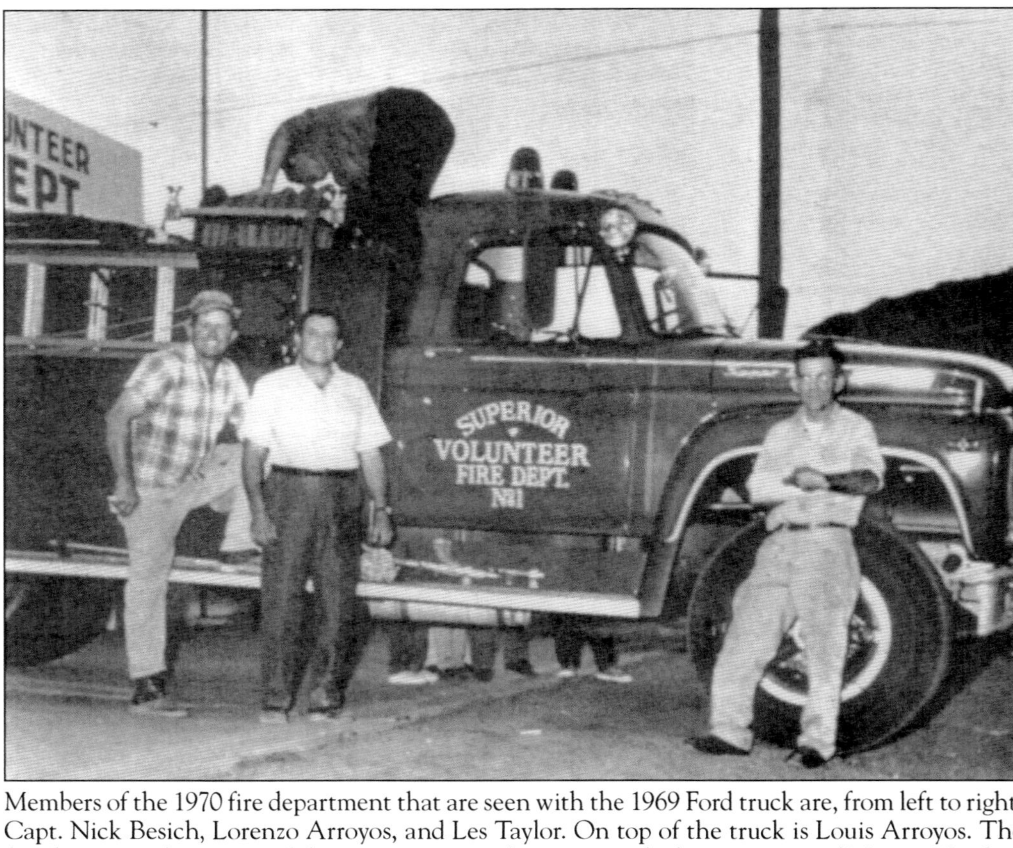

Members of the 1970 fire department that are seen with the 1969 Ford truck are, from left to right, Capt. Nick Besich, Lorenzo Arroyos, and Les Taylor. On top of the truck is Louis Arroyos. The fire district took in most of the community at that time, with the exception of Magma Heights. (*Superior Sun.*)

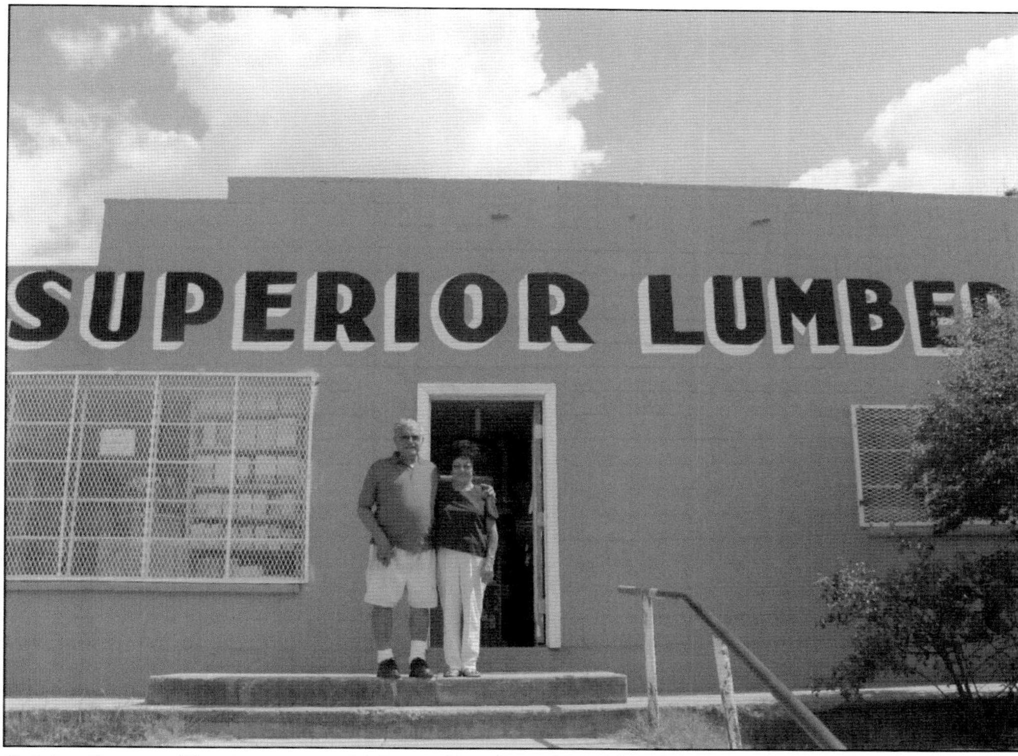

Originally owned by Antonio and Maggie Sanchez, Arnold and Margaret Salazar of Queen Valley purchased Superior Lumber and reopened it on Labor Day 1966. Providing a critical service to the community, they are well known for being helpful and patient, even with those looking for a left-handed hammer!

The 1969 Superior High School basketball team included the following members: Danny Real, Mike Mitchell, Donnie Palacios, Joe Sanchez, Gary Antilla, Hank Gutierrez, Elias Alonzo, Manuel Pelayo, and Bobby Fontes. Shown holding the basketball, Manny Ruiz coached football and basketball for 10 years. He spent 17 summers working underground in the Magma Mine and served as mayor and city council member several times. (SF.)

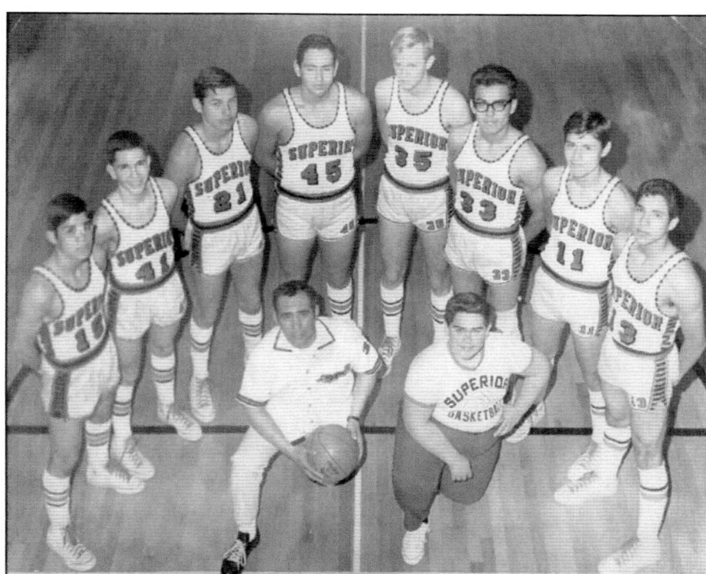

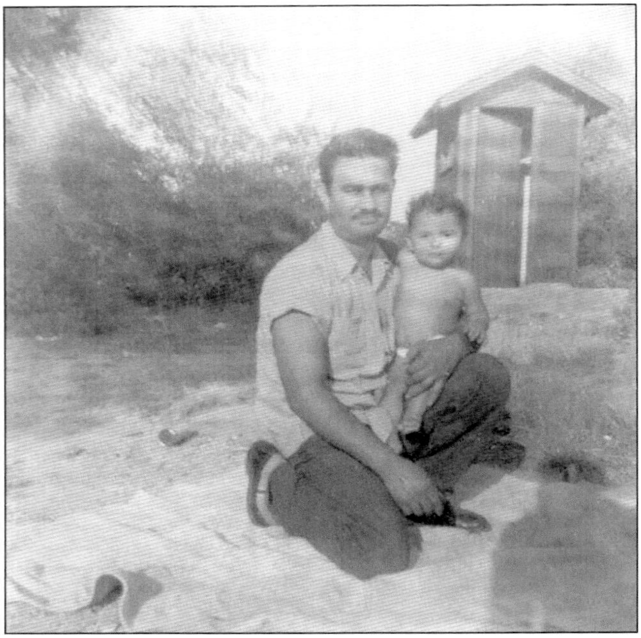

The townspeople worked hard and also played hard in the nearby Tonto National Forest. Shown here is Mary Gomez as an infant with her father at the Oak Flats campground. Many Superior families share fond memories of family outings at the Oak Flats campground. Tonto National Forest was a close getaway for camping and day trips for people of Superior. (Mary Gomez.)

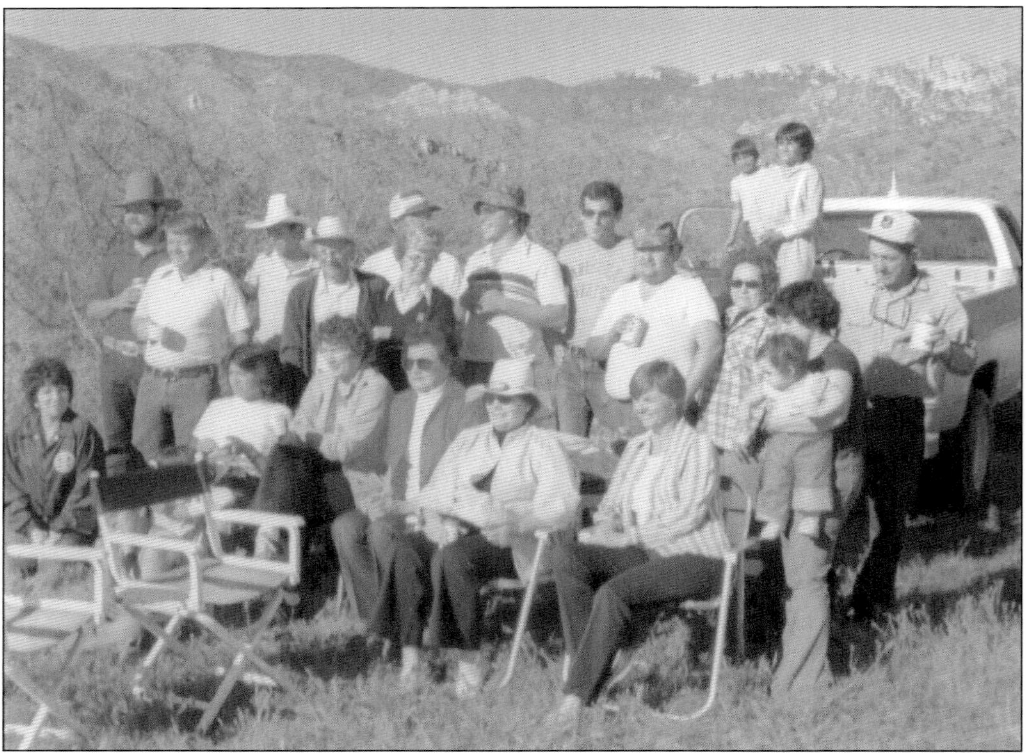

The area around Superior has wonderful recreation opportunities. This photograph shows the Besich, Martinez, and Nuñez families on a picnic and four-wheeling trip to the nearby Tonto National Forest. These are the kinds of activities that bind both friends and communities through the ages. (Besich family.)

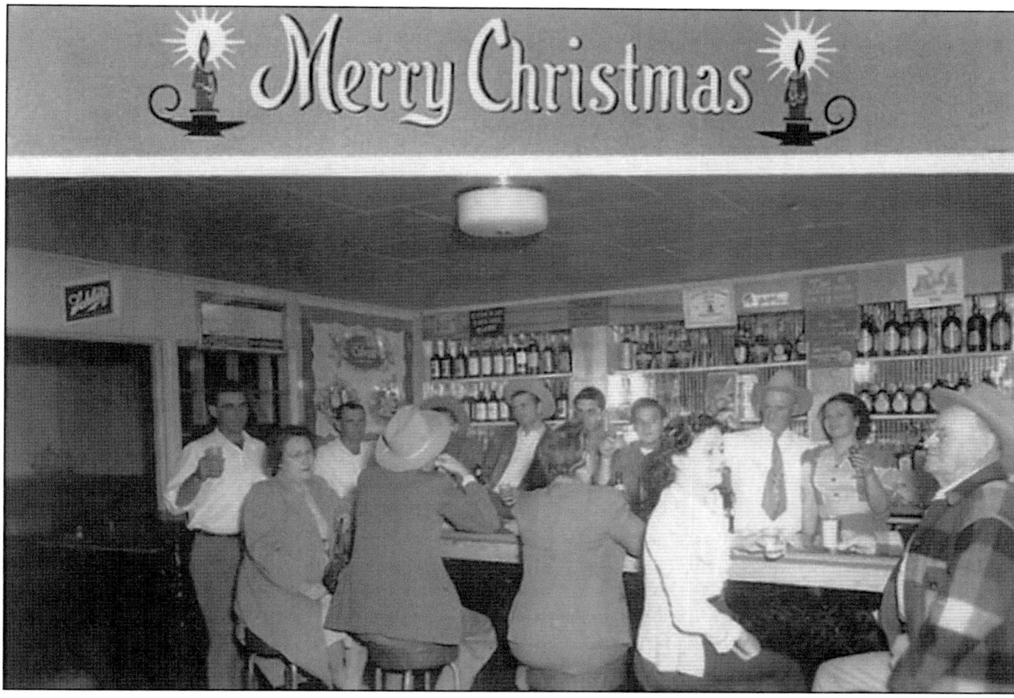

Other folks choose to relax by visiting with friends over refreshments in comfortable settings, such as this business in Superior. The Lamina Bar was so popular that it created its own Christmas card for patrons. The Lamina Bar was owned by Elaine Haddad's grandfather. Shown here are bartender Kelly Haddad, her father, and her great uncle Frank Haddad. Other patrons are unidentified. (SF.)

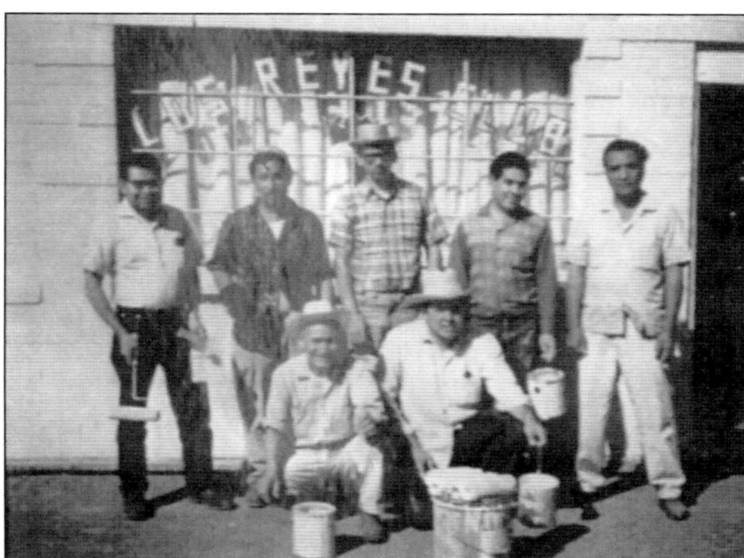

The Los Reyes of Superior started on May 15, 1955, for the purpose of serving the community with a wide variety of projects. Shown here are unidentified members preparing to go paint a building. (Mila Lira.)

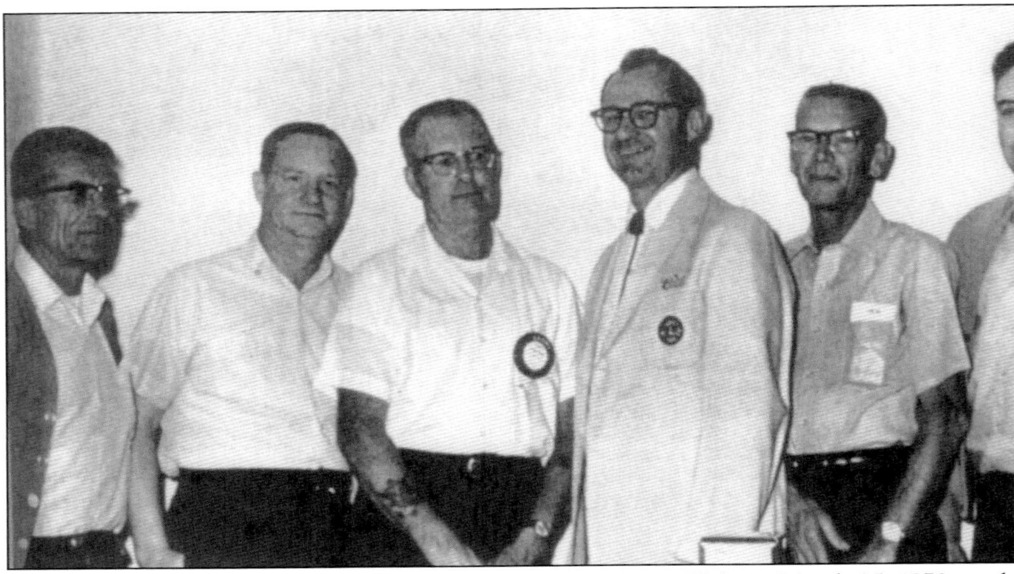

Here new members are being inducted by the Superior Lions Club on March 25, 1970, at the Triple X bar. Those shown are, from left to right, Les Taylor; Merle Lumley; Andy Hight; Bill Turnbull, District 21V governor; Clen Haynes, president of the Superior Lions Club; and Bill Salazar. (*Superior Sun.*)

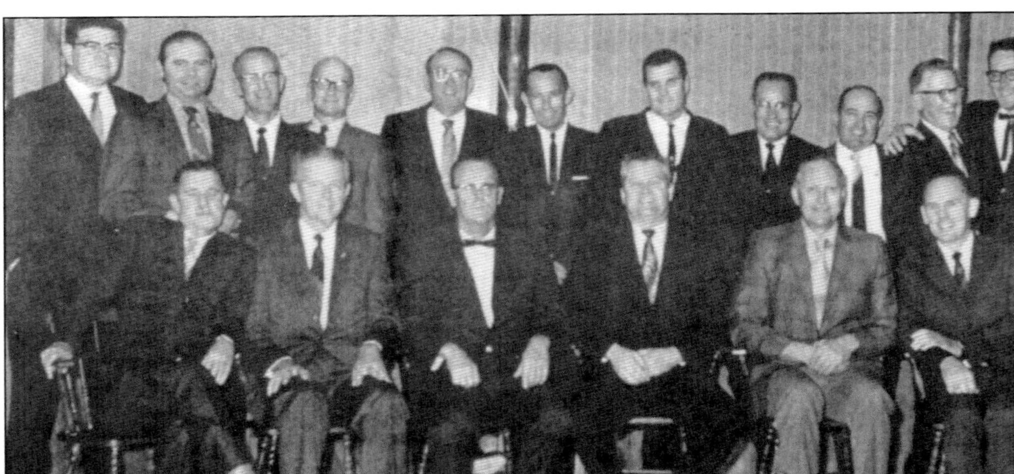

Magma Mine Managers received American Management Association certificates at a dinner in the Queen Valley Steakhouse in March 1970. Pictured here are, from left to right, (first row) Howard Johnson, Frank Spalding, Zach Coxon, Jack Flanagan, Curtis Sundeen, and Ira Medlock; (second row) Frank Florez, Dan Porter, Bob Mc Anany, Roland Moxcey, Claude Soule, Joe Patrick, Gene Sargent, Tom Kerich, Bud Cooksley, George Towsend, and Bill Hales. (*Superior Sun.*)

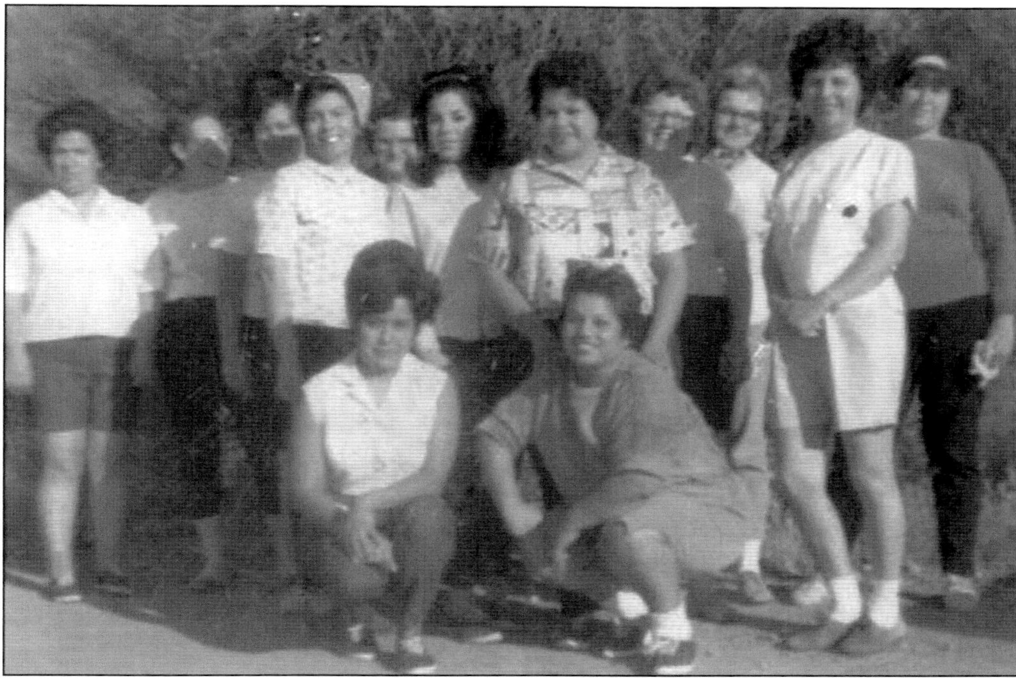

The Apache Tear Tops Club met on Monday evenings in the community room of the Superior Public Library. Traditionally, they sponsored the children's section of the July 4th parade, winning awards several years in a row. This close group encouraged healthy living and nutrition long before it became a national imperative. (Mary Gomez Collection.)

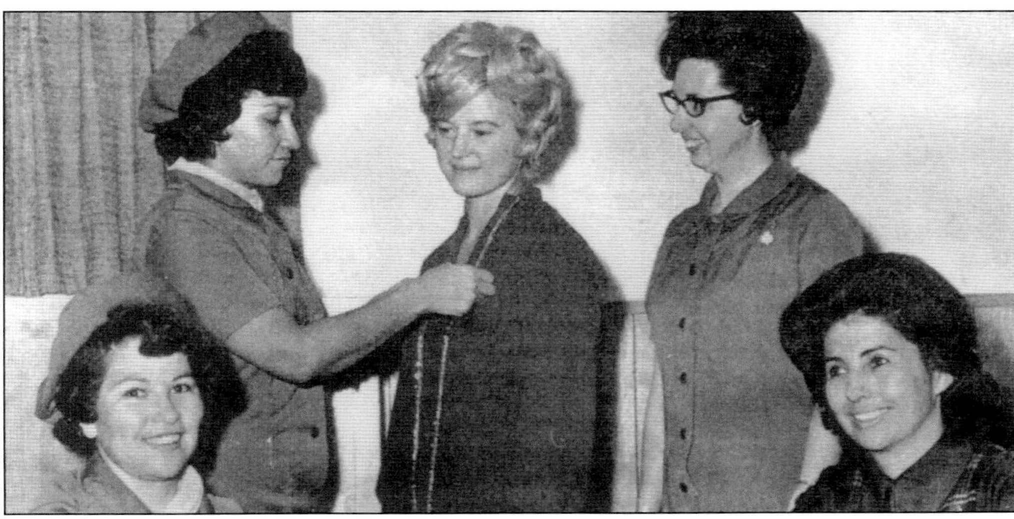

The Girl Scouts of America names new committee heads for the Superior area in this 1970s picture. Standing are, from left to right, Mary Baltierra who is placing a pin on Marcia Murry, a new service chairman, while field director Phyllis Hartley looks on. Seated is Brownie leader Frances Lewis (left) and troop organizer Tessie Haro. (*Superior Sun*.)

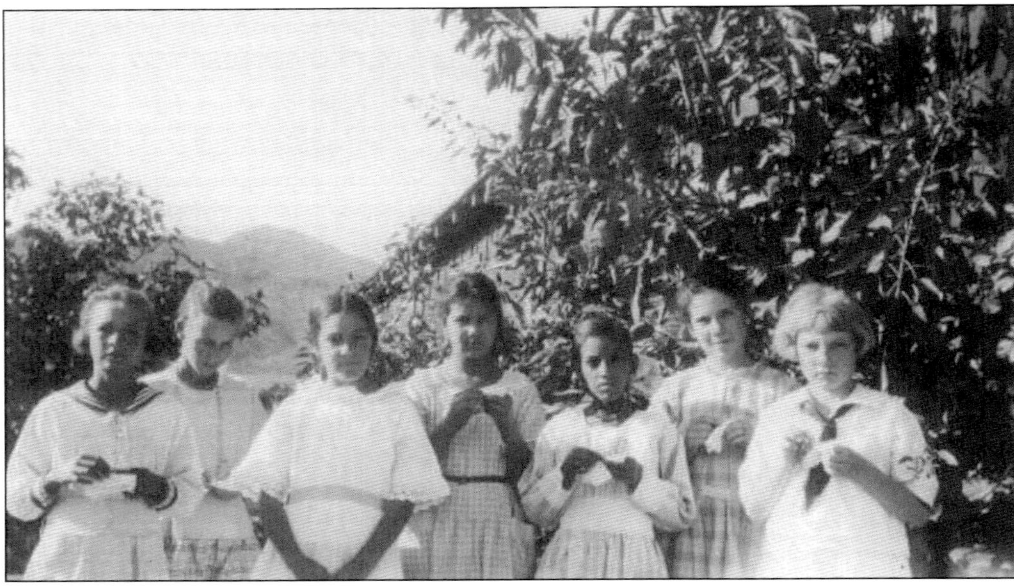

This 1921 photograph shows the Superior garment-making club that worked under the guidance of Ellen Cardon. Those in the photograph are unidentified. In photograph below, the Superior 4-H Club members continue the tradition of learning homemaking skills such as sewing. This photograph shows the project leader Molly Zapeda with the girls, who had just completed several years of clothing making. Those pictured are, from left to right, (first row) Becky Rivera, Yolanda Guzman, and Angie Jimenez; (second row) Diane Palacio and Magda Jimenez. All were attending the 34th Annual Pinal County Dress Review held at the 4-H Fair in 1970. (Above, courtesy of Mary Gomez; below, courtesy of *Superior Sun*.)

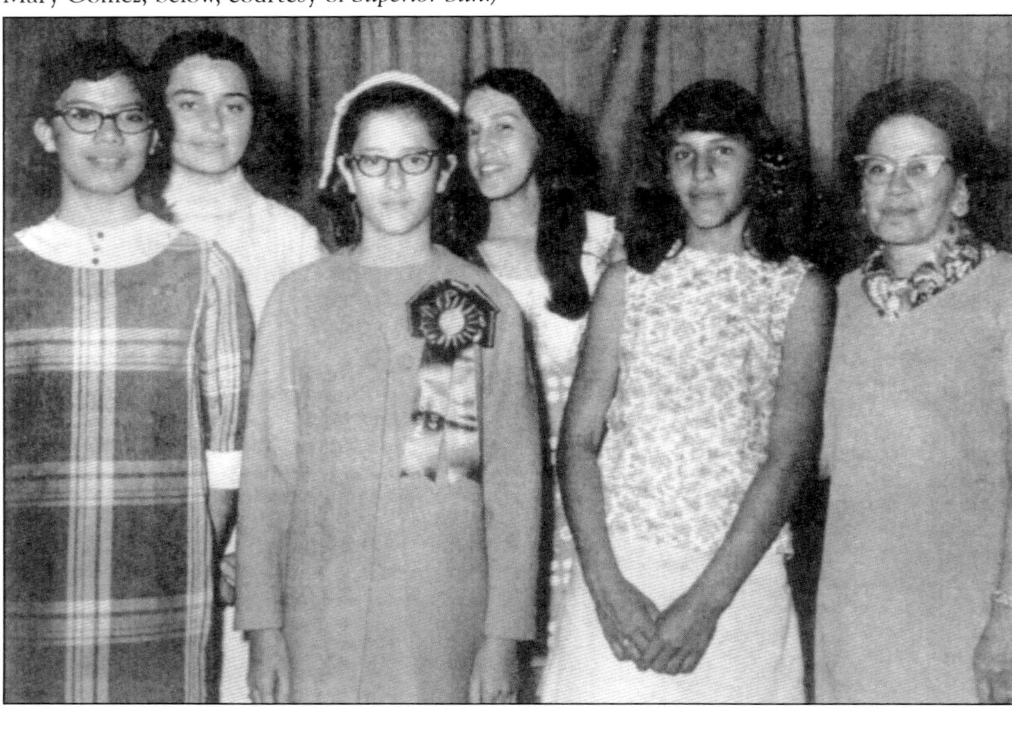

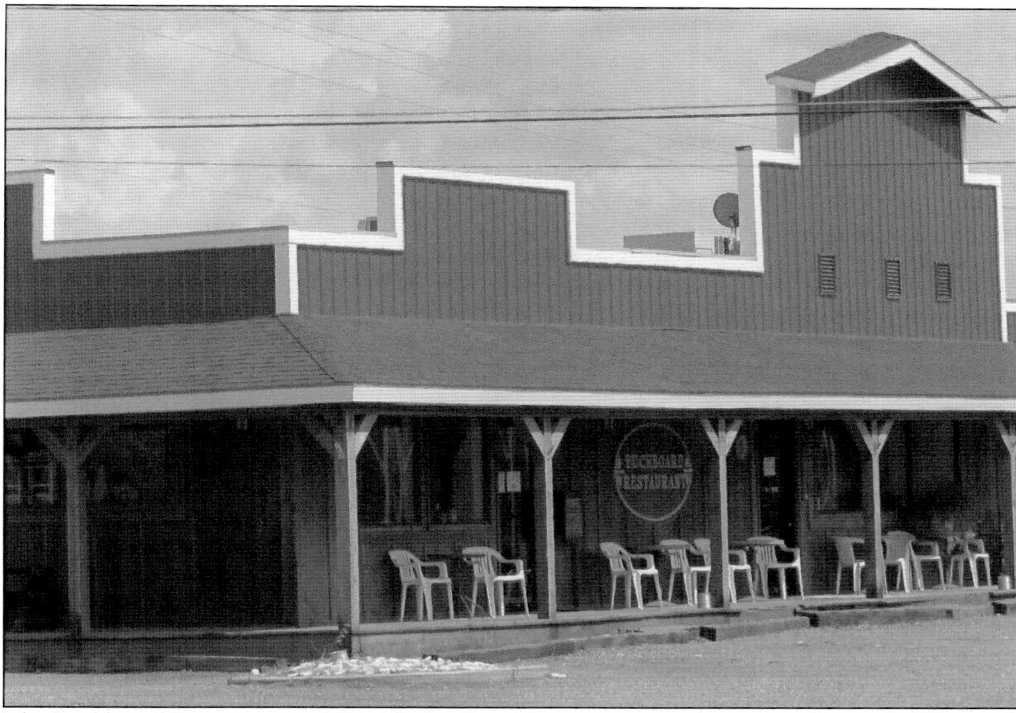

The Buckboard Restaurant and World's Smallest Museum is a popular stop on Route 60. Weekends see visitors coming to Superior on motorcycle tours, classic car road trips, and Sunday drives from all over the state. This unique museum showcases "artifacts of ordinary life" that honor the world's workforce. It has a mere 134 square feet under roof and only 80 square feet to display artifacts.

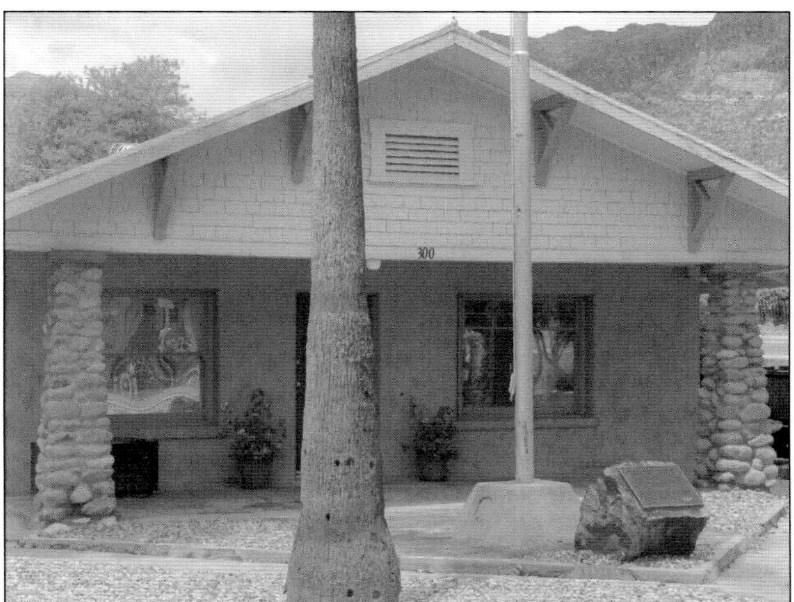

A visit to Bob Jones Museum, operated and managed by the Superior Historical Society, is also a must-see in Superior. Located at the home of Arizona's sixth governor, Robert "Bob" Taylor Jones, visitors explore the rich history of Superior, including its culture, relation to mining, minerals, and pioneer families.

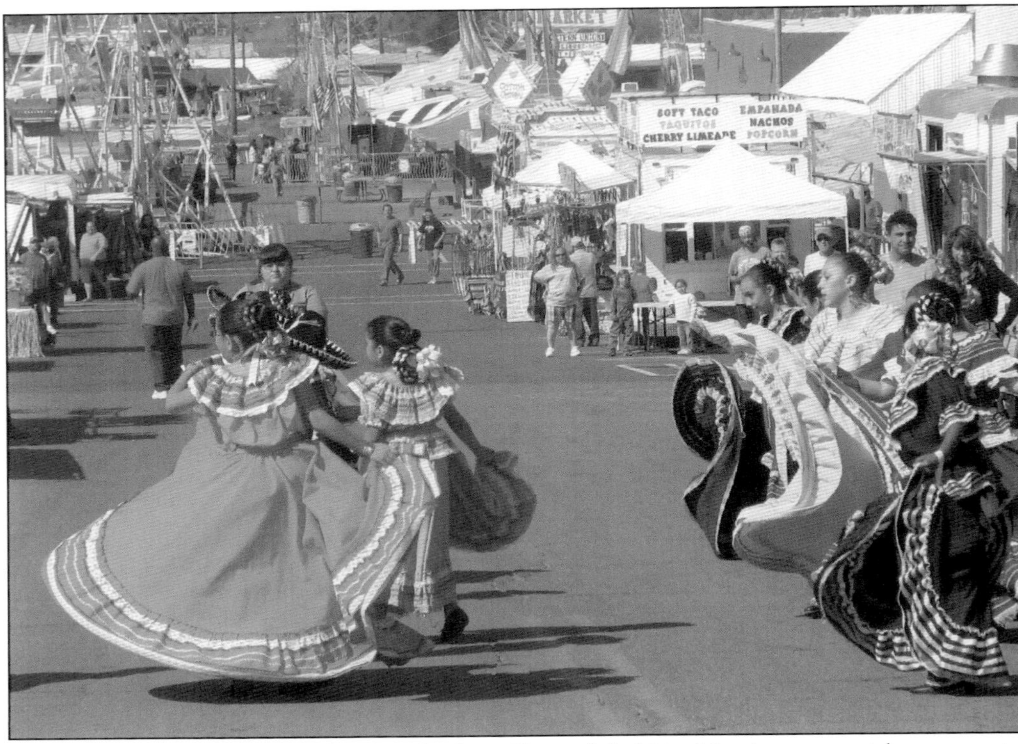

An annual three-day event, the Apache Leap Festival, held in March, opens with ceremonies honoring several of Superior's legendary residents and offers local entertainment. On Saturday morning, the festival begins with a parade, and some main features include mining competitions, salsa contests, horseshoe tournaments, Chihuahua races, live performances, and carnival rides. This is one of the town's biggest celebrations that showcases its rich and diverse history, and residents and visitors enjoy it each year.

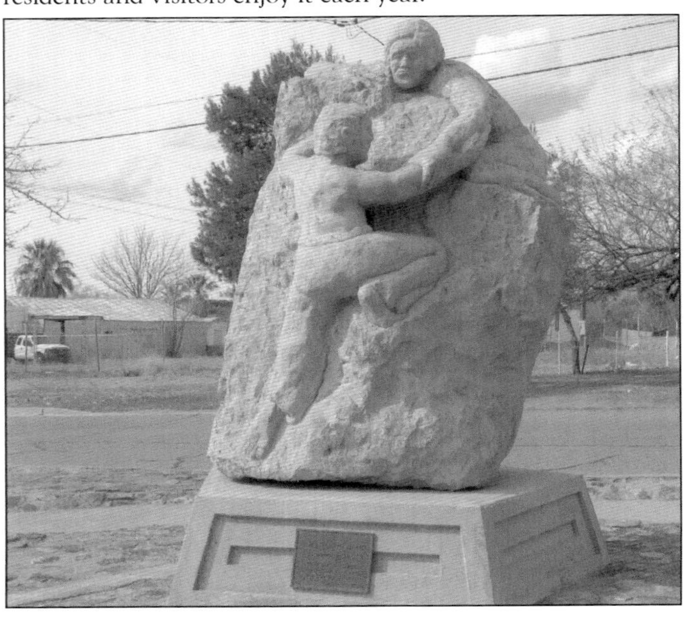

The *Helping Hands* statue by sculptor Tom Macias is a very fitting testament to the culture and attitudes of the residents and business people of Superior. The town developed from a spirit of pioneers working together to tease precious minerals from the earth. They will continue into the future helping each other through town charity events, celebrations, and simply by living in harmony in this very special hometown.

Six

Queen Valley

Queen Valley is the "Jewel of the Sonoran," according to those that have discovered this hidden treasure. It will celebrate its centennial in 2015 and has strong connections to the town of Superior.

Queen Valley is in a beautiful valley, strategically located along Queen Creek, with Superior to the east, 15 miles; Florence to the south, 18 miles; and Apache Junction to the west, 22 miles away. In the 1800s, the town was the center point for travel by the military, miners, and pioneers, as it was in the direct route from New Mexico to California. It became the path for stagecoaches, wagons, and eventually trains that were connecting shipping routes.

As the mining towns of Silver King, Pinal, and Superior began to develop, so did ranching. The Whitlow Ranch was established in 1874 near Elephant Butte, a few miles north of Queen Valley. The ranch provided milk, butter, and cheese to Superior and Florence. A freight hand working the Superior route fell in love with the area and built a home in October 1915. He filed the first homestead to officially begin what Hart Mullins called "Peaceful Valley."

The town gained several other homesteads like those that belonged to the following families: the Baldwins in 1918, Mattinsons in 1923, Olsons in 1932, and the Espinozas in 1934. These settlers farmed and ranched the valley, harnessing Queen Creek with irrigation canals that are still in use today. Hart Mullins loaded his vegetables and fruits onto a mule wagon and took them to Superior weekly, filling orders from the previous week's delivery. He and his wife, Margaret, had six children while living in the valley. When they retired to Superior, they sold the land to Pete Allen, whose dream of building a resort retirement community was then launched. The town's ability to sustain development was sealed with the building of Whitlow Dam in 1960 to protect Williams Air Force Base and to control floodwaters that once ravaged the valley.

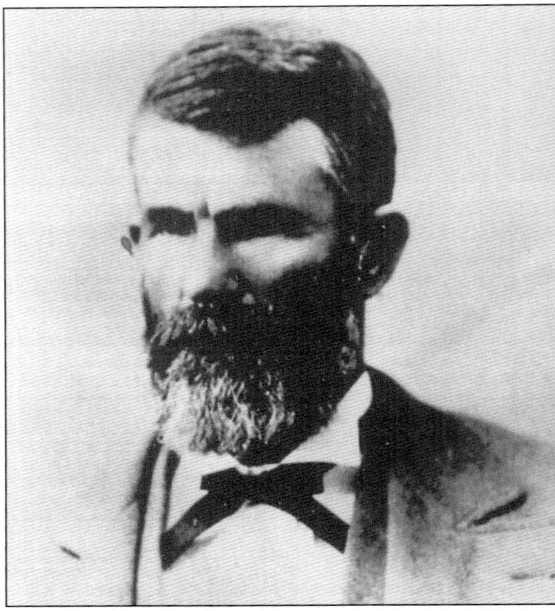
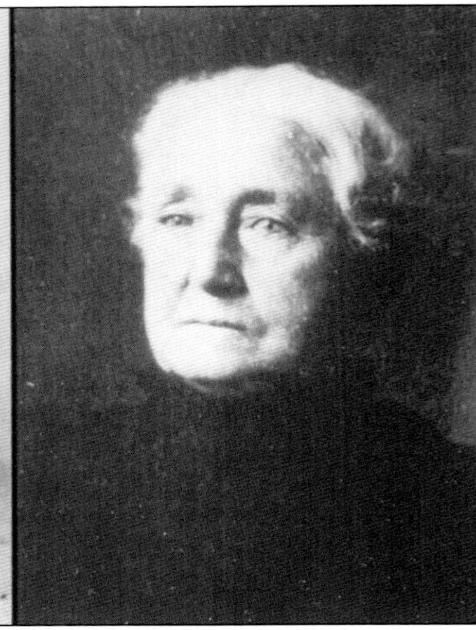

Charles Whitlow married Sara Jane McKee, shown above in 1850, and Allen Whitlow married Josephine McKee. The brothers and sisters moved by wagon train to Texas, California, and finally Arizona. In the 1860s, Whitlow opened a settlement store near Fort McDowell and, in 1873, was appointed postmaster. He named the town Marysville after his daughter Mary Elizabeth Whitlow. She later married William Long, a founder of Silver King Mine. (PCHSM.)

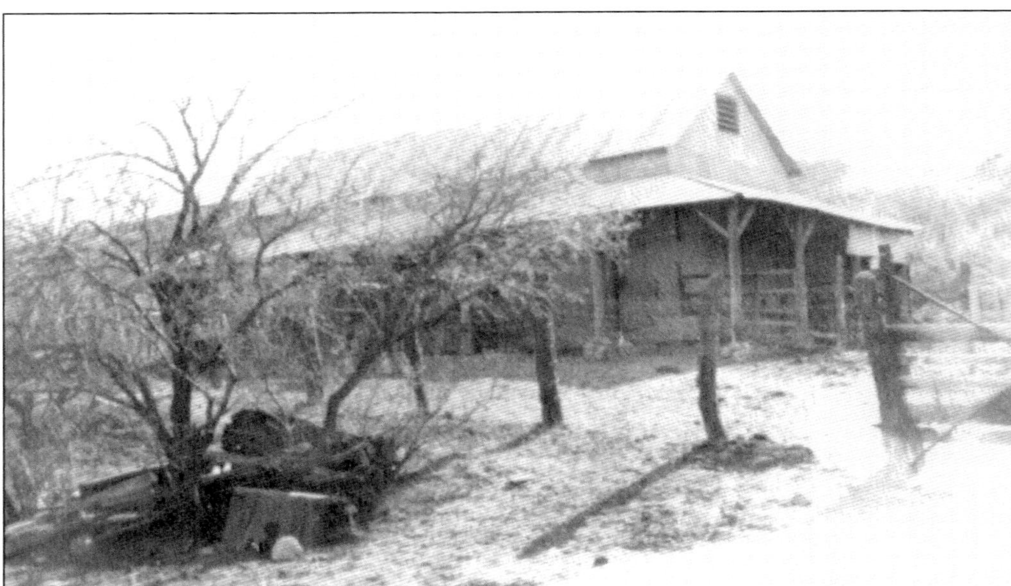

Leaving Maryville when Fort McDowell closed, they moved to the Queen Valley area and settled the first Whitlow Ranch on Queen Creek in Pinal County in 1874. They also had a nearby stage station and trading post. Descendents report stories that were passed down of a visiting Dutchman, named Jacob Waltz, who had to sleep outside, because Sara thought he smelled. (USACE.)

Charles Allen "Slouch" Whitlow, a son of Charles and Sara, was born in 1871 and came to Arizona via Butterfield Stage with his parents. The family established the Whitlow Milk Ranch, located 4 miles away from the original ranch in Queen Valley in 1885, with around 60 head of cattle. Slouch married Dorcas Phy, and soon the ranch was producing 40 pounds of cheese per day and butter in colder months. (PCHSM.)

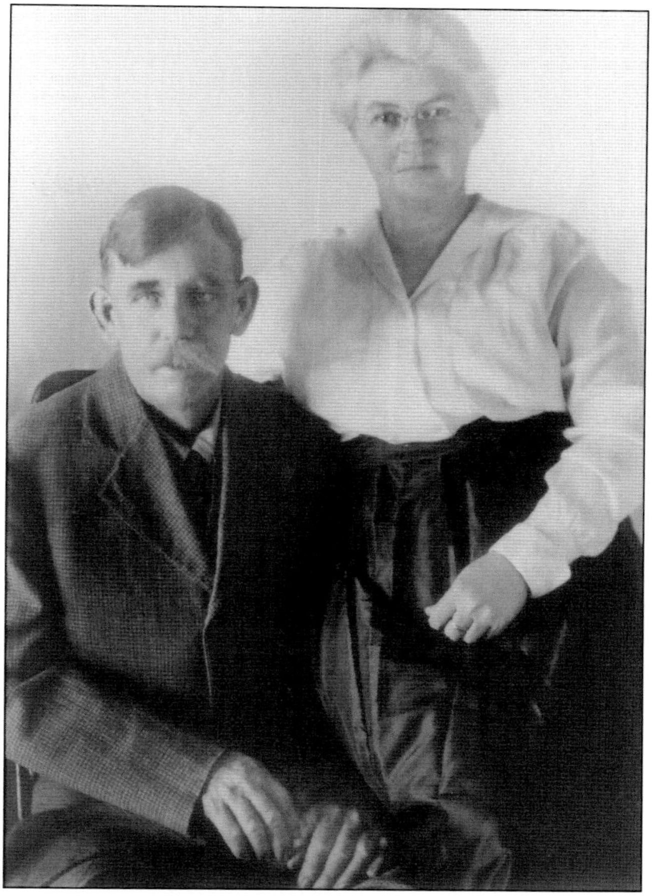

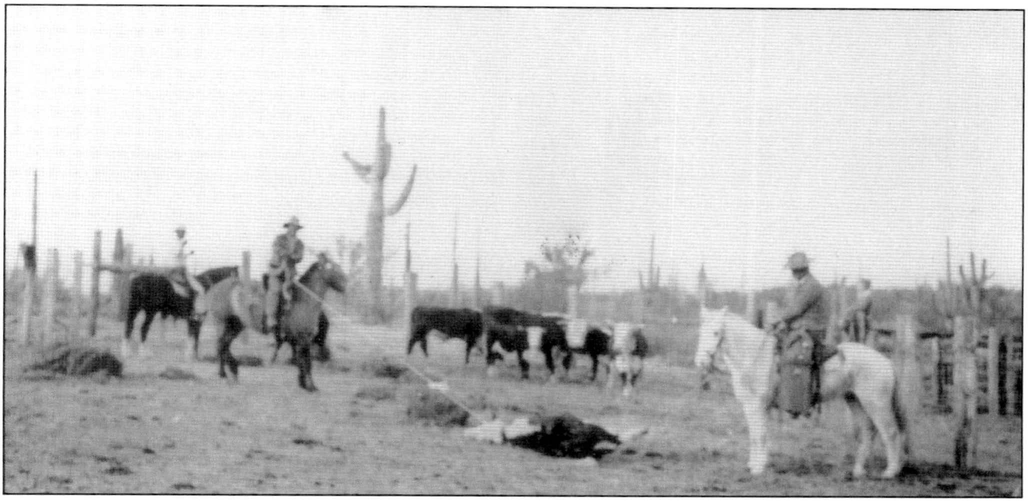

The *Arizona Weekly Enterprise* on January 17, 1885, reported, "Mr. Whitlow came near losing his entire 12-mule team yesterday, crossing the river. They got into quicksand and five of the mules got down, and it was only by the united efforts of his brother teamsters that the team was got out." By 1910, the creek-side ranch was sold. (PCHSM.)

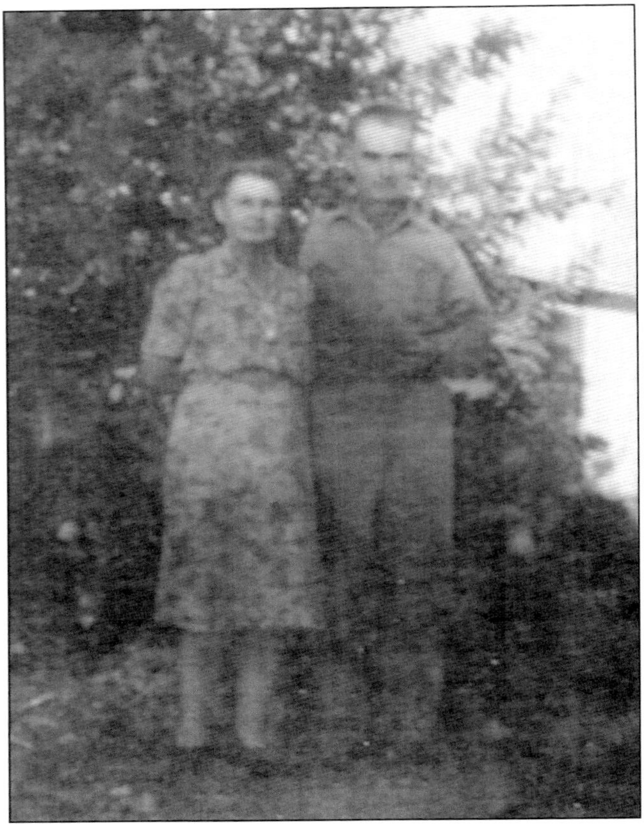

Brothers Hart and Jesse Mullins discovered an area that "seemed near a paradise" while delivering furniture to Superior. Hart brought his bride, Margaret (both shown at left), to the area to establish a homestead in October 1915. They filed final proof documents in the Phoenix Land Office, obtaining their 160 acres on April 11, 1922. His is the first legally documented settling of the area that became Queen Valley. (Fran Olson Harkey.)

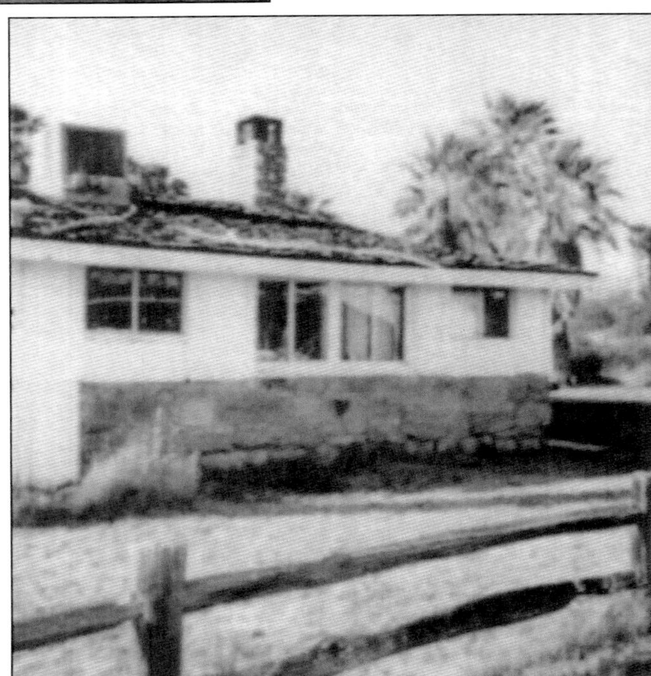

The Mullins family lived in the then abandoned Whitlow cabin, while Hart was building the stone house that still stands on the original homesteaded land. Family members tell wonderful stories of the hardships and joys of settling what Hart called "Peaceful Valley." (Fran Olson Harkey.)

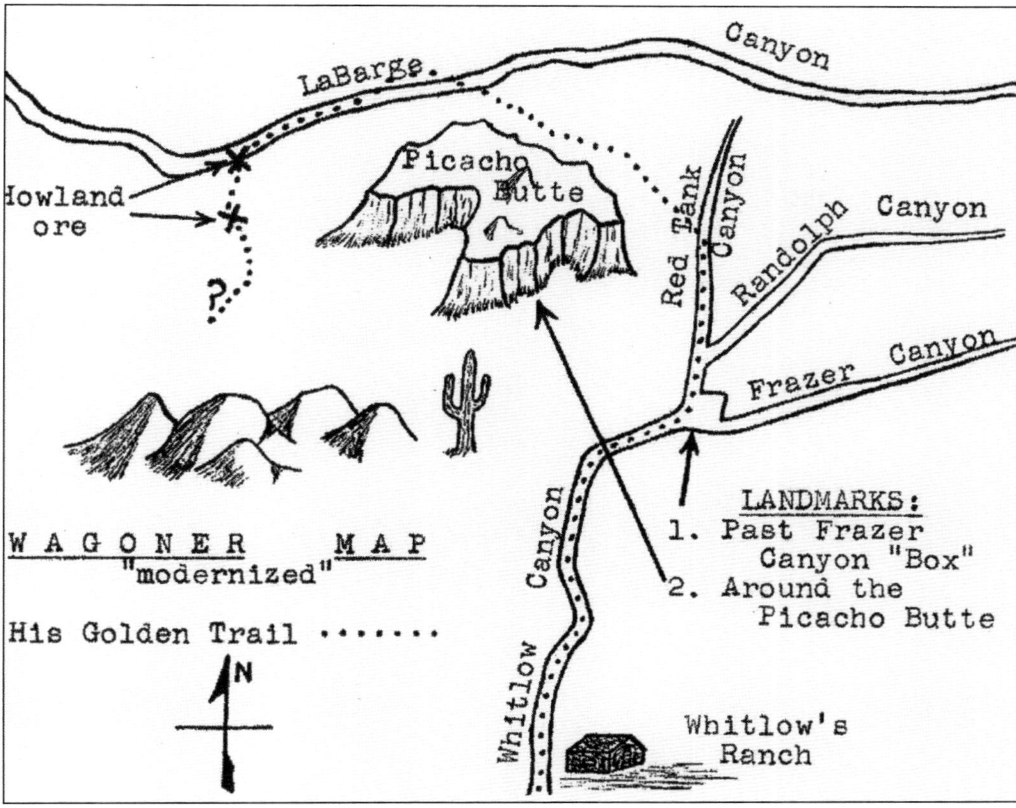

At the age of 15, Jesse Mullins drove a freight wagon for his father, Fredrick, and ran delivery from Phoenix to Florence and the Magma. He once picked up Jacob Waltz, south of the Superstitions. He also talked of stage driver Hebe McDonald picking up Wagoner who regularly got off near Queen Valley and would return to the stage three days later with a suitcase of gold. (Jack San Felice.)

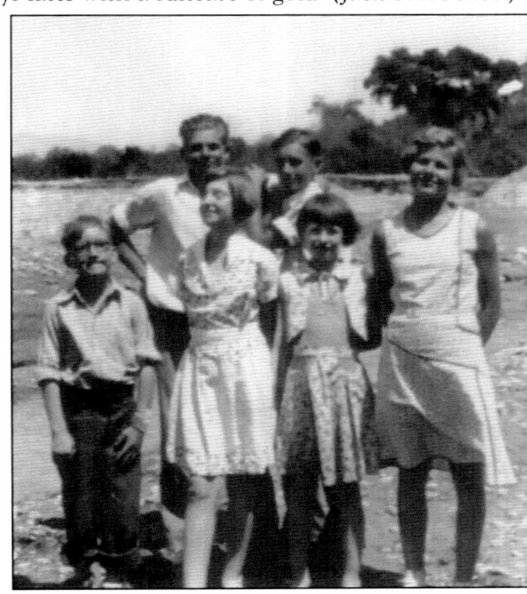

Hart and Margaret Mullins had six children, Jessie Ann, Gordan, Joyce, Rosemary, and twins Harry and Jerry. Harry only lived six days. When Gordan was 16, he was injured trying to jump over a fence when a bull was chasing him. He severely injured his intestines, leading to an early death. Living in rural areas could be dangerous for everyone, but especially children. (Fran Olson Harkey.)

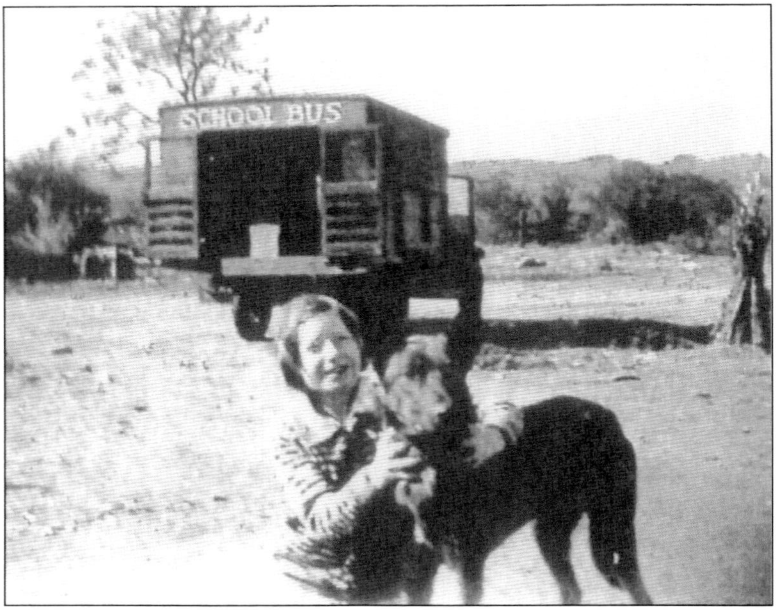

Margaret Mullins drove the children to the Hewitt Station School in this horse-drawn school bus, built by Hart Mullins. When they got older, it was mounted on a truck, and they were then able to make the trip to Superior, which is where Margaret became well known as the bus driver. Shown at left is a Mullins child. (Bill Moser and Fran Olson Harkey.)

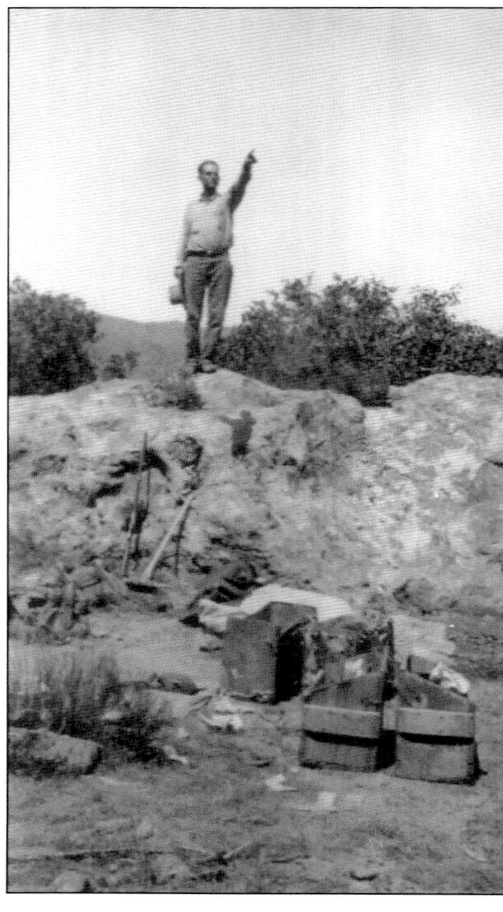

Hart and Jesse spent years searching for the lost Dutchman's gold. The Mullins brothers filed claims on the Elephant Butte and Whetrock Mine in 1951. Hart and another partner filed on the Whetrock and Buzzard's Roost area; both mines produced copper and silver. This photograph of Hart has the caption of "looking for the lost mine, which is still lost." Hart is shown here preparing for another trip into the mountains. (Fran Olson Harkey.)

Hart Mullins's brother Jesse, left, lived in Queen Valley when not prospecting in the Superstition Mountains. Robert Garman, right, came to Arizona to prospect with his uncle who was a friend of Jacob Waltz back in 1877. Garman was friends with Travis Tumlinson who found the Peralta Stone Maps in Queen Valley in 1947. Garman spent many years unsuccessfully searching for the Dutchman's gold. (SMHS.)

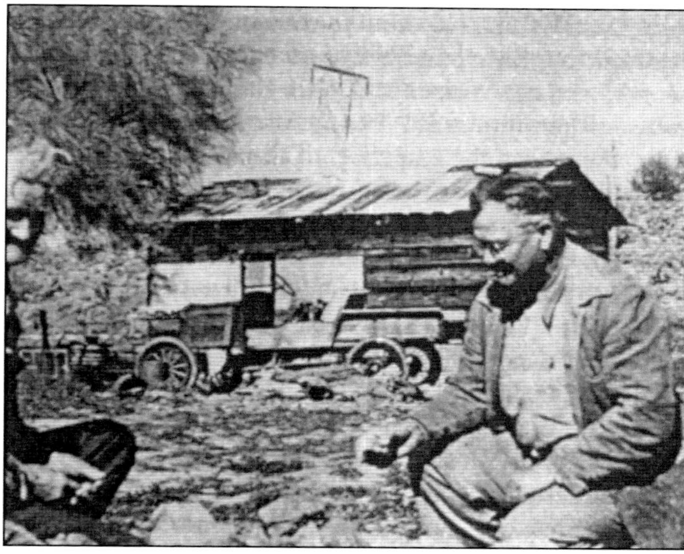

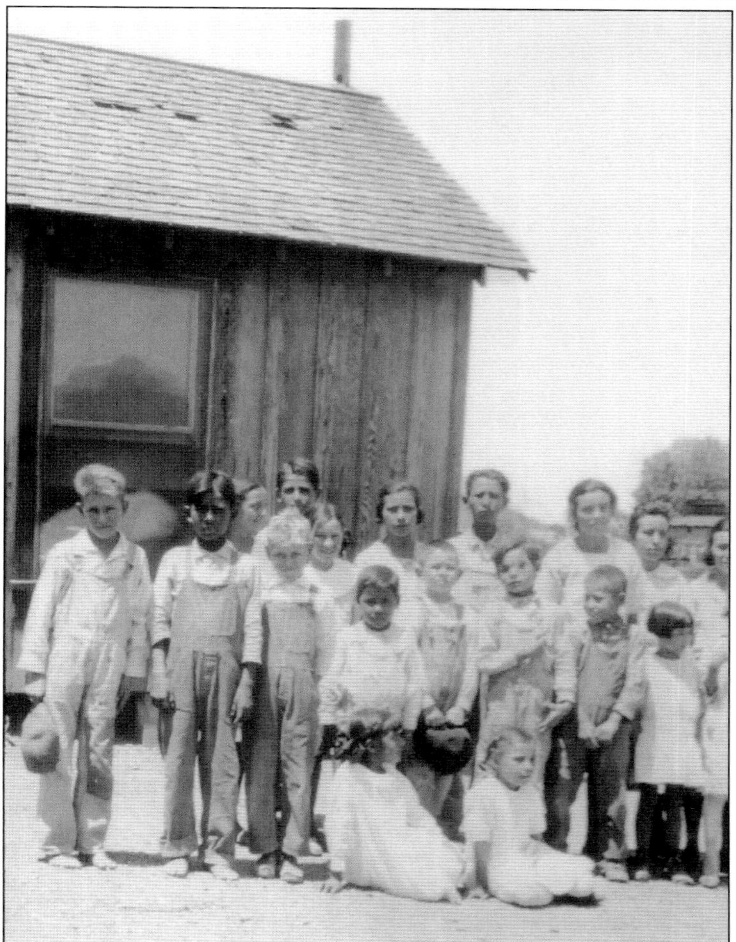

Children of Mexican railroad line workers attended the Hewitt Station School while the Superior to Magma Flats track was built. Other children like John ("Jack") Woodward Olson, pictured on the far left, also attended Hewitt. Jack later became a Queen Valley homesteader. (Fran Olson Harkey.)

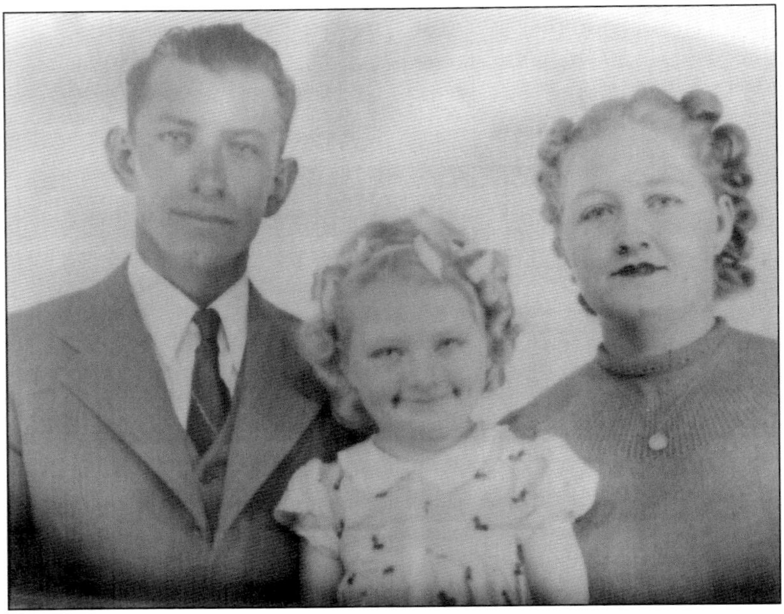

Hart and Margaret's daughter Jessie grew up in Queen Valley and married Jack Olson. In February 14, 1938, their stock-raising homestead of 640 acres of property, located 4 miles north of the Mullins' home and off Elephant Butte Road, was signed by F. D. Roosevelt. Jack and Jessie are shown with daughter Fran, whose grandfather was Bill Martin Sr. (Olson Harkey.)

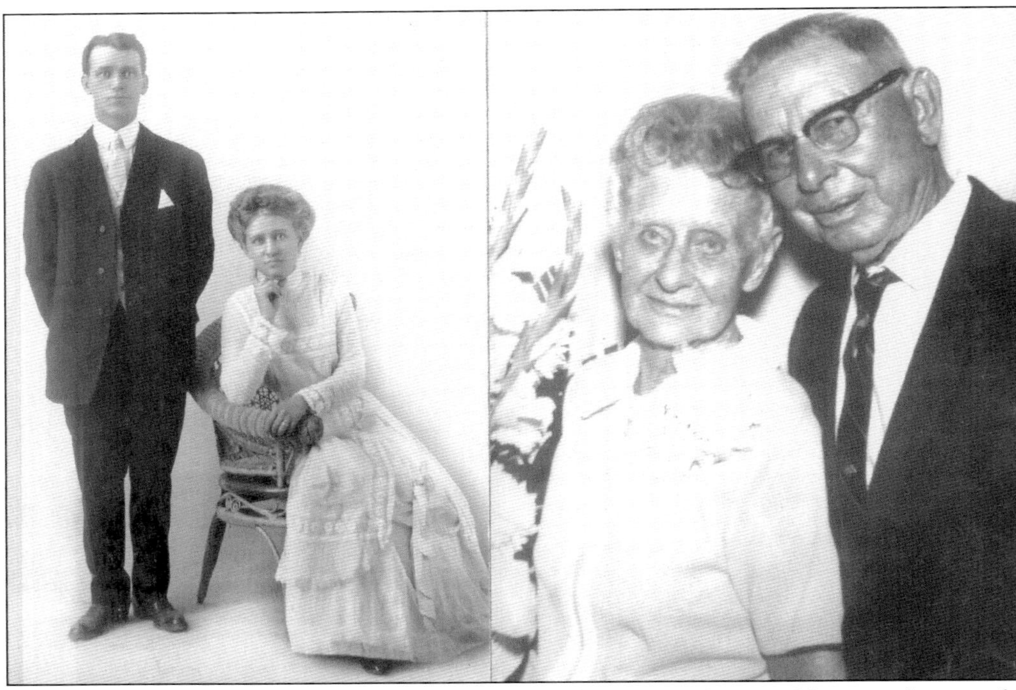

Bill Martin Sr. and wife, Lenora Olson Martin, lived in Hewitt Station. He was a foreman for both the JF Ranch, which ran from Iron Mountain to Queen Creek, and the Clemens Cattle Company, which ran from Reavis Canyon to the Salt River. Clemens had bought the old Reavis Ranch from Jack Fraser. During roundups, the cattle were driven from the range, through Queen Valley, to stockyards on Baseline and Dobson Roads.

Herman Petrash, shown here, lived on Hewitt Station Road next to Bill Martin Sr. and spent 50 years looking for the lost Dutchman's gold in the Superstition foothills. (Bill Moser.)

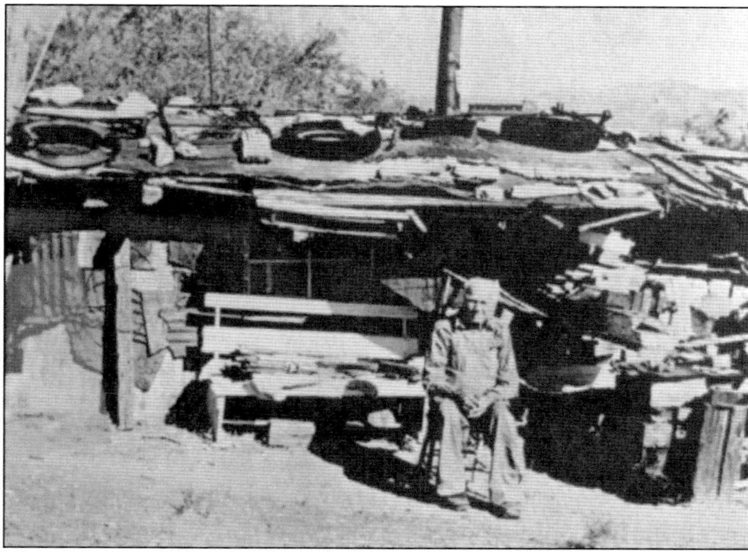

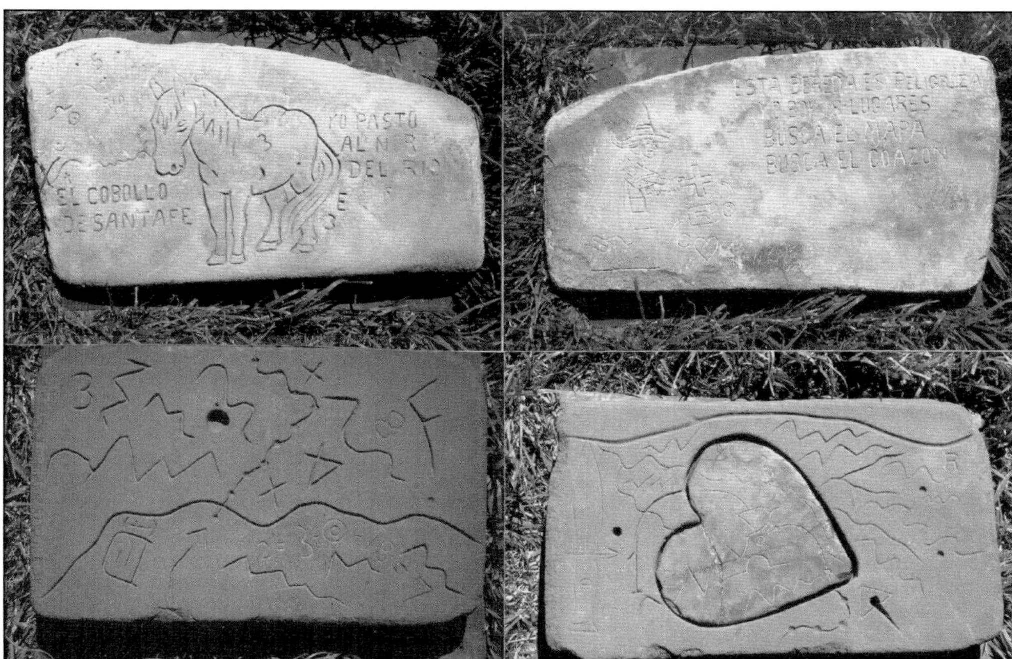

The Peralta Stones were found near Queen Valley, and the mystery of origin still continues. One story is that Don Miguel Peralta left the maps directing descendants to the mines while mining the areas around the Superstitions. Others believe it's a hoax by someone, perhaps James Reavis, trying to prove claim to Mexican land grants. For more details, one can read *Treasure Trails of the Superstitions* by Jack San Felice. (Jack San Felice.)

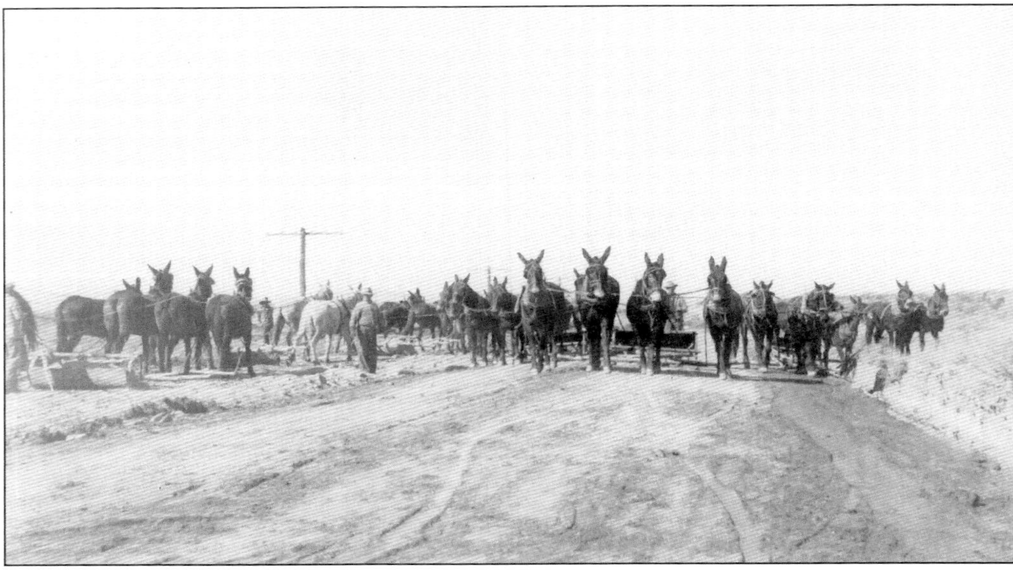

This early-1900s photograph shows the original methods for surfacing and flattening roads, which were done with the help of mule teams. Here the Florence Superior Route 60 is being more fully developed from a wagon trail to a more direct and sustainable roadway. Hart Mullins worked for the Arizona Highway Department whenever a Democrat was in office but was out of work when a Republican became governor. (Arizona State Library.)

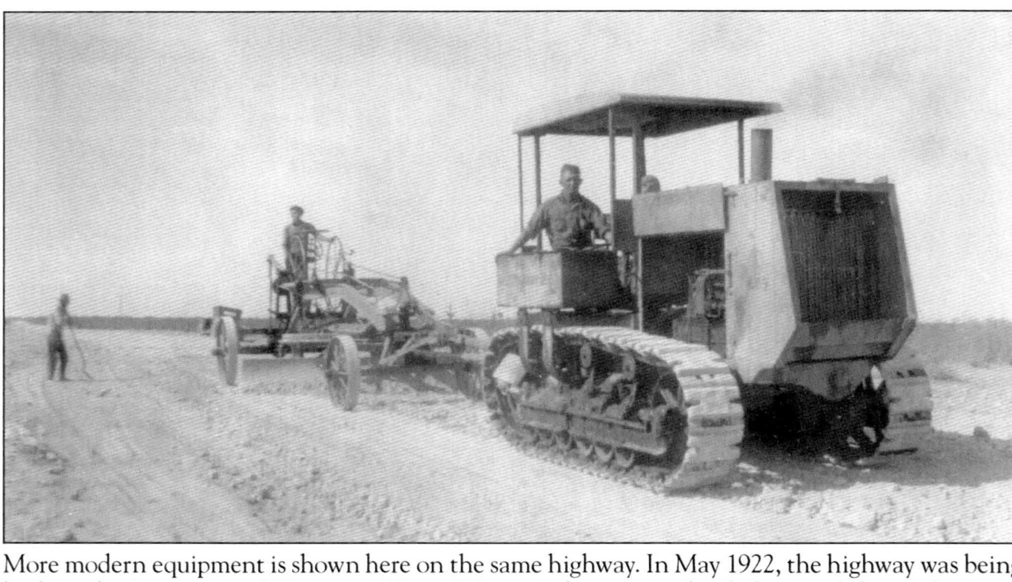

More modern equipment is shown here on the same highway. In May 1922, the highway was being built at the insistence of Governor Hunt. Water to the site was hauled in, and the workers and travelers no doubt took advantage of the nearby refreshment stop at Florence Junction. (Arizona State Library.)

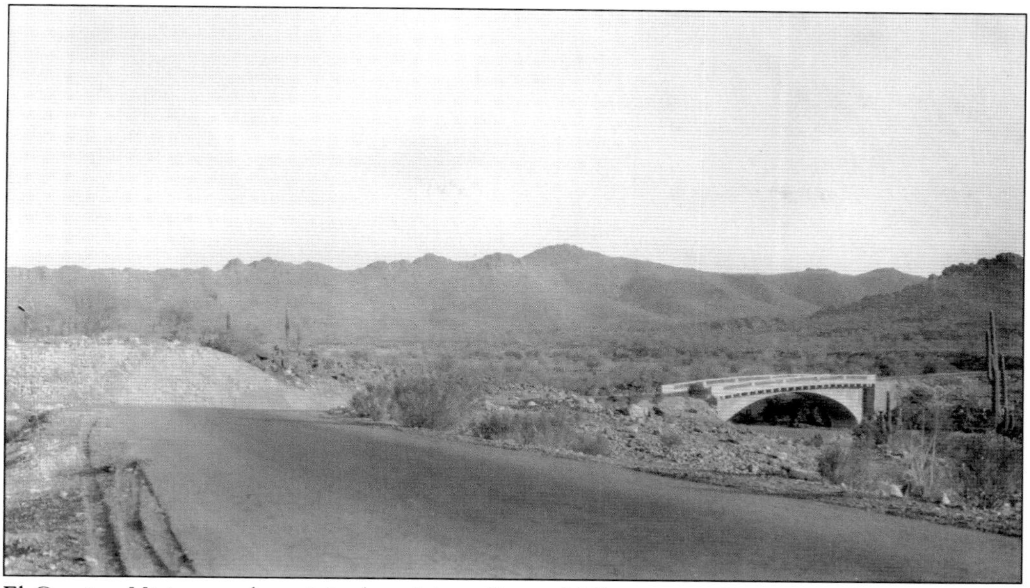

El Camino Viejo was the original road into Queen Valley, across Queen Creek. Wagons once traveled this route before U.S. Route 60 was paved and rerouted south of the town. The bridge was built in 1938. Florence Junction's gas stations had a prime location for serving interstate travelers, but over the years, competition from nearby towns created the ghost town of Florence Junction. (Arizona State Library.)

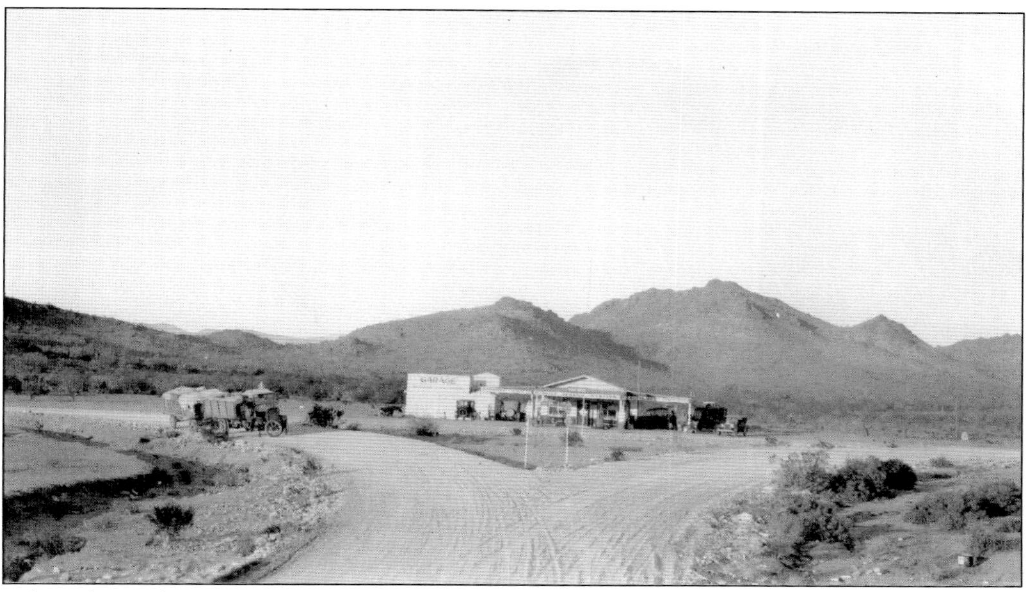

When the road was rerouted south of Queen Valley, there were both cars and wagons traveling the area. The 4-mile trip into Queen Valley was still on the west mountainside, via the El Camino Viejo Road. The road from Florence and Tucson came to a "Y" shape there and then split off toward to Superior and Phoenix. (Arizona State Library.)

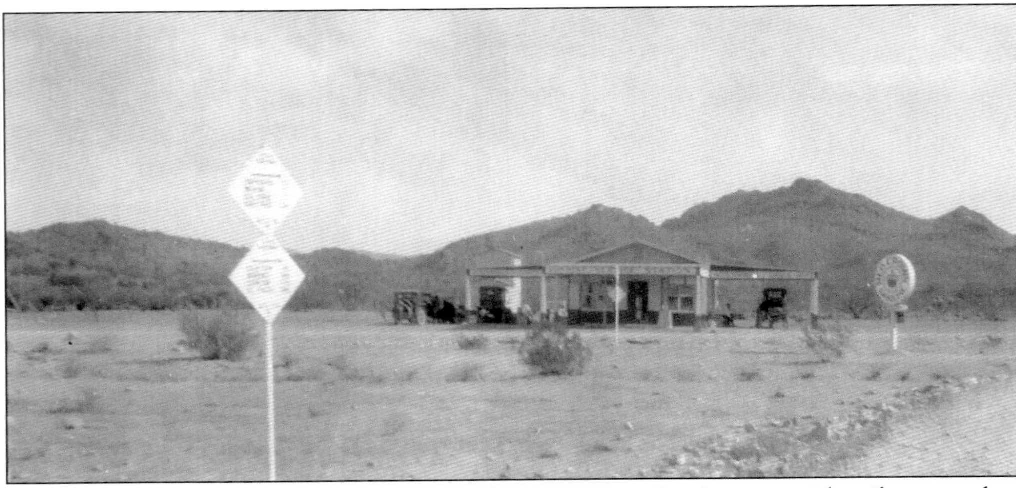

This view shows Joyce and Harold Willoughby's station in the distance with mileage markers directing traffic to nearby towns. Joseph Willoughby, who was from Superior, pioneered Florence Junction. He also opened the station that is pictured above in 1923. The Willoughbys were relatives of the Olson family. The station burned down in 1970, and by then, Bertha Barnett owned it. (Arizona State Library.)

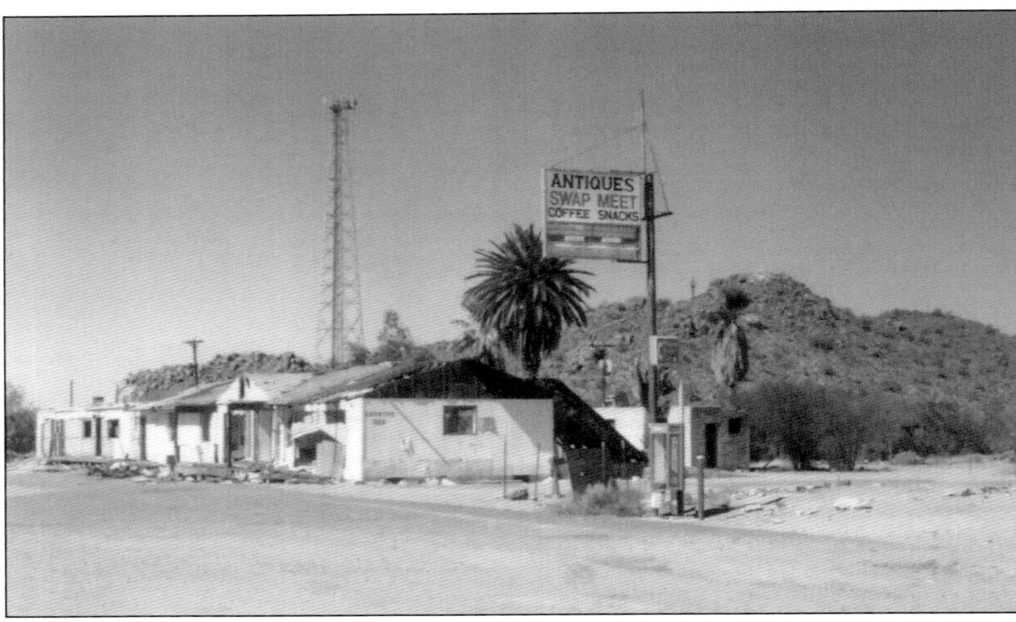

Florence Junction served as a truck rest stop and transcontinental bus stop in the 1940s and 1950s. It was also called Coyote Crossing or the Crossroads and had a number of small shops to attract tourists. Shown is the antique store and café. The buildings were still standing in the early 1970s but were torn down for safety. Today the lot remains for sale. (SMHS.)

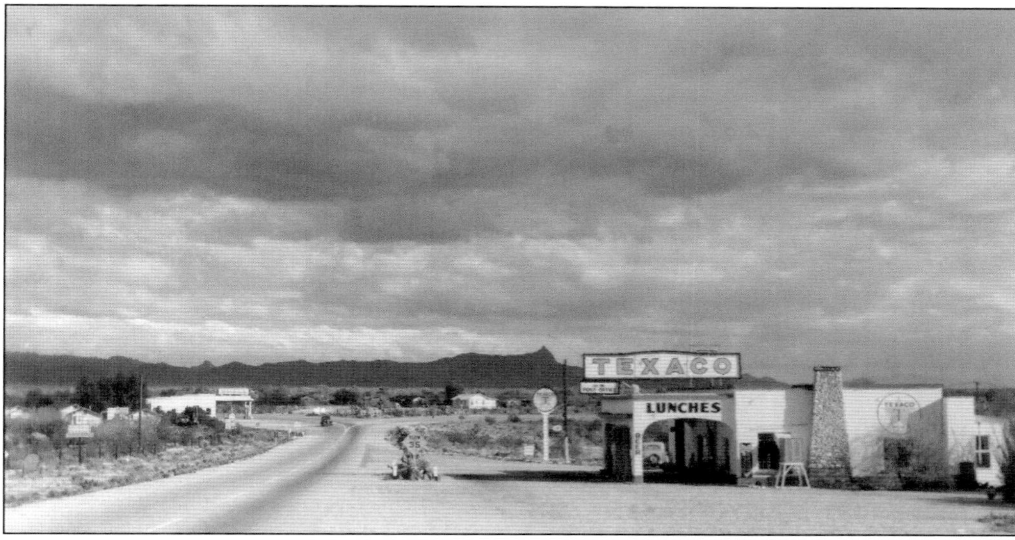

The original Texaco at Florence Junction was built in 1932 by C. E. Caldwell and purchased by J. W. Parr in January 1939. The Parr family helped raise Lenore Olson Martin after her mother's early death. Queen Valley resident Cecil Fendley's father, J. T. Fendley, leased and ran the station from 1964 to 1966. (SMHS.)

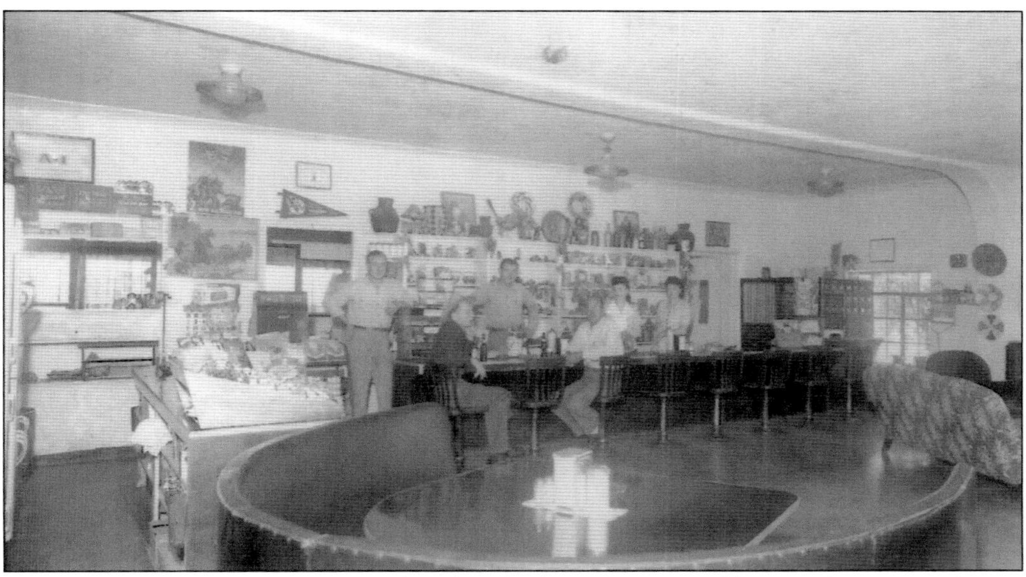

When Cecil Fendley, now Queen Valley's fire chief, was four years old, a traveler came in for gas, and in an effort to help his father, Cecil removed the traveler's license plate unbeknownst to both the car owner and Cecil's father. The traveler was later stopped in Gonzales Pass for not having a license plate. The traveler, knowing he had it last at the station, returned, and the plate was discovered laying in a pile with others that Cecil had "helped dad with." (SMHS.)

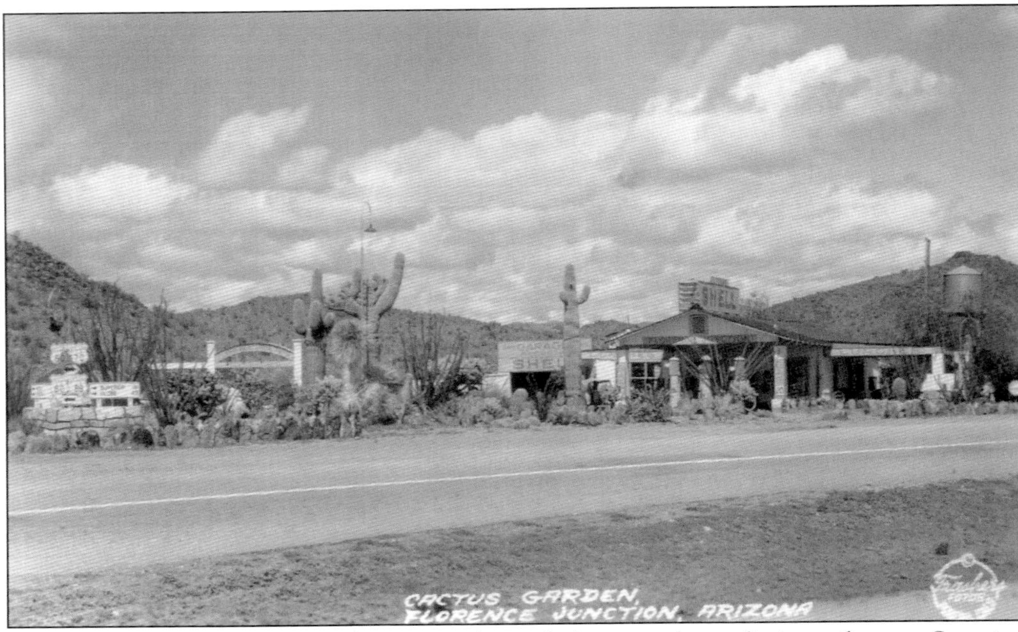

Florence Junction had a beautiful cactus garden with directional signs listing mileage to Superior, Globe, Florence, Tucson, and Phoenix. It was a popular stretch point along the highway, showing off the local cactus varieties. This postcard, courtesy of the SMM, shows the Shell station and water towers. (SMHS.)

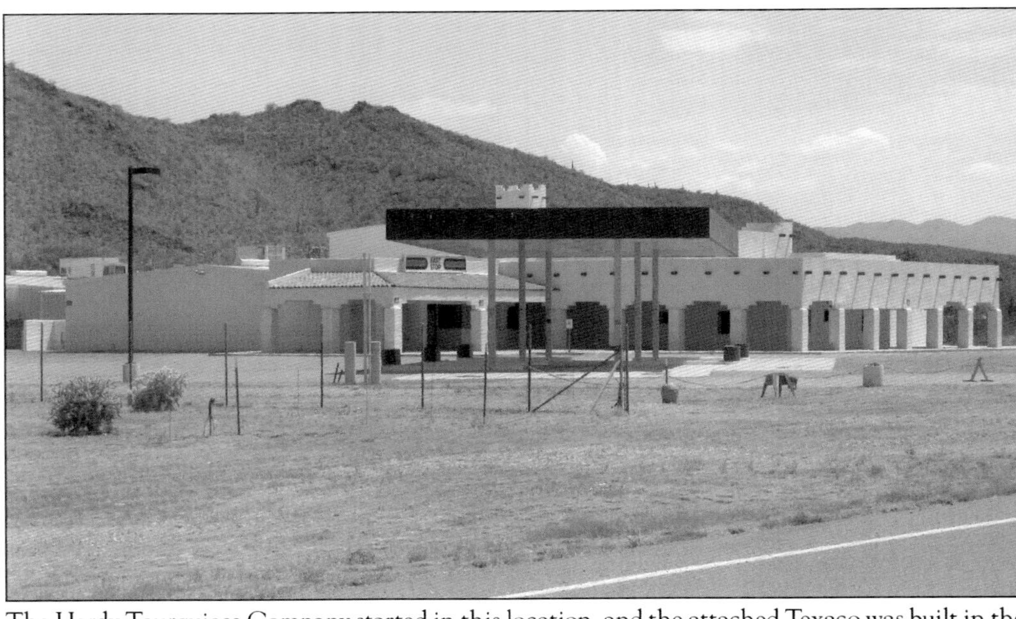

The Hardy Tourquiose Company started in this location, and the attached Texaco was built in the 1970s. At one time, there was a TasteeFreeze restaurant and rooms for rent for truckers upstairs. Hardy had a private airstrip on the north side of Route 60 and flew to Kingman frequently. Route 60 was rerouted in 2003, and the Texaco closed soon after. The town disappeared like many along Route 66.

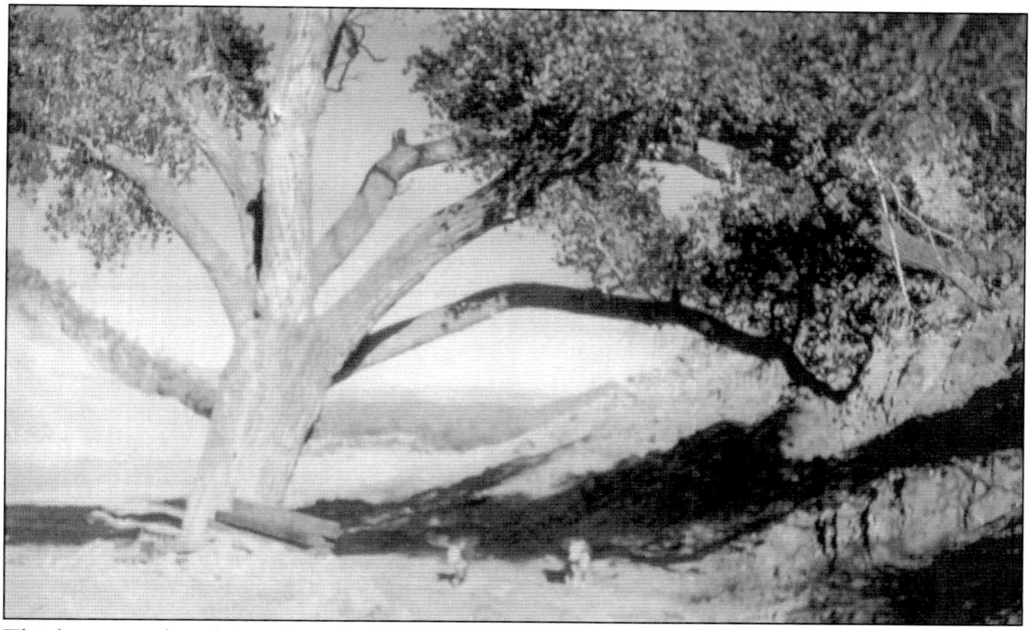

This huge tree dwarfed cattle in the Queen Creek riverbed. According to homesteader Mullins, the tree was used in the early part of the 20th century as a hanging tree for cattle rustlers. Geronimo once traveled through the area hunting for thieves who had rustled horses from the tribe. The rustlers were not found, and Geronimo passed through peacefully. (Bill Moser.)

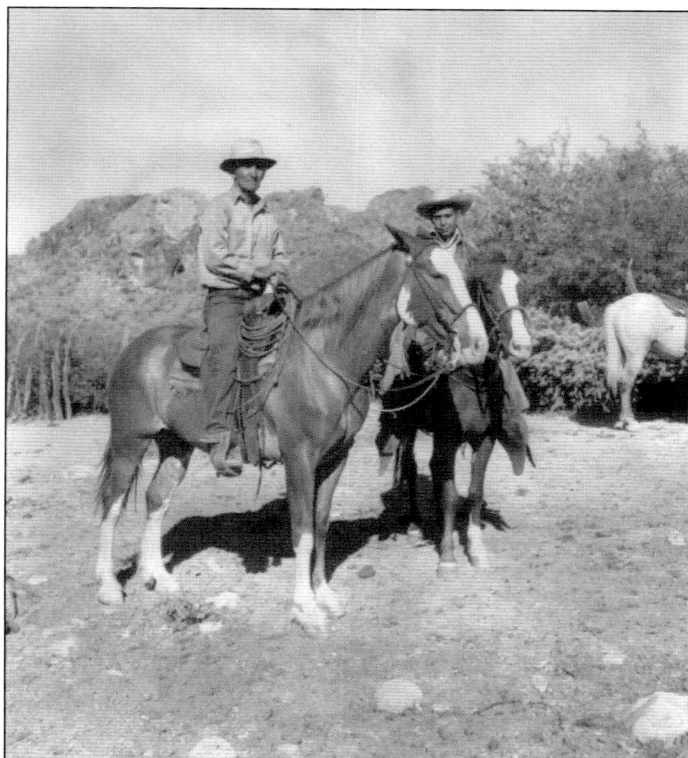

Documents signed by Pres. Franklin D. Roosevelt on November 18, 1940, show that the area around Queen Valley was opened to grazing under the Taylor Grazing Act of June 1934. It states that, in total, 5,672 acres were open to grazing by local ranchers. Manny Ruiz's family has grazed around Queen Valley for many years. He is shown here in 1947 with his grandfather Phil Ruiz in Queen Valley.

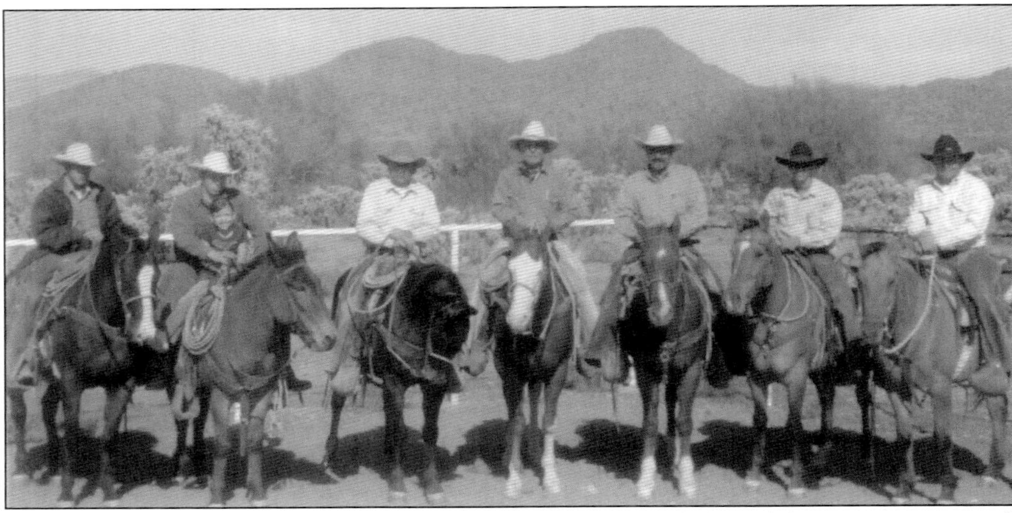

At the age of 12, Manny Ruiz's father already worked for his father, Phil Ruiz, running cattle bought from George Lobb of Superior. When Manny was nine, Bill Martin Sr. gave him gifts of three motherless calves. A Superior resident, Manny later purchased grazing rights and, in 1991, bought land in Queen Valley. He is shown (center) with his ranch hands from the Martinez and Castillo families in a Queen Valley roundup. (Manny Ruiz.)

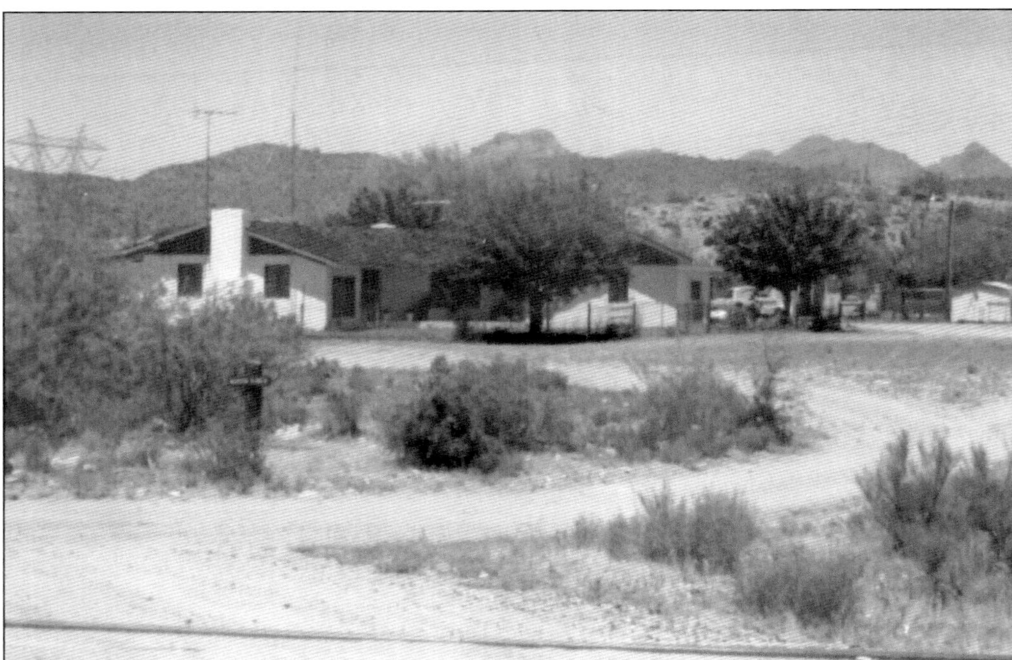

Bill Martin Jr.'s ranch, located along Hewitt Station Road, allows him to run cattle to the east side of town. When Whitlow Dam was built, his father's family ranch was moved east toward Superior. The Espinoza Ranch was where the Queen Valley Sewer Treatment Plant is now. Dee Johnson runs the J Bar P Ranch, situated just west of Queen Valley, and his cattle graze near Queen Valley West. (SMHS, Martin Collection.)

This photograph shows Hart and Margaret Mullins in 1958. They sold their homestead to Pete Allen and retired to Superior. Hart had known before moving to Queen Valley that a flood control dam had been planned in the late 1880s. It was not built by the time this photograph was taken, and after one last frustrating flood, they decided to move to town.

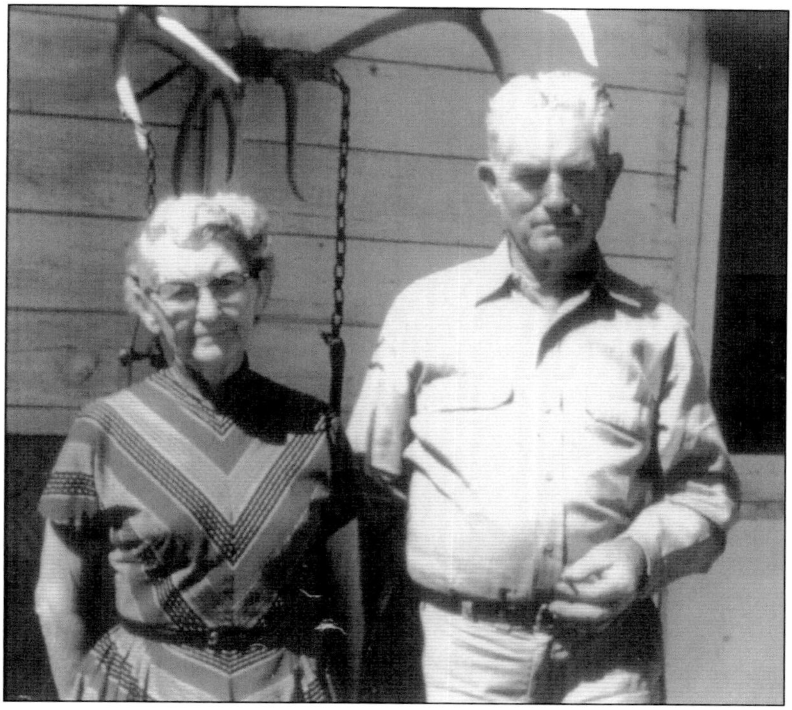

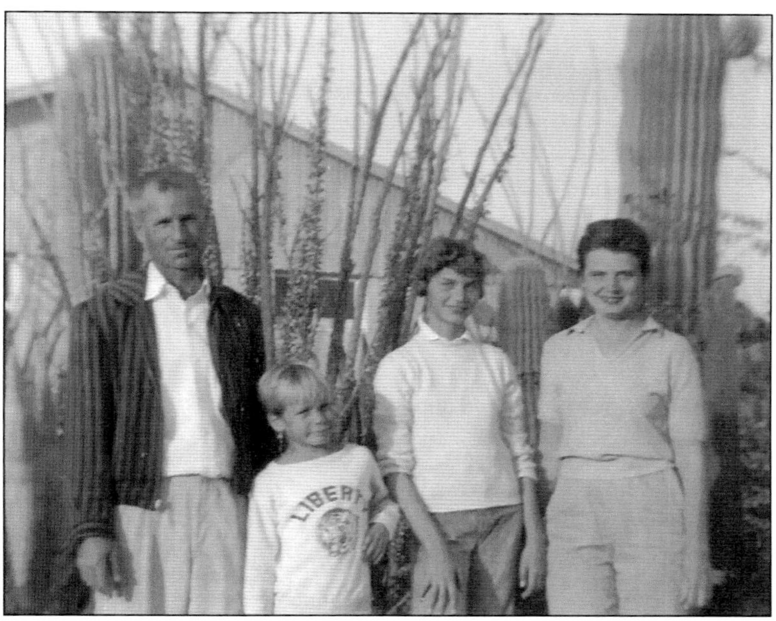

Developer Pete Allen and his family are shown in 1957 in front of the recreation hall at the Anchor P Trailer Park. He was owner of this trailer park, which was in Mesa on Higley and Main Streets. The park is still there but is under the name of X Bar B. Allen often brought groups of guests out to see his Anchor P Cattle Ranch in the beautiful desert of Queen Valley. (Bill Moser.)

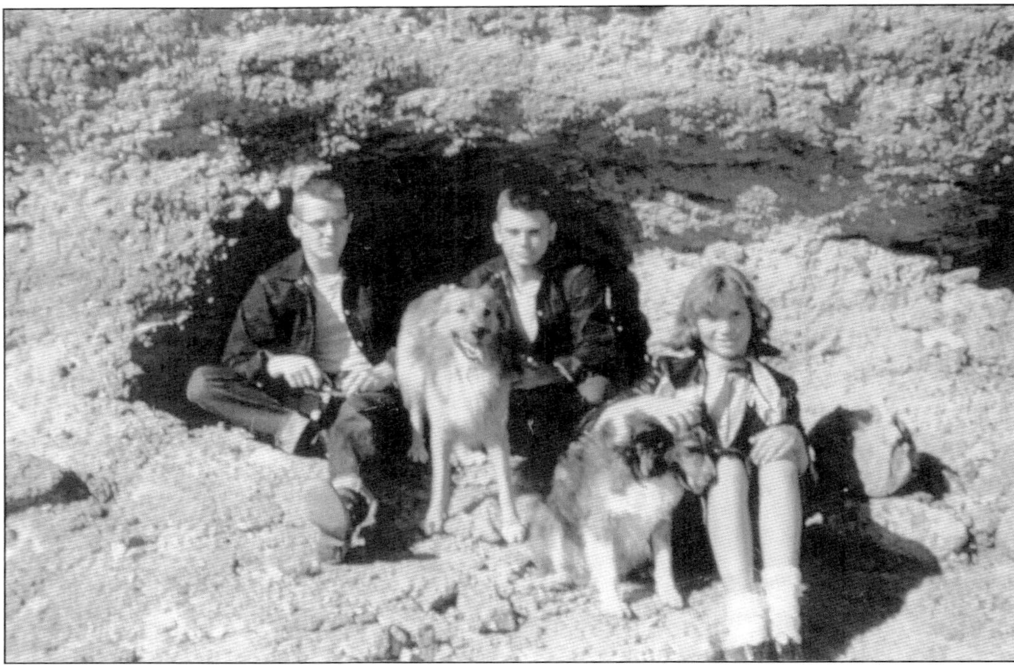

In January 1958, Bill Moser, left, came to Queen Valley to visit his parents' friends the Allens. As shown in this picture, he spent time exploring the caves and Native American ruins in the hills around Queen Valley with Pete's children Rob and Barbara and dogs Bob and Pepper. (Bill Moser.)

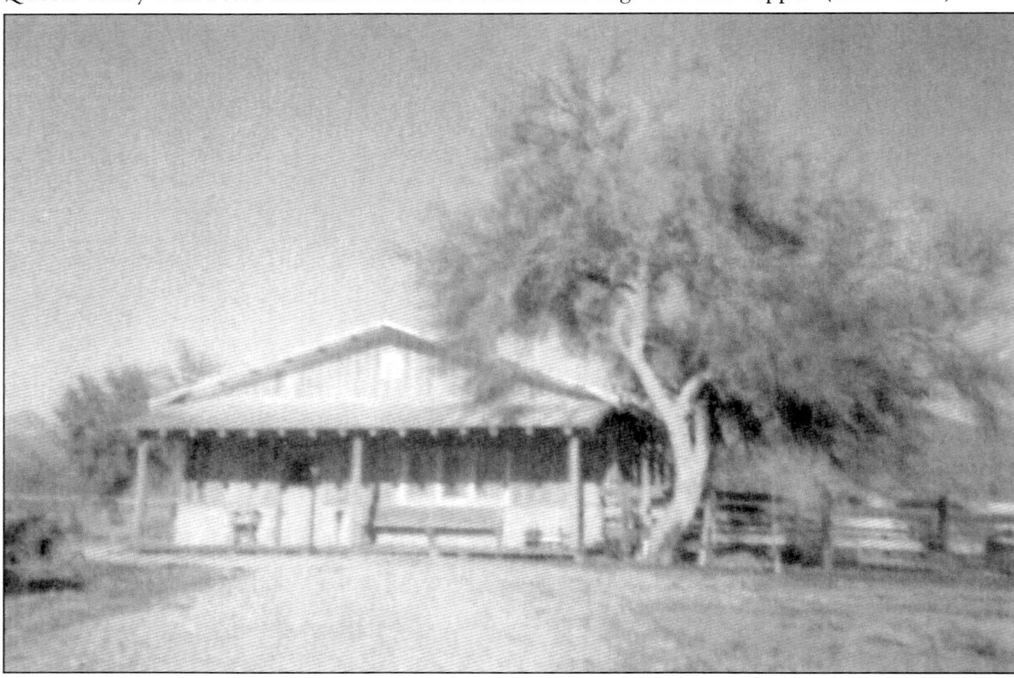

This building had a bunkhouse on the east and a livestock barn on the west. A double-sided fireplace kept them both warm. Allen kept the Anchor P brand upon purchasing the ranch from Hart Mullins. The town was originally called "Peaceful Valley." (*Superior Sun.*)

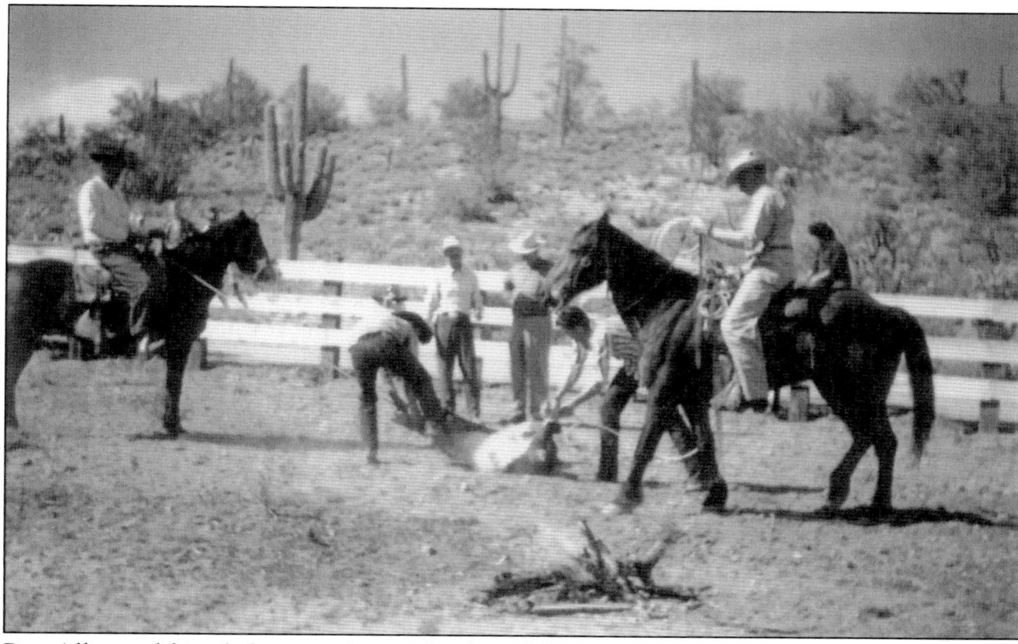

Pete Allen and friends from nearby ranches brand the Anchor P cattle. It was not uncommon for the ranchers to work together to bring in cattle for castrating, birthing, branding, and de-horning activities. These cowboys were from the ranch south of Queen Valley, called the Horse Track Ranch run by Mr. Block. (Bill Moser.)

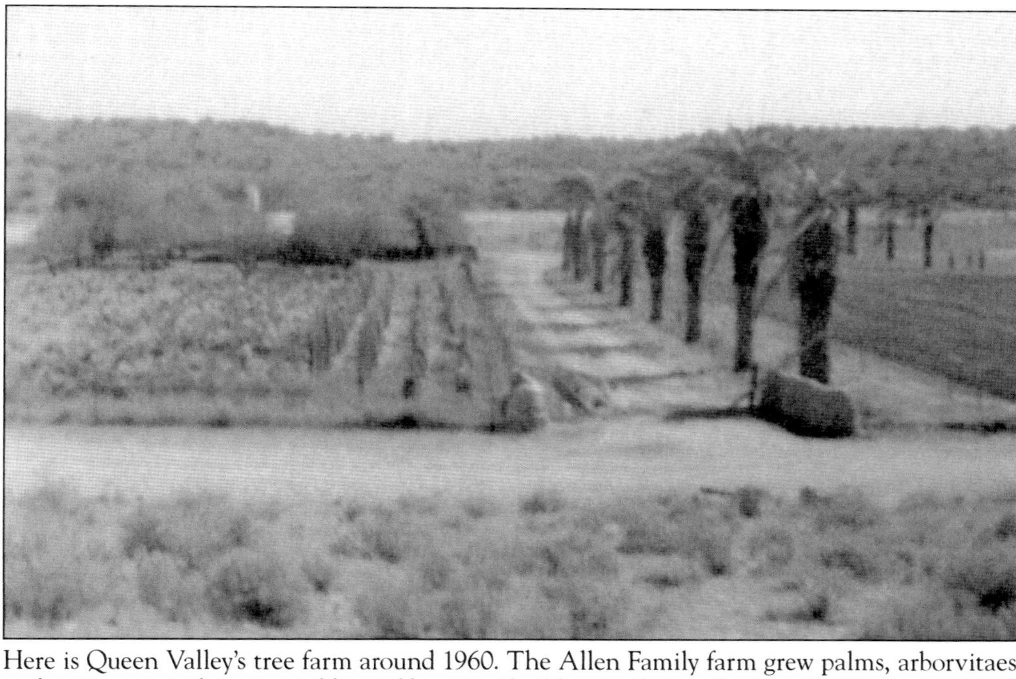

Here is Queen Valley's tree farm around 1960. The Allen Family farm grew palms, arborvitaes, and cypress trees that were sold to golf courses, builders, and even the Apache Greyhound Race Track. Evidence of this tree farm can be seen all over the existing golf course that was built over the former tree farm property. (Bill Moser.)

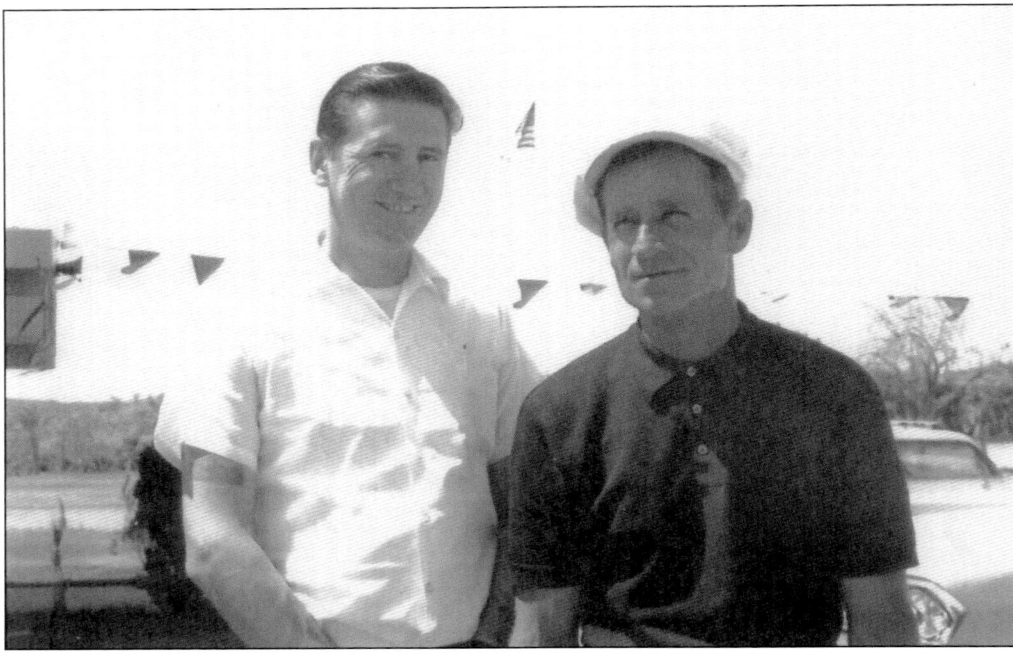

The property transferred ownership to Kenneth Gietz in 1962, before the course actually opened to the public. Gietz, left, began building homes and selling them, and the development of Queen Valley was in full swing around 1963. Gietz was killed in a front-loader accident while clearing property for building a home. (Bill Moser.)

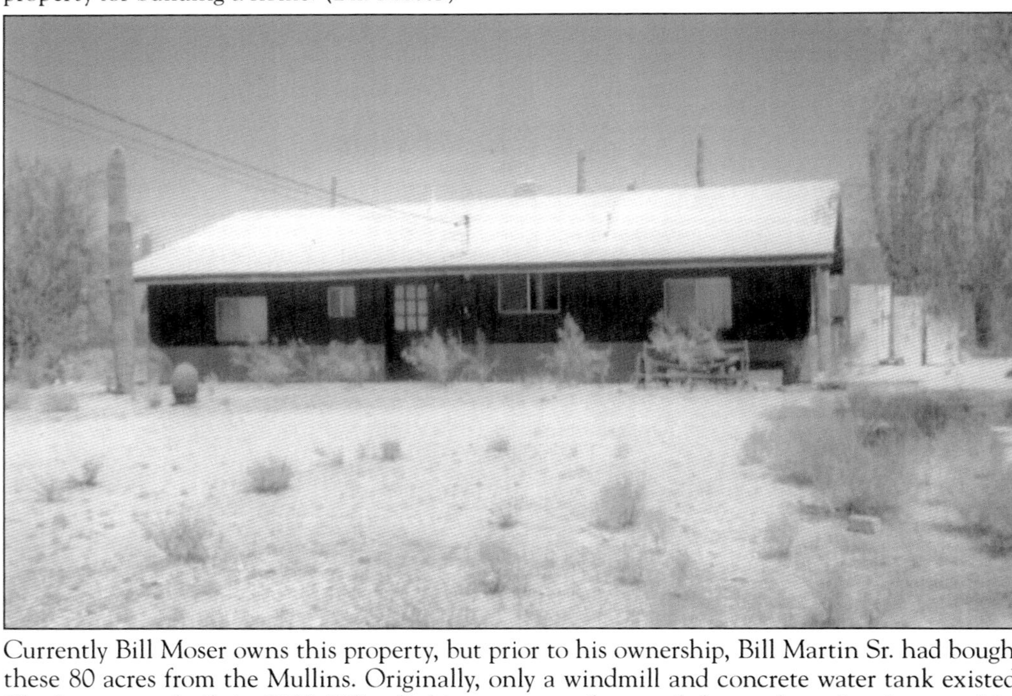

Currently Bill Moser owns this property, but prior to his ownership, Bill Martin Sr. had bought these 80 acres from the Mullins. Originally, only a windmill and concrete water tank existed. The house was built in 1963. Bill split his acreage and created the roadway that is named Jay Street. (Bill Moser.)

Some of the land for the golf course was purchased from the Espinoza and Baldwin Ranches. This original application for membership to the Queen Valley Golf Course shows fees were $50 to join and then $5 monthly dues. Many of the charter members in the early days of the course were from the town of Superior. (Bill Moser.)

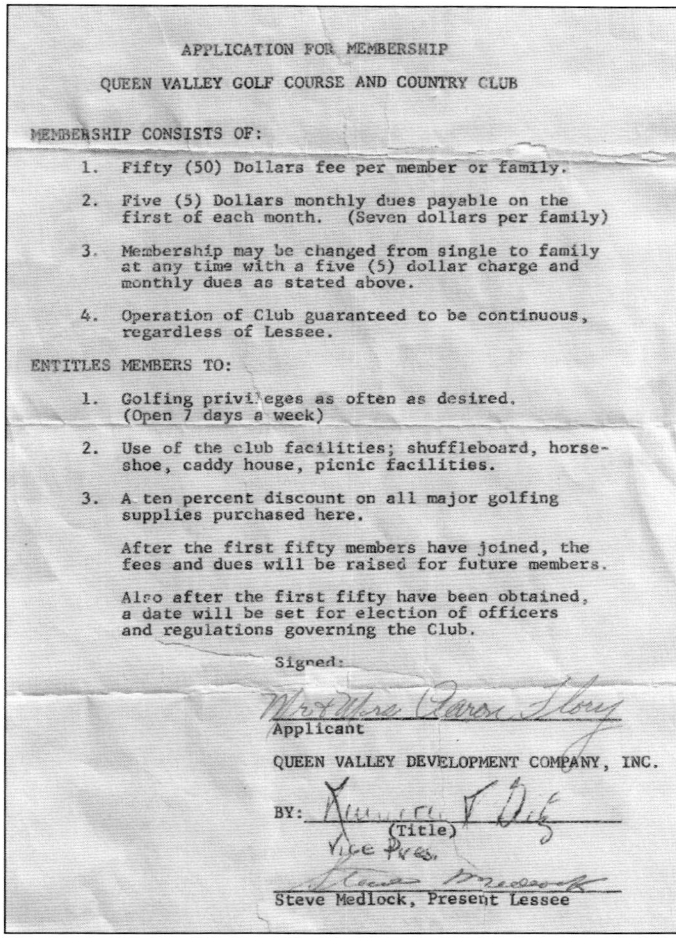

APPLICATION FOR MEMBERSHIP

QUEEN VALLEY GOLF COURSE AND COUNTRY CLUB

MEMBERSHIP CONSISTS OF:

1. Fifty (50) Dollars fee per member or family.
2. Five (5) Dollars monthly dues payable on the first of each month. (Seven dollars per family)
3. Membership may be changed from single to family at any time with a five (5) dollar charge and monthly dues as stated above.
4. Operation of Club guaranteed to be continuous, regardless of Lessee.

ENTITLES MEMBERS TO:

1. Golfing privileges as often as desired. (Open 7 days a week)
2. Use of the club facilities; shuffleboard, horseshoe, caddy house, picnic facilities.
3. A ten percent discount on all major golfing supplies purchased here.

After the first fifty members have joined, the fees and dues will be raised for future members.

Also after the first fifty have been obtained, a date will be set for election of officers and regulations governing the Club.

Signed:

Mr & Mrs Aaron Story
Applicant

QUEEN VALLEY DEVELOPMENT COMPANY, INC.

BY: ______________
(Title)
Vice Pres.

Steve Medlock
Steve Medlock, Present Lessee

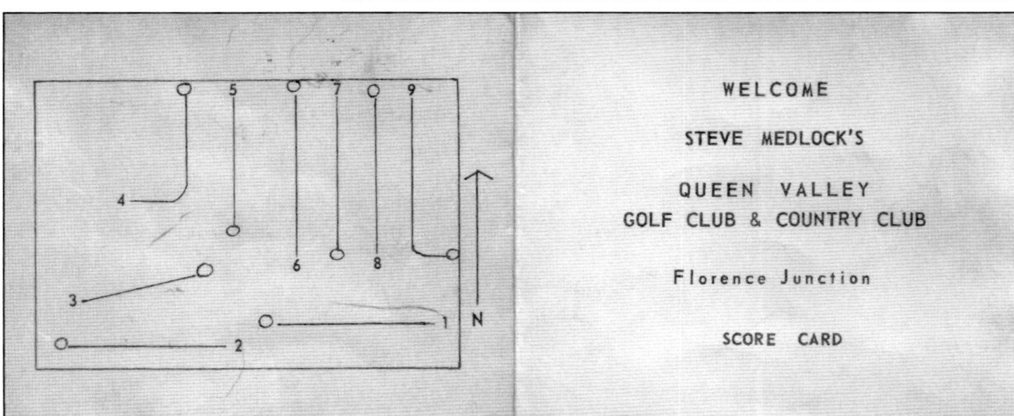

Here is a golf scorecard from the Queen Valley Golf Course in 1964. Only 9 holes existed at that time, and Steve Medlock ran the golf course. The address is listed as Florence Junction since that was the nearest post office at the time. Few knew where Queen Valley was actually located. Now people come from all over the United States and Canada to play the beautiful course. (Bill Moser.)

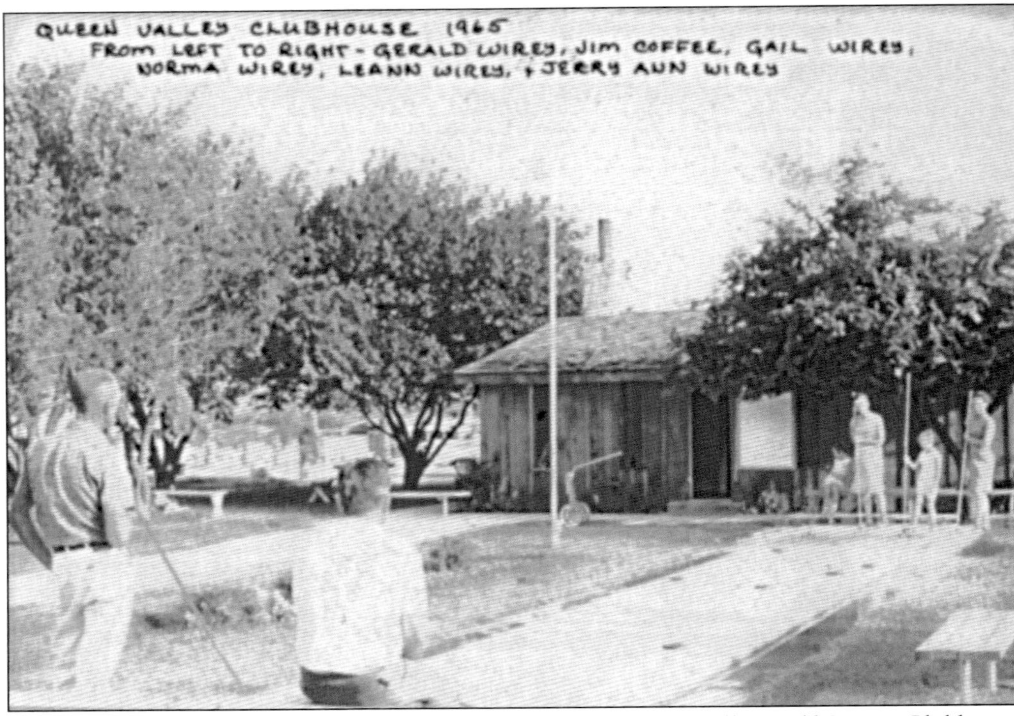

Hart Mullins's original stone house was later used as the Queen Valley Golf Course Clubhouse. Shown here is a family playing shuffleboard. There were also tennis courts, but the upkeep and minimal use caused their demise. The stone house now serves as a bar owned by Emilio Palacio. (QVHS.)

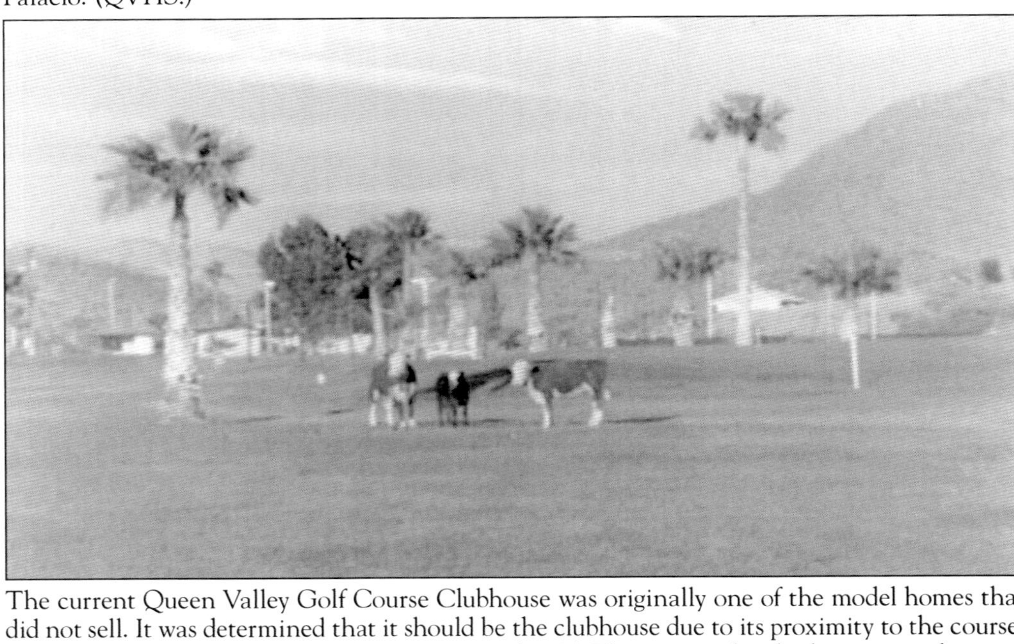

The current Queen Valley Golf Course Clubhouse was originally one of the model homes that did not sell. It was determined that it should be the clubhouse due to its proximity to the course, and the clubhouse moved to this location around 1966. The course often had unexpected animal visitors. (Laura Dean-Lytle.)

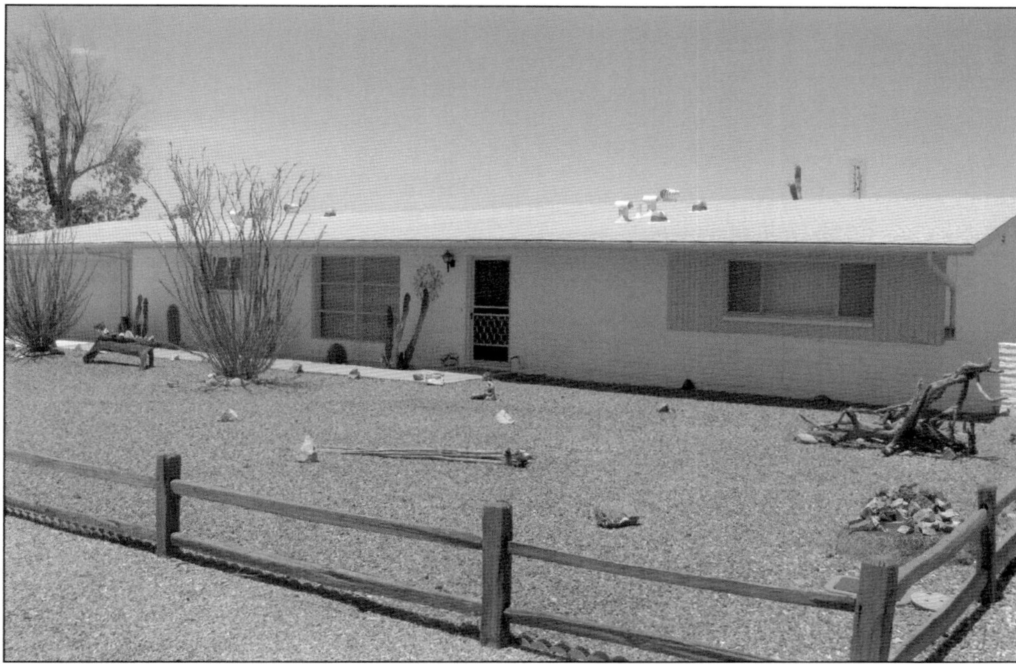

The Sahara Land and Realty Company was marketing homes placed on the hills rather than down in the valley floor due to the fear of flooding by potential buyers. This model home was used as the real estate office. Bill Moser sold the first couple lots for around $1,700 each.

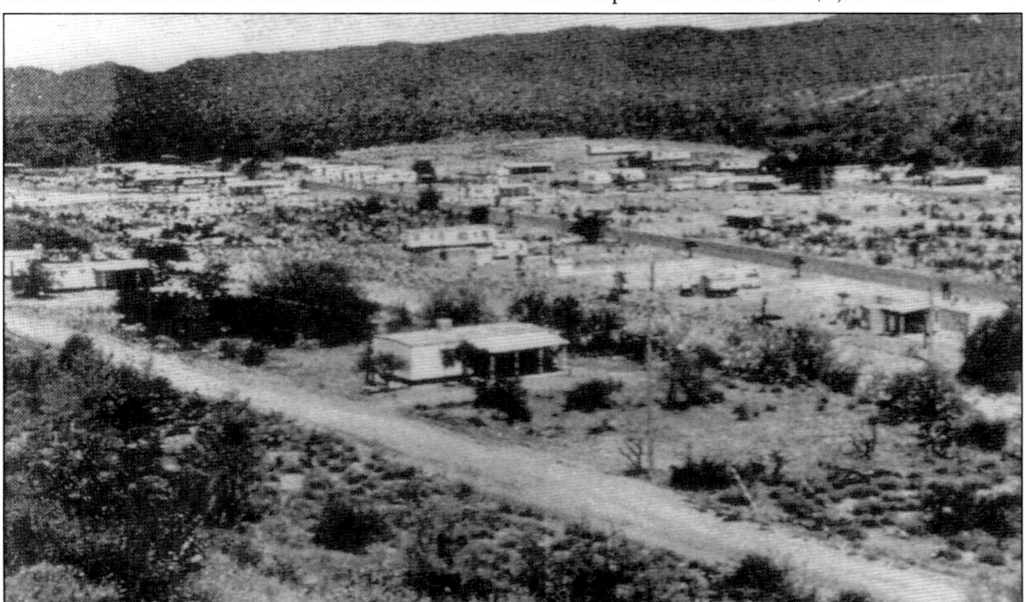

Originally, no mobile lots were planned, but the developers changed their minds as requests came in. Sales began as an "experiment" to see if flooding was a problem. Eventually, the west side of Queen Valley developed into mobile home lots that now dot the western hills and valley. Many of those residents remain today in their original mobile homes or houses that they subsequently built in Queen Valley. (*Superior Sun*.)

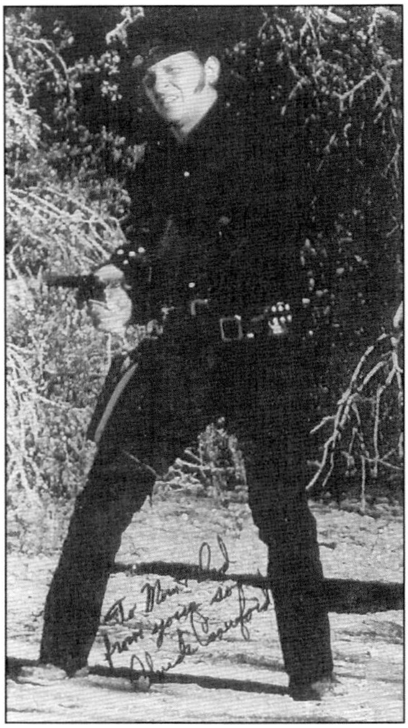

As the town developed, a richly diverse group of people made the town their home. This included some very unusual people like convicted arsonist and accused murderer Marjorie Hagen and prospector Charlie Crawford. Charlie was an avid gold seeker and got involved in politics but was never elected to office. He sometimes worked at the Apacheland Movie Studios as an extra and called himself "Black Bart." (Jack San Felice.)

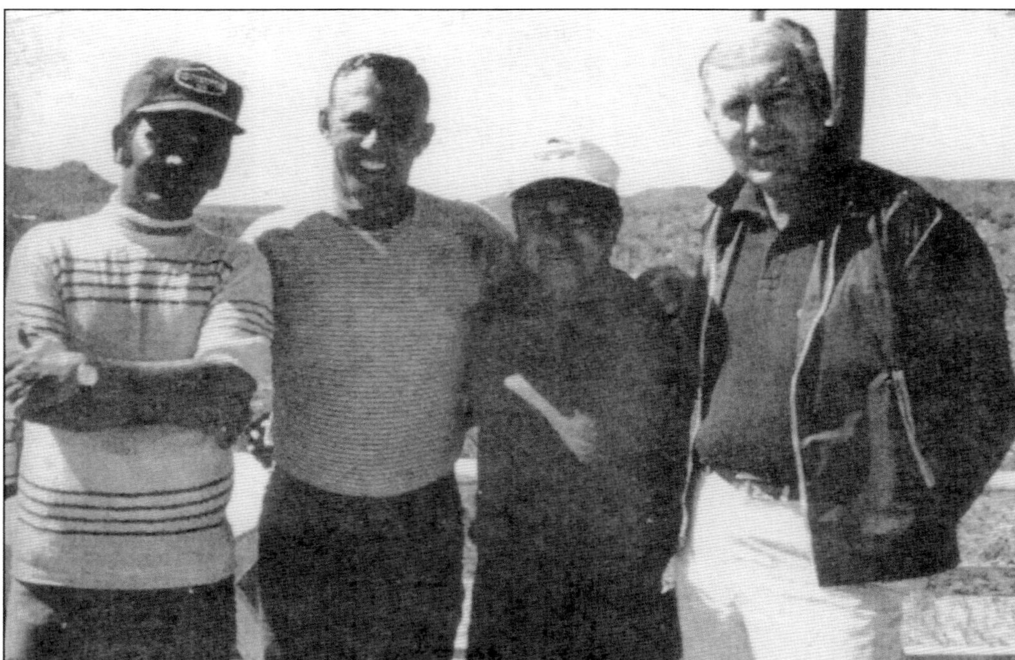

The Queen Valley Golf Course was heavily marketed and drew visitors from everywhere. This 1970 photograph shows unidentified members of the San Francisco Giants baseball team. In 1971, the course held an Amateur Classic Tournament including celebrities from baseball. Host Willie Mays brought his baseball friends. The committee included Alvin Dark, manager of the Cleveland Indians; Larry Smith, scout for the Atlanta Braves; and several managers of Harrah's Lake Tahoe. (*Superior Sun.*)

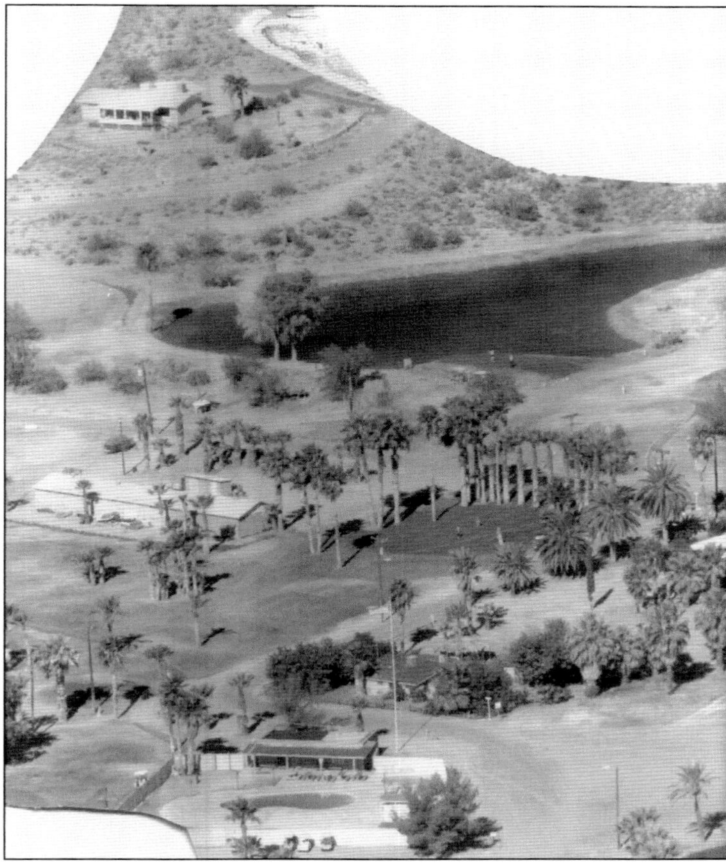

The house at the top of the picture was one of the first built by Pete Allen and served as a ranch house for the Anchor P. The original stones in the foundation and ponderosa pine rafters have now been covered over. The golf course, Oasis Room, pool, and maintenance shed are shown, and the town's development was fully underway. (QV Properties, Inc.)

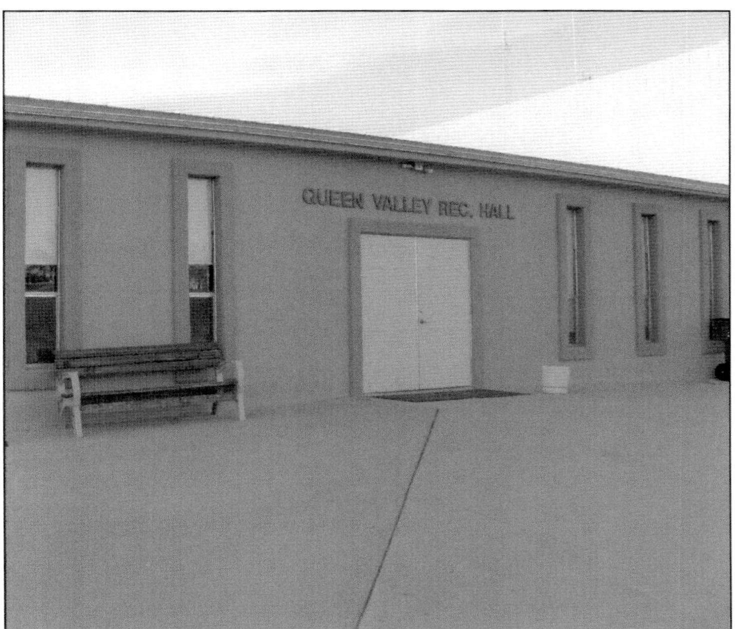

Gietz started the Queen Valley Homeowner's Association, but upon his death, it evolved into an unofficial HOA. With $20 yearly dues, the HOA keeps Queen Valley residents in touch through dances, road cleanups, blood drives, and charity activities. This group is the social connection that binds the community and serves as liaison to Pinal County and state officials.

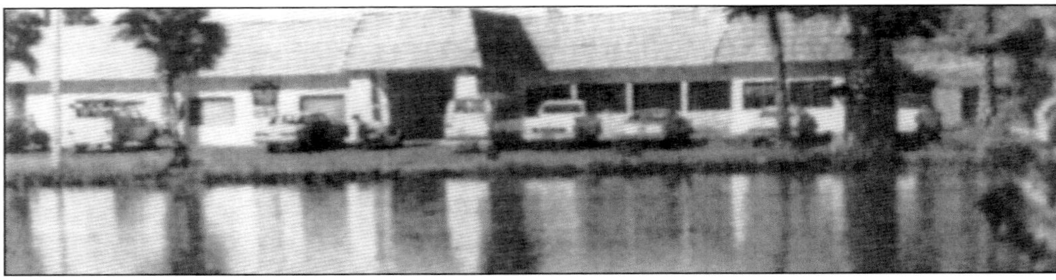

The Anchor P bunkhouse was expanded and converted in 1968 to a steak house, with a dance floor located where the barn once stood. It changed owners and managers several times over the years but remained a very popular place. People came from miles around to party or have business meetings in Queen Valley. Resident Jane Blackburn wrote a song about Queen Valley to the tune of "The Battle Hymn of the Republic"; it was always sung at evening's end when friends said goodnight. The last owner, Emilio Palacio, displayed a collection of liquor decanters as well as pictures of the people who came to enjoy the food, drinks, and good company of neighbors and town visitors. Sadly, everything was destroyed in a 1988 fire. (QV HOA.)

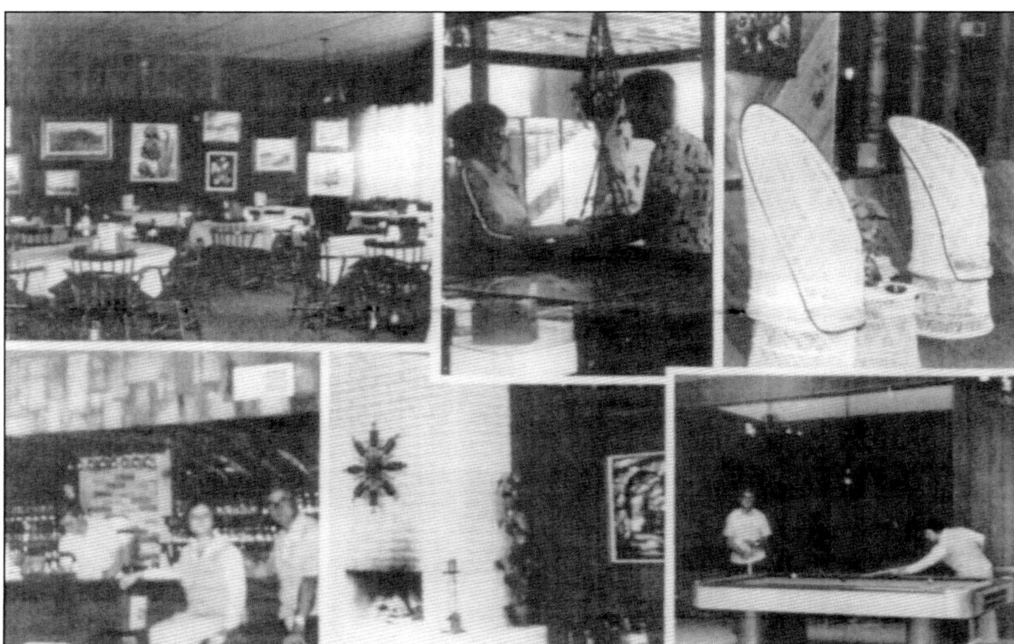

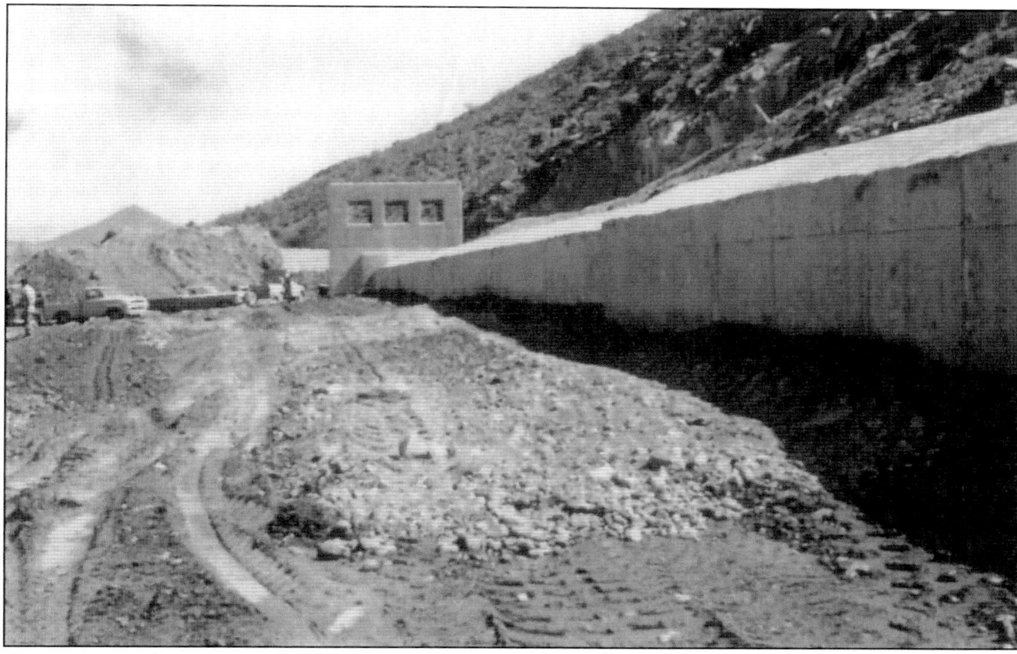

Construction began on Whitlow Dam in 1959 and took one year. The work was done by the U.S. Army Corps of Engineers. It took many years to get funds for the dam. Queen Creek's flooding caused damage to the town of Queen Valley and to the runways at Williams Air Force Base. Prior to the dam being built, there was only one way into Queen Valley, and when it flooded, townspeople were stranded. By 1961, negotiations allowed the town to utilize the road built for the dam construction as a second road into town. With the help of the dam, floods that now occur are much smaller and seldom impede travel. That road has now become the main road into town, and the original road is considered "the back way out." (Bill Moser.)

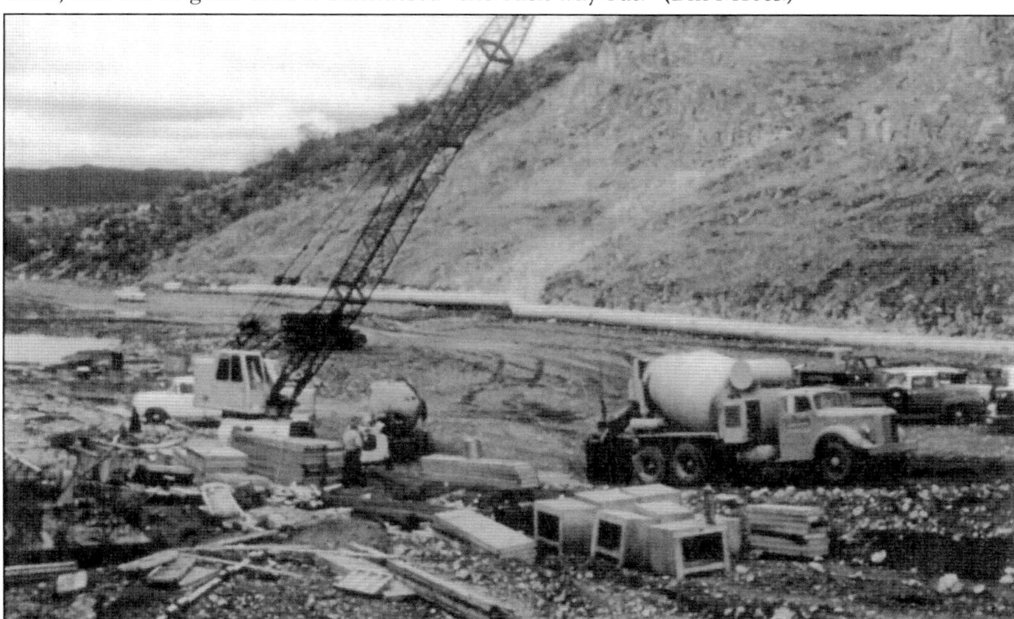

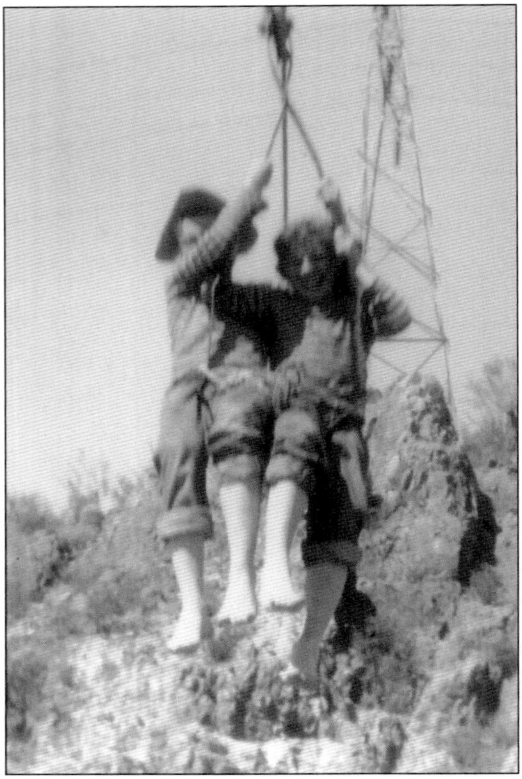

The building of Whitlow Dam allowed Queen Valley to become a viable town. Prior to that time, the town's buildings and agriculture were at the mercy of heavy rains and flooding. Homestead records speak of years of drought and floods, both of which damaged crops. Rob and Barbara Allen used to play in the construction zone and once got caught in the aerial bucket that traversed the dam and needed to be rescued. (SMHS.)

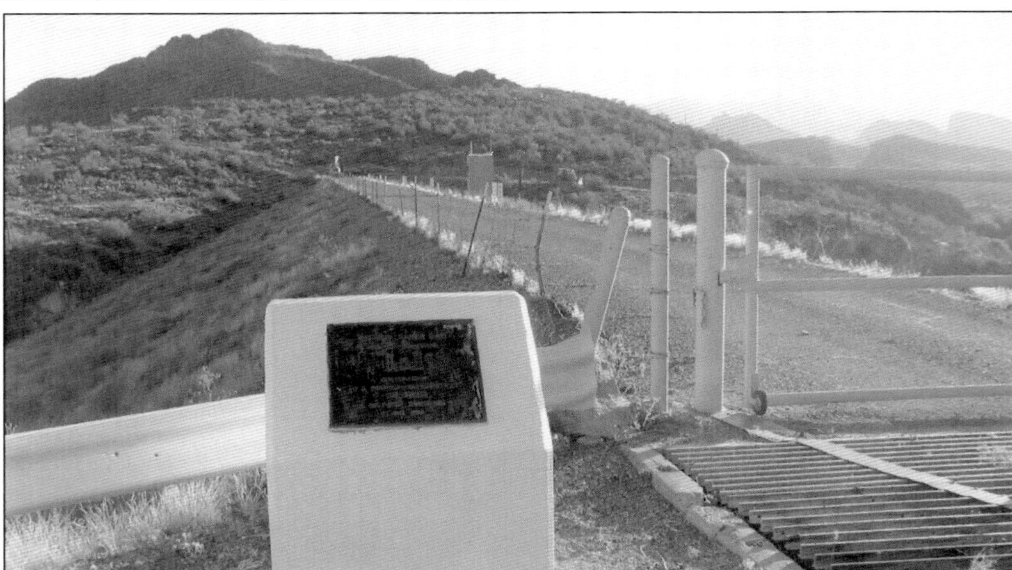

Whitlow Dam was dedicated on October 1, 1960, and included a number of speakers in the ceremony, including Sen. Carl Hayden, Congressman John Rhodes, Supreme Court Justice Jesse Udall, and Gov. Paul Fannin. The Army Corps of Engineers continues to inspect the dam every five years and performs routine maintenance on it yearly. The dam is also used as a weather-monitoring station, with daily records being sent electronically.

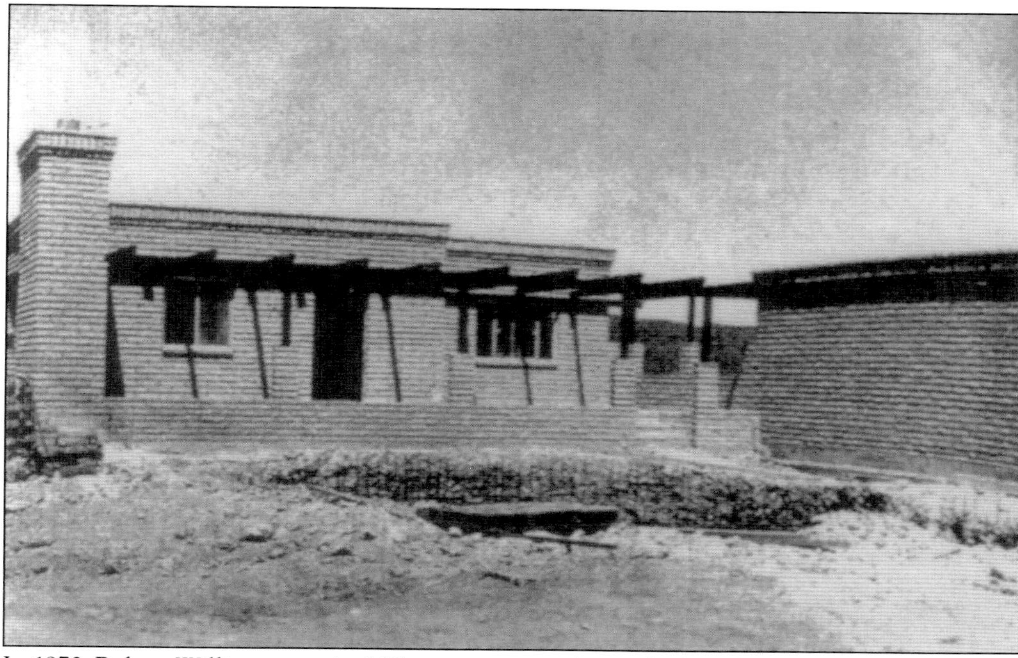

In 1970, Robert Williams, a retired Chevy engineer who worked on the first Corvette, built this Spanish-style house on the hill overlooking town. It included a pool and workshop where he ran his welding business, "Valley Forge." (*Superior Sun*.)

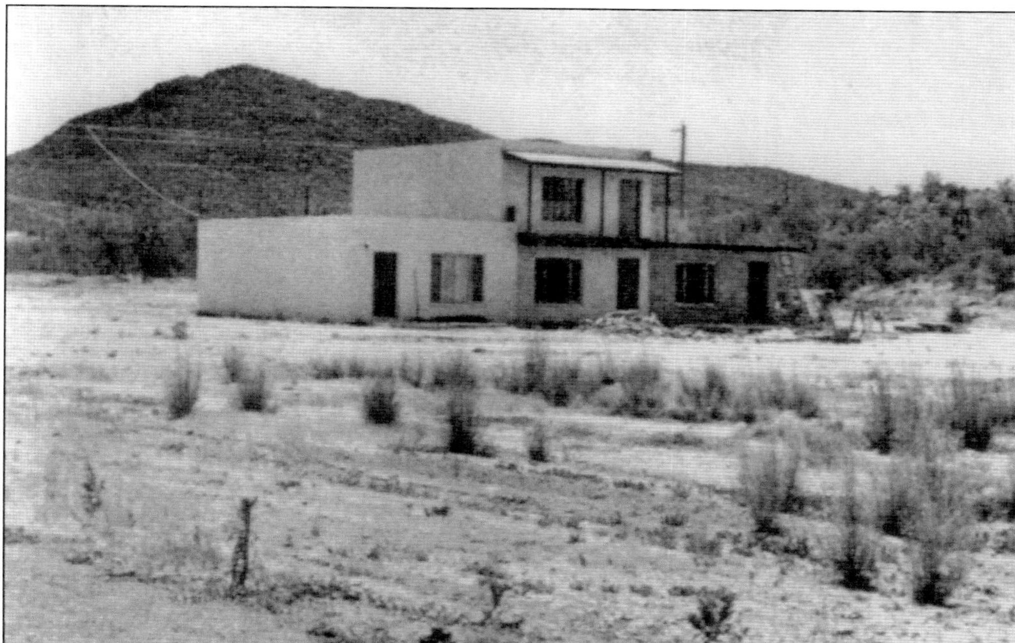

This unit, built in 1970, was the first of what was to be 10 units of one-bedroom apartments. Marketed as ideal for younger people or retired persons wanting more leisure time, they were easily rented, but only three units were built. They were later converted into the Queen Valley Guest House. (*Superior Sun*.)

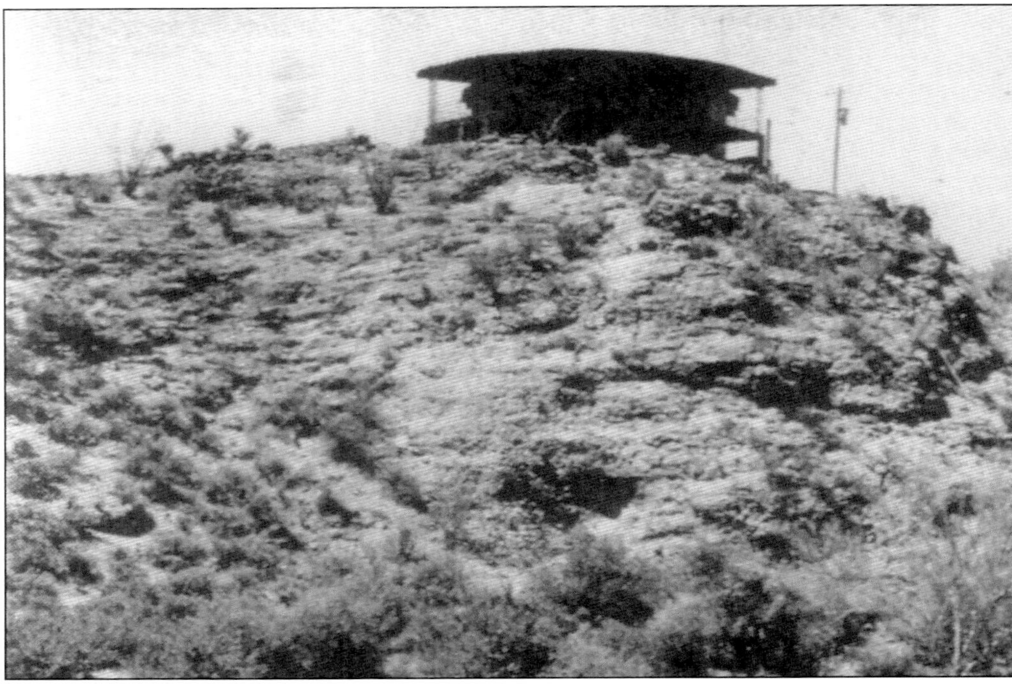

Tag Glover, a golf instructor and real estate sales person for the Queen Valley Development Corporation, sold lots from $2,400 to $4,500 in 1970. His home sits perched on a 100-foot cliff that overlooks town. The 16-sided home, with a covered patio, provides a panoramic view of the back nine holes of the golf course and also views of the foothills of the Superstition Mountains. Others soon copied Glover, building their homes there too. (*Superior Sun*.)

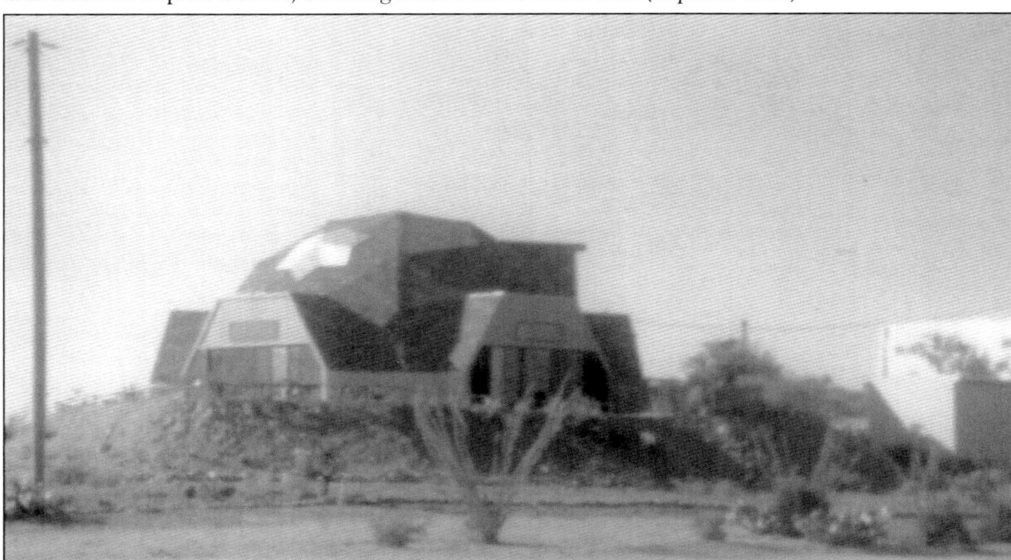

Queen Valley became an area known for its custom homes, and one of the most unusual homes to be built was that of D. L. and Connie Smith. They were looking for a place to escape from California earthquakes and fell in love with Queen Valley. Built in 1980 on the first lot they viewed and bought on the spot, this geodesic dome is an icon in the valley. (Smith Collection.)

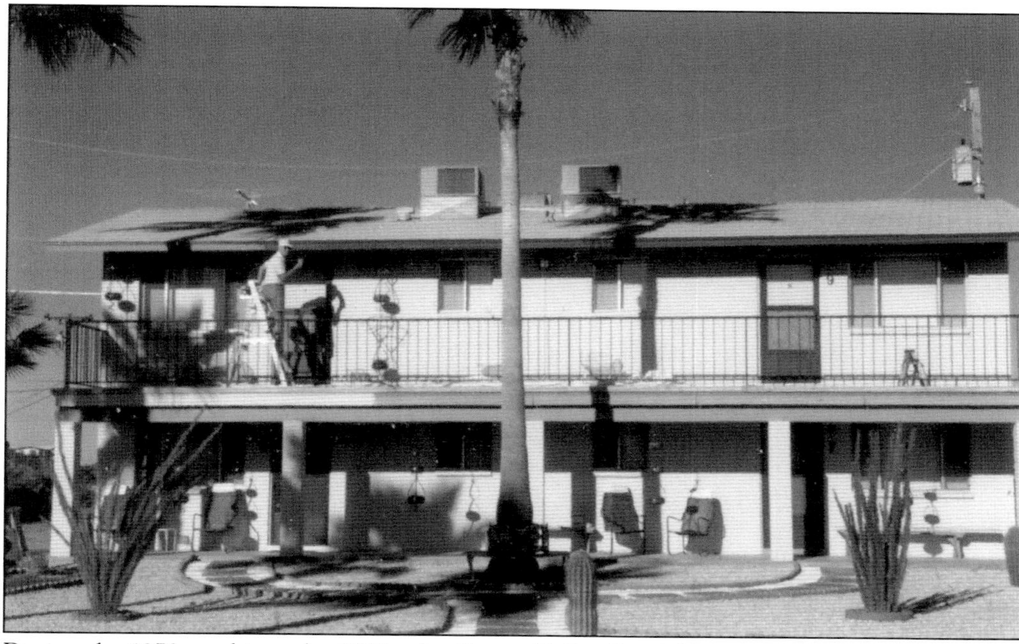

During the 1970s and into the 1980s, the Queen Valley Guest House was a very popular rental property with a waiting list and reservations made years in advance. Many people returned year after year to this beautiful valley for the golf, the climate, and the friendships. (Bob Deem, shown here painting it soon after purchase, provided this photograph.)

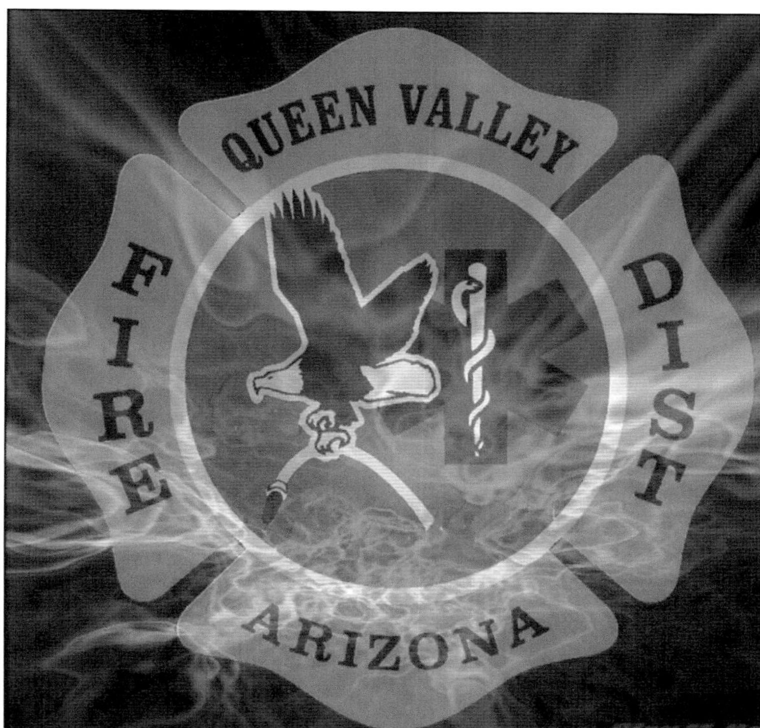

The Queen Valley Fire District was formed in 1986 with O. E. Jones as first chairman, Cecil Fendley as fire chief, and Steve Joyce as deputy fire chief. The fire department has an active fire auxiliary that raises funds for the purchase of equipment and other firefighting efforts.

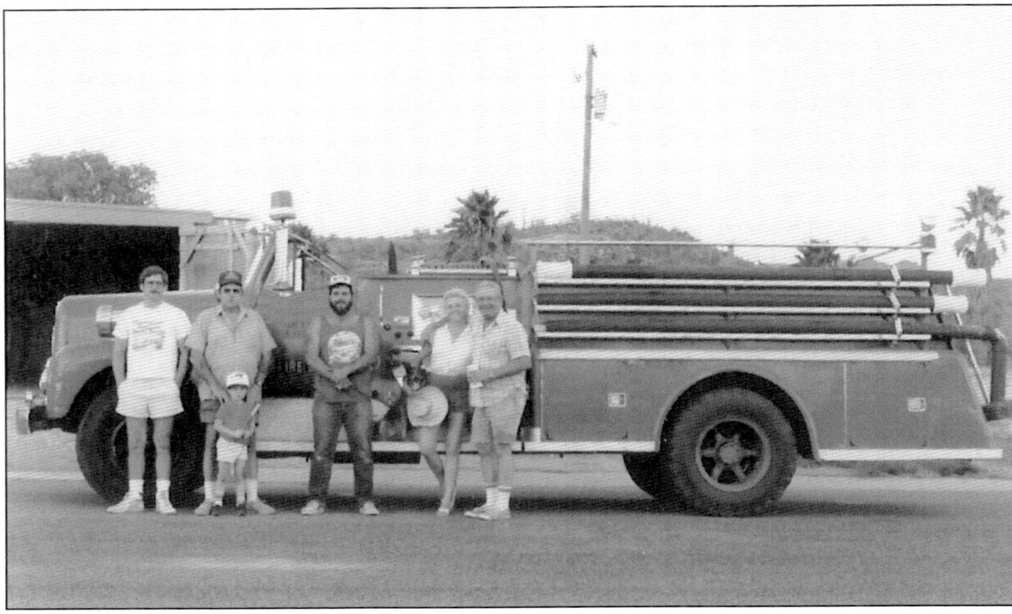

Queen Valley had a seven-member volunteer fire department beginning in 1986. That tradition continues today with around 20 volunteers and 10 explorers. Shown here with the 1959 Hale Pumper are, from left to right, Steve Joyce, John Smith, Cecil Fendley, and the Barnetts. The child in front is John's grandson. (QV Fire Department.)

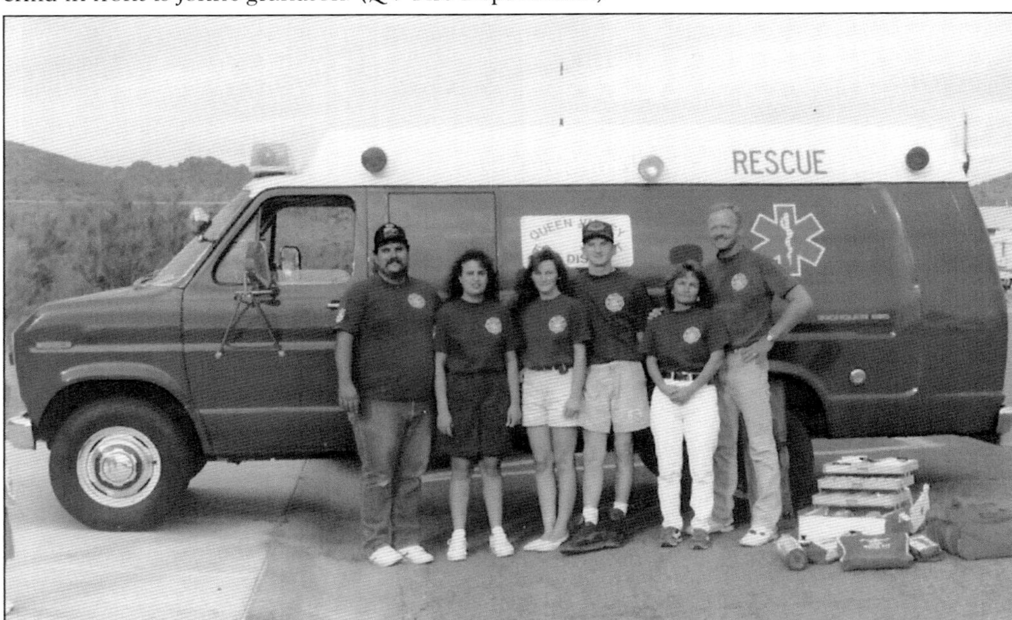

In this 1990 photograph, the Queen Valley Fire Department is receiving its new rescue vehicle. Shown are, from left to right, Cecil Fendley, Penny Fendley, Kim Weires, Jessie Weires, Charlene McKinney, and Deputy Chief Russ McKinney. The volunteers monitor all of Queen Valley and Route 60, from Florence Junction to Superior, and halfway to Florence, covering car accidents, water rescue, and medical emergencies. (QV Fire Department.)

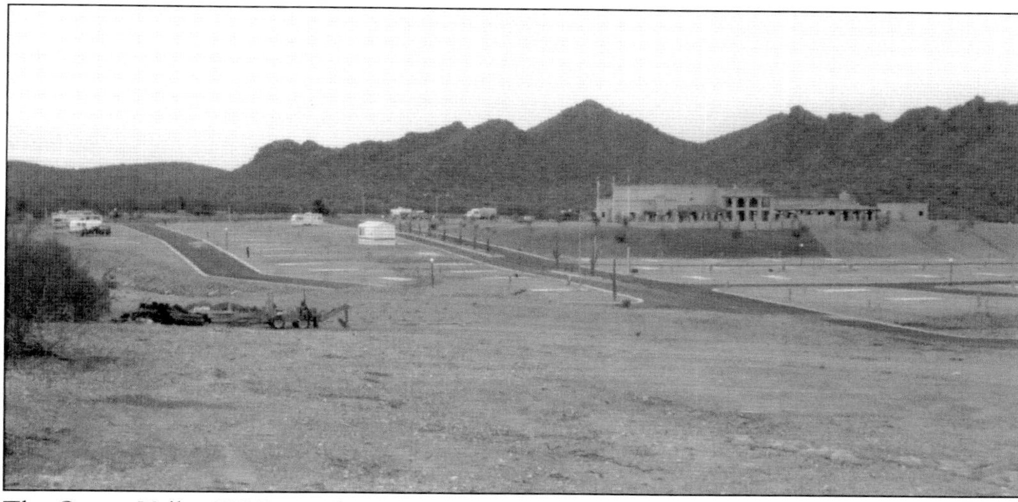

The Queen Valley RV Resort began construction in 1982 and moved into its new offices on October 1, 1984. In this photograph, the streets are being installed and the clubhouse and office are already completed. Manager Sally Phillips has been with the resort since its inception. While a few heat-loving folks live there year-round, during the winter season guests fill the park to capacity. (Bill Moser.)

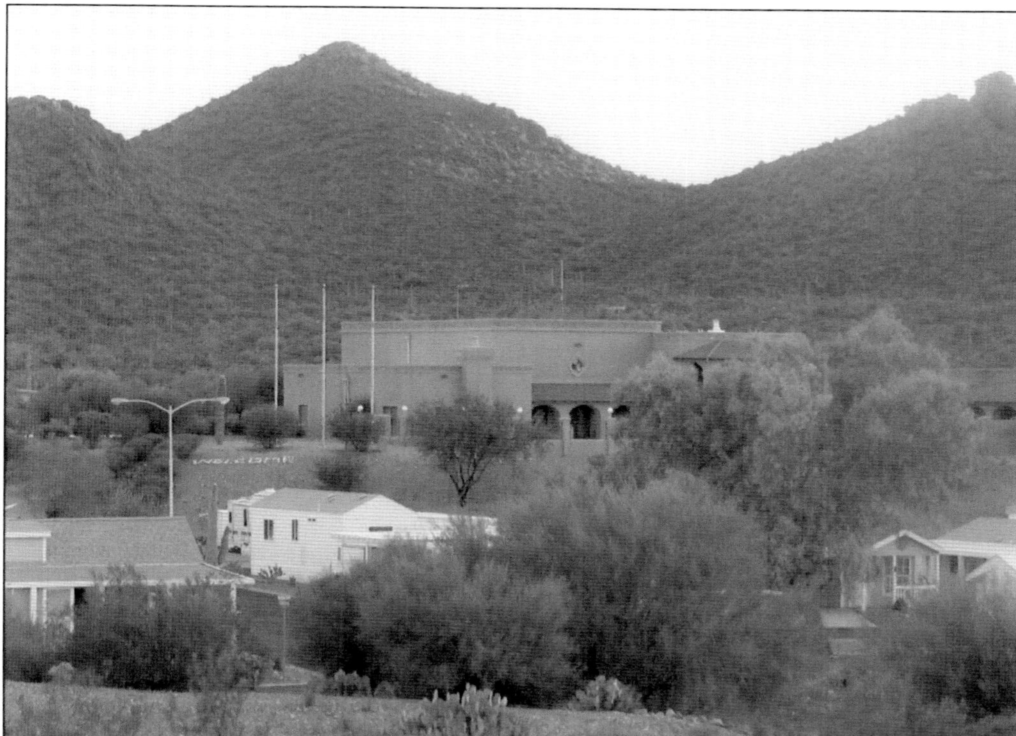

Ownership changed in 2005, and it is now the McGavin Queen Valley RV Park. Almost 400 visitors come to stay for a few nights to a few months, annually. Park models have annually returning residents. The park residents and visitors are a big part of the social life and fun in Queen Valley, sharing activities with the townspeople. Many have formed lifelong friendships.

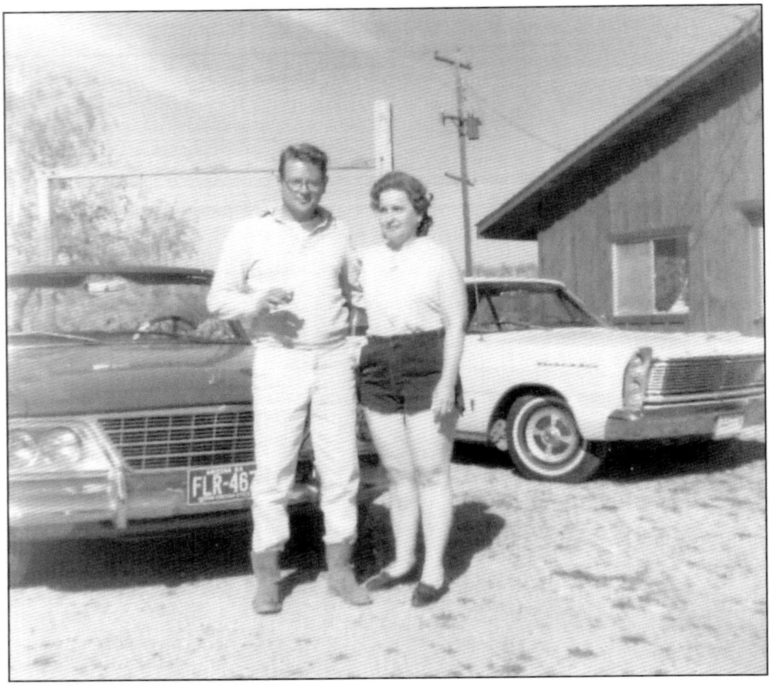

Bill Moser was a real estate salesman in Apache Junction and Queen Valley and became Pete Allen's business partner. He began to develop the west side of town along the El Camino Viejo Road in the 1960s. He is shown here with Thelma Allen, Pete's sister. (Bill Moser.)

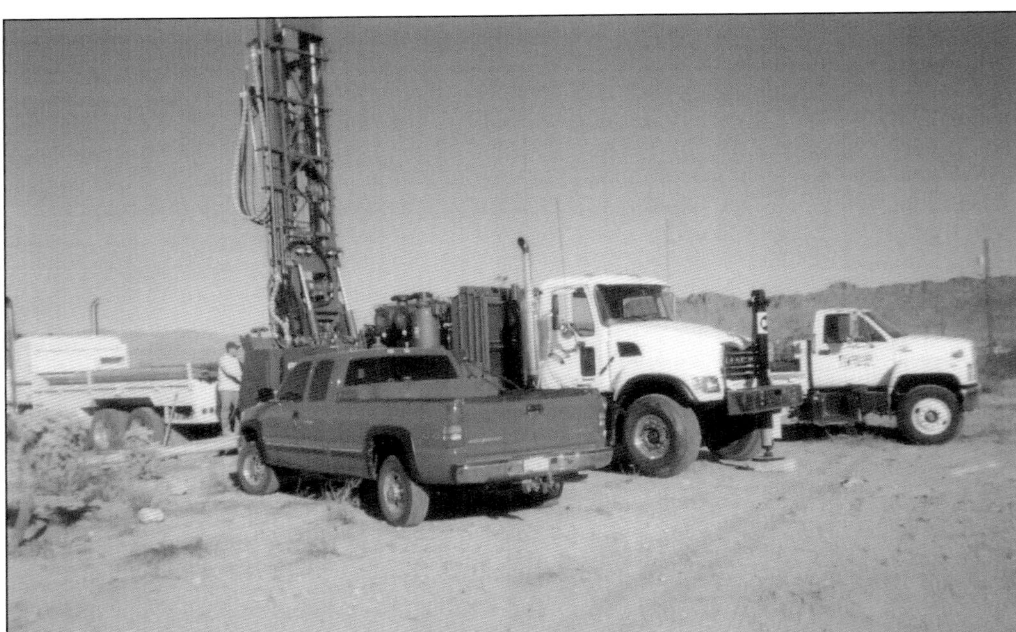

The development on the west side of the mountain, which is now called Queen Valley West, is due in large part to the efforts of Bill Moser. He drilled wells and began selling parcels of land he had purchased from Joyce Mullins. Several ranches and houses now exist on that original property. For several years, a nudist park was being developed, but it did not last. (Bill Moser.)

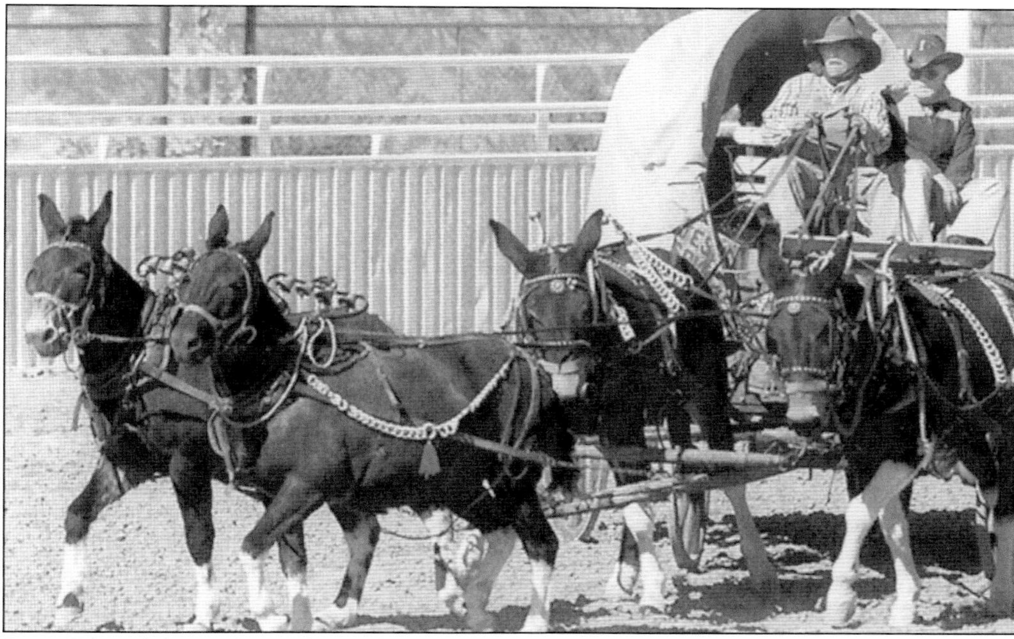

Steve Edwards began his mule ranch in the foothills of the Superstitions but moved here in 1997 for the peace and quiet. His bunkhouse was the original headquarters for the Ruiz Ranch. The Queen Valley Mule Ranch offers training for mules, donkeys, and their owners through clinics, apprenticeships, and individualized programs. (Steve Edwards.)

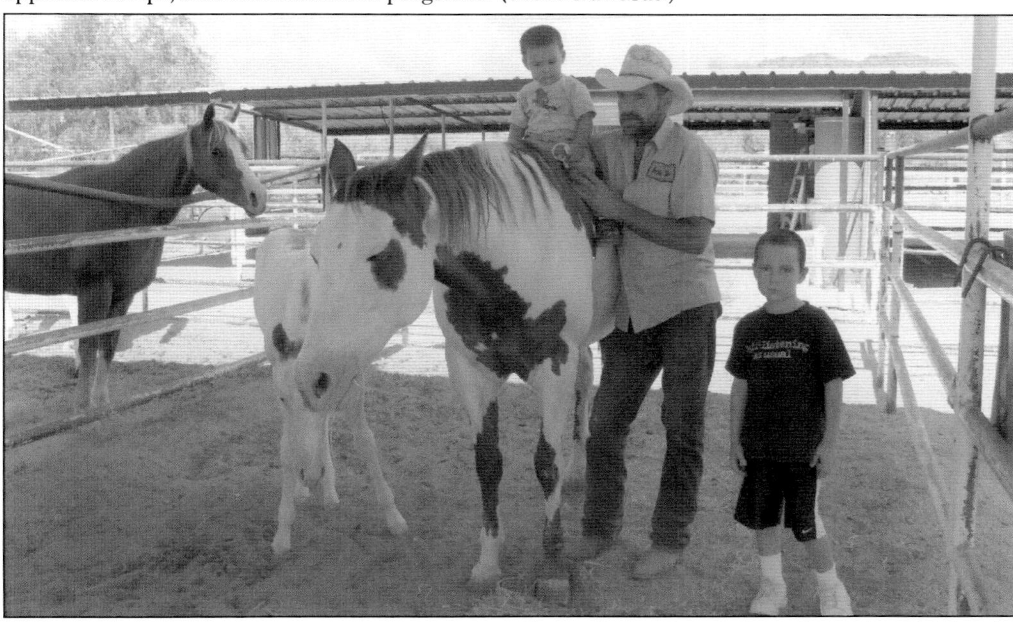

The Superstition Paint Horse Ranch in Queen Valley West, run by Merle and Marilyn Ehlebracht, is a horse-boarding facility, with various sizes of pastures and enclosures. They also offer recreation vehicle spaces, with attached private horse pens and tack rooms, and "RV'ers are welcome whether or not they are bringing horses!" Shown here are Merle and grandsons Cameron and Ryan, sitting on one of the fourth-generation thoroughbred paint horses.

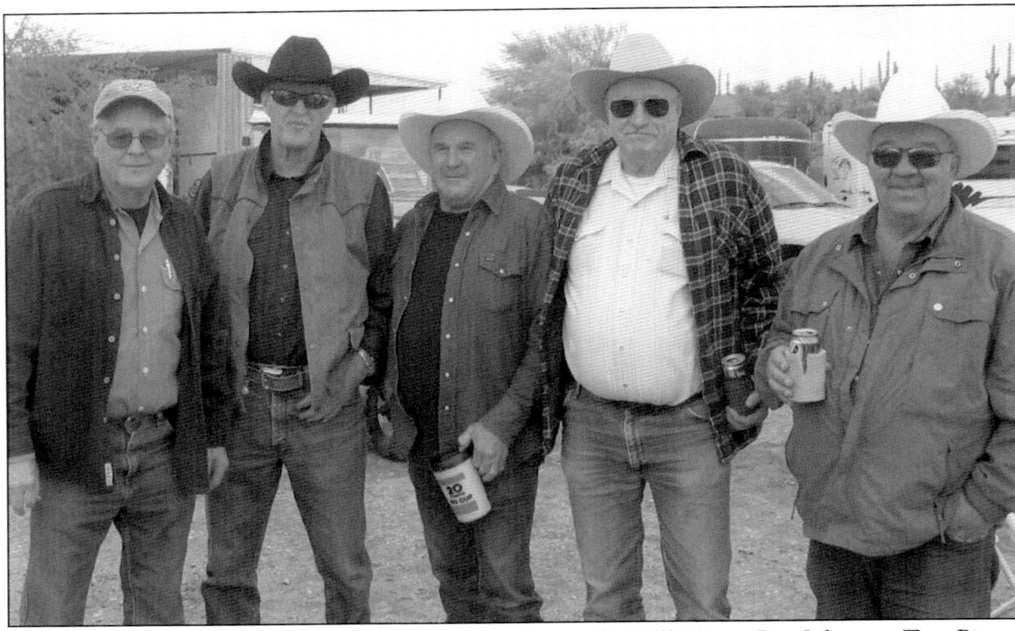

These Queen Valley cowboys include, from the left to right, Bill Moser, Dee Johnson, Tom Pierce, Doug Lewis, and Donnie Ells at the Superstition Paint Horse Charity Event. Yearly, friends and family of Cameron, a former pediatric intensive-care unit patient at St. Joseph's Children's Health Center, sponsor a fund-raiser to thank the hospital staff for his care. The fun includes Western events, bands, and horseshoe, poker, and volleyball tournaments.

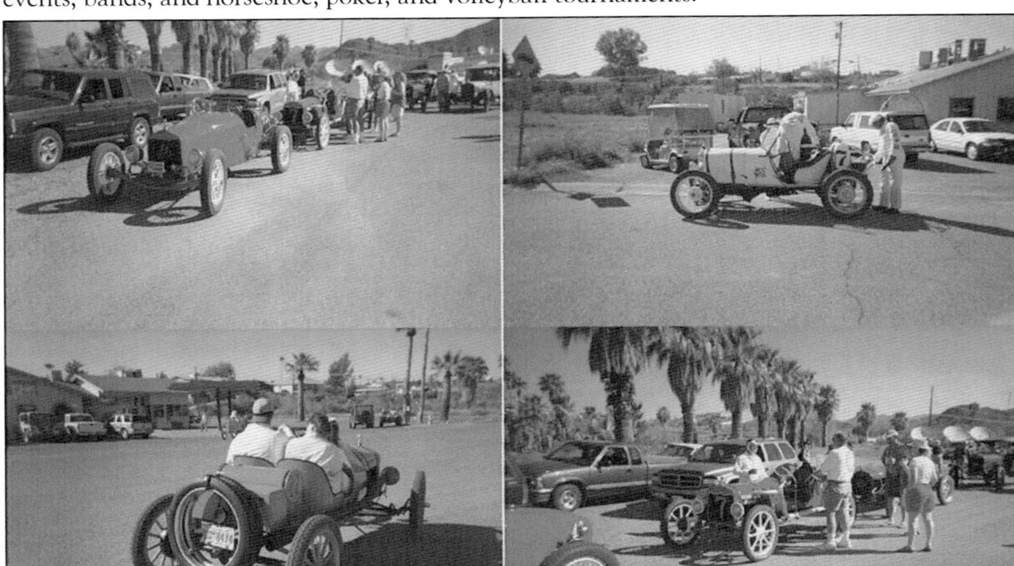

Queen Valley is increasingly becoming a favorite pass-through destination for motorcycle touring clubs, road rallies, and tourists. The ever-changing shadows of light on the surrounding mountains and the "Peaceful Valley" atmosphere welcome everyone who visits. Shown here is the memorial poster for the Sun Country Model T Club that visited in March 2001. (Sun Country Model T Club.)

Seven

Scenic Draw

Just as people in the late 1800s saw inviting places where they could make their homes in the East Valley, so do families of today. The undeveloped area between Phoenix and Superior is quickly becoming smaller as Pinal County continues its rapid growth. The natural desert beauty, wide open spaces, clean air, quiet, relaxed lifestyles, and star-filled night skies are drawing people away from the city and into the small towns of the East Valley. There are solid houses now from downtown Phoenix through Gold Canyon, with the demarcation lines between Tempe, Mesa, Apache Junction, and Gold Canyon becoming difficult to identify without signs. Gold Canyon is home to past and present county supervisors, and as Pinal County's planned economic development is achieved, it will continue growing. State Trust Land south and just west of Queen Valley has already been sold for development. It is the hope of the town that the nearness of services and businesses will improve the economy of the county, while allowing Queen Valley to maintain its small town closeness and unique beauty.

Superior's future is bright, as it has several efforts underway to improve economic development for its townspeople and businesses. The Copper Corridor Consortium and the Superior Chamber of Commerce are working diligently to attract tourism and appropriate sustainable development to the area. A part of this development will be, as it has been in the past, through the mining industry. Exploration has uncovered what may be one of the largest copper resources ever found in North America. If the mine is developed, projections of employment for up to 1,200 mine employees are forecast for several decades. This could have a very significant impact on Superior and surrounding towns like Queen Valley. As of the publishing of this book, the townspeople have mixed feelings about the balance between economic growth for the Cooper Corridor area and the environmental and cultural impacts. Whatever decision is ultimately made, it will most certainly impact the culture, economy, and long-term future of this very special mining town.

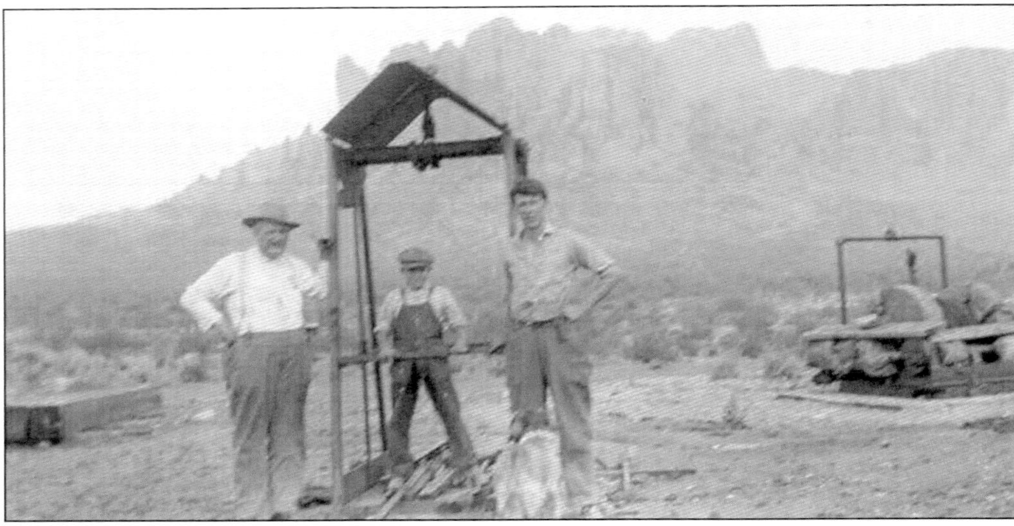

In 1892, Goldfield began when gold ore was found. Soon the town boasted three saloons, a boardinghouse, general store, post office, brewery, blacksmith, butcher, and school. For five years, 1,500 people were residing there. The town was abandoned by 1898, when the ore played out. A rebirth happened from 1921 to 1926, but that died too. Today visitors can travel back in time in this re-created ghost town. (ADMMR.)

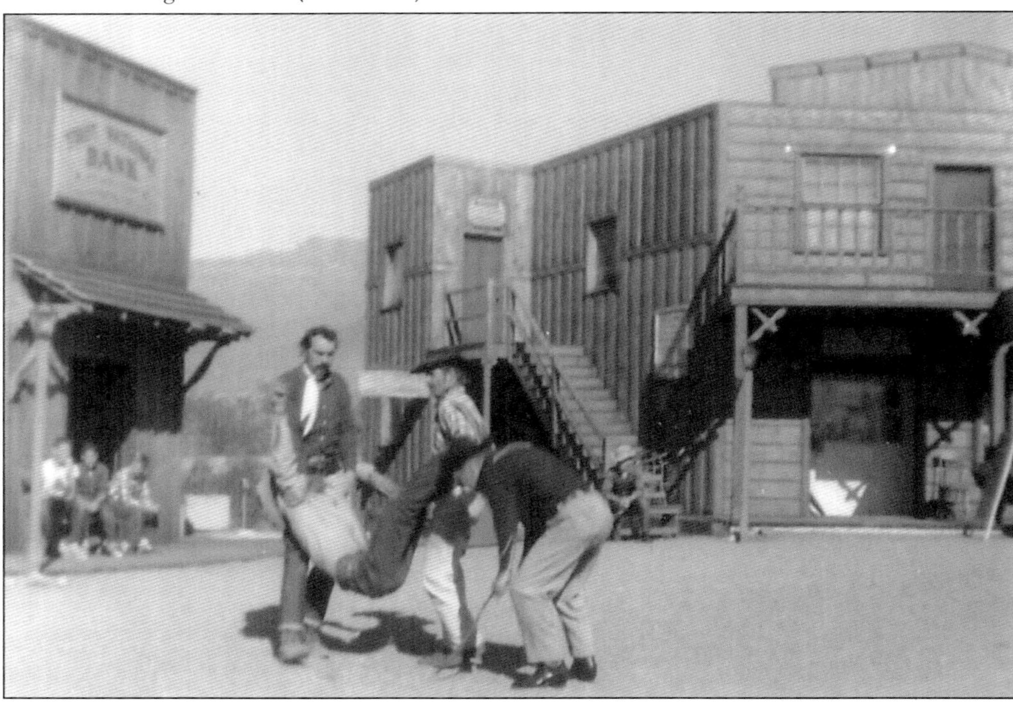

Apacheland Studio was opened for business June 1960 and filmed the television show *Stagecoach West* and movie *The Purple Hills*. Actors such as Elvis Presley, Jason Robards, Ronald Reagan, Steve McQueen, Clint Eastwood, and Audie Murphy filmed Westerns here. In 1969, a fire destroyed most of the ranch. The sets were soon rebuilt, but in February 2004, a fire once again destroyed Apacheland, and it closed its doors to the public permanently. (Bill Moser.)

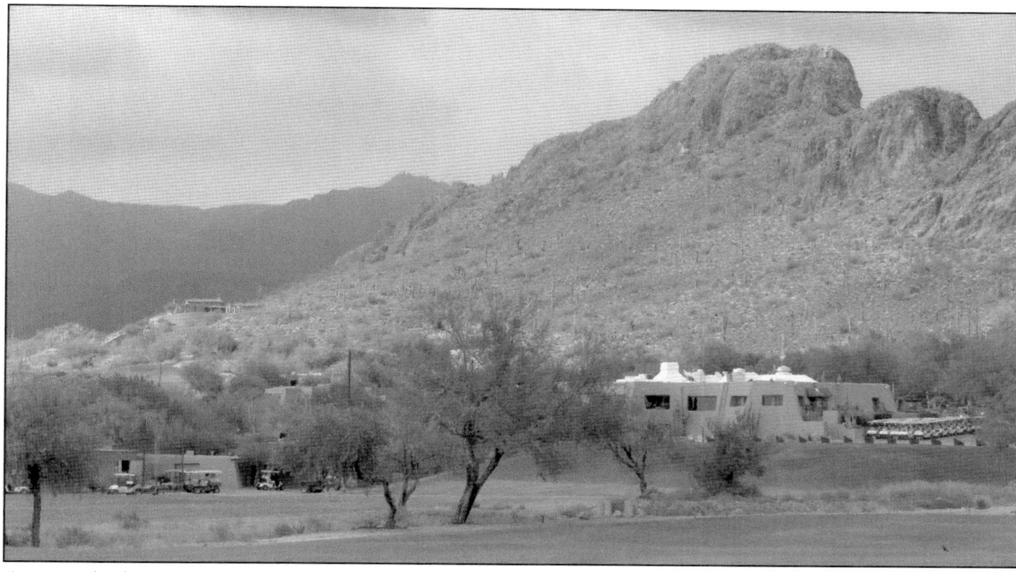

As people from the city began coming to the East Valley to see its attractions, they discovered the beauty and quiet of the Superstitions. In the early 1980s, Harold Christ began building a 3,300-acre, master-planned community named Gold Canyon Ranch. It also included a 60-guest villa resort and featured golf and equestrian activities. Today Christ's dream is a reality with the beautiful community of Gold Canyon.

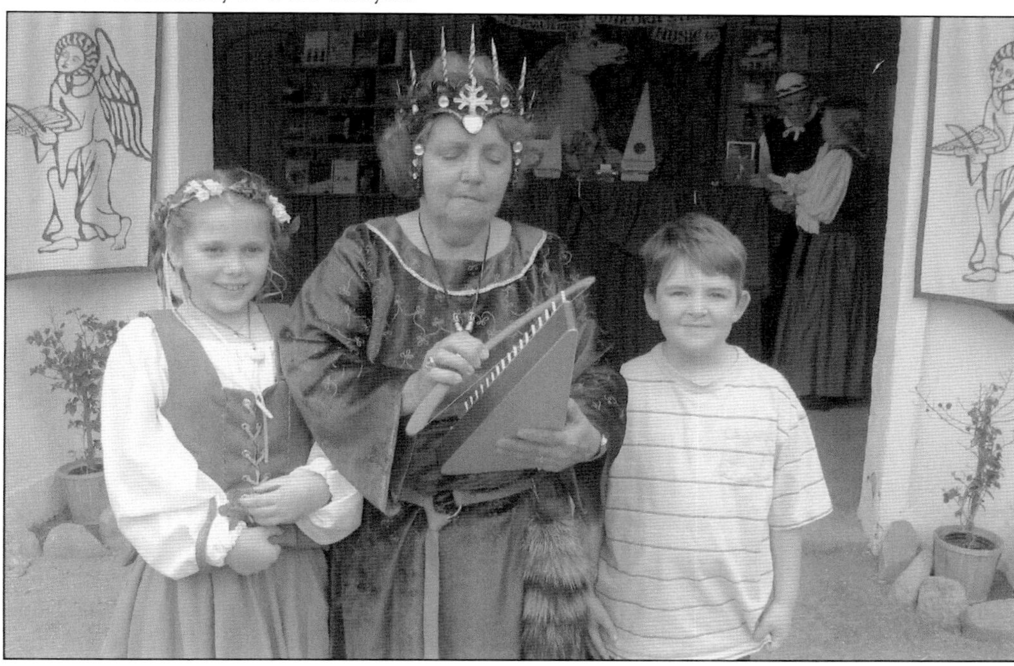

People have been attending the Renaissance Festival on the Highway 60 for 22 years now. Half a million people from all over Arizona and the Southwest attend this fun trip back to the Middle Ages. A Queen Valley resident since 1980, Connie Smith worked for five years for Unicorn Strings. She is shown here playing the bowed psaltery for her granddaughter Sarah Harber and the author's son Connor True.

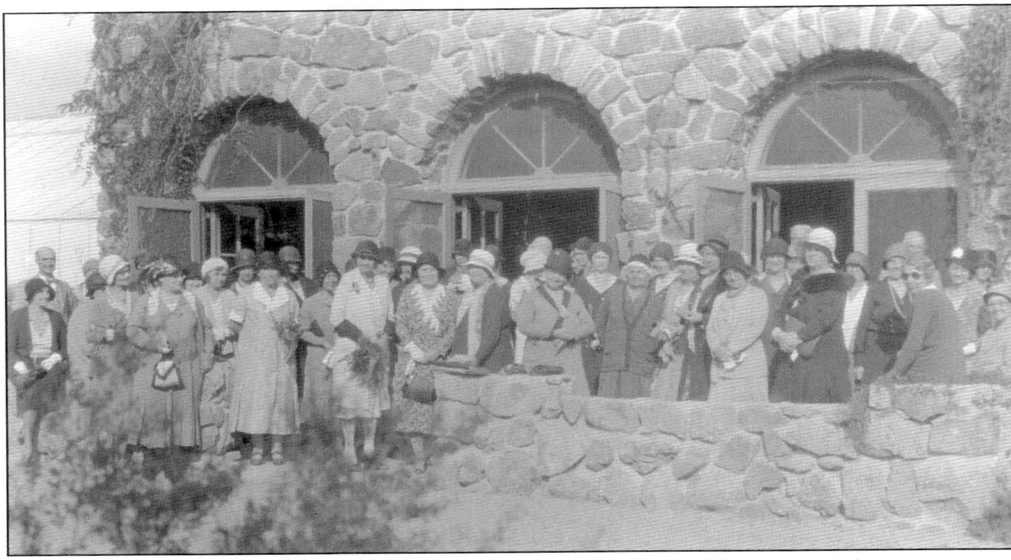

Ladies from the Phoenix Garden Club made a visit to the Boyce Thompson Arboretum around 1930. It has long been one of the most interesting and beautiful places to visit in the Superior and Queen Valley area. People come from all over the world to visit Boyce Thompson's desert biology education center and former home. (BTA.)

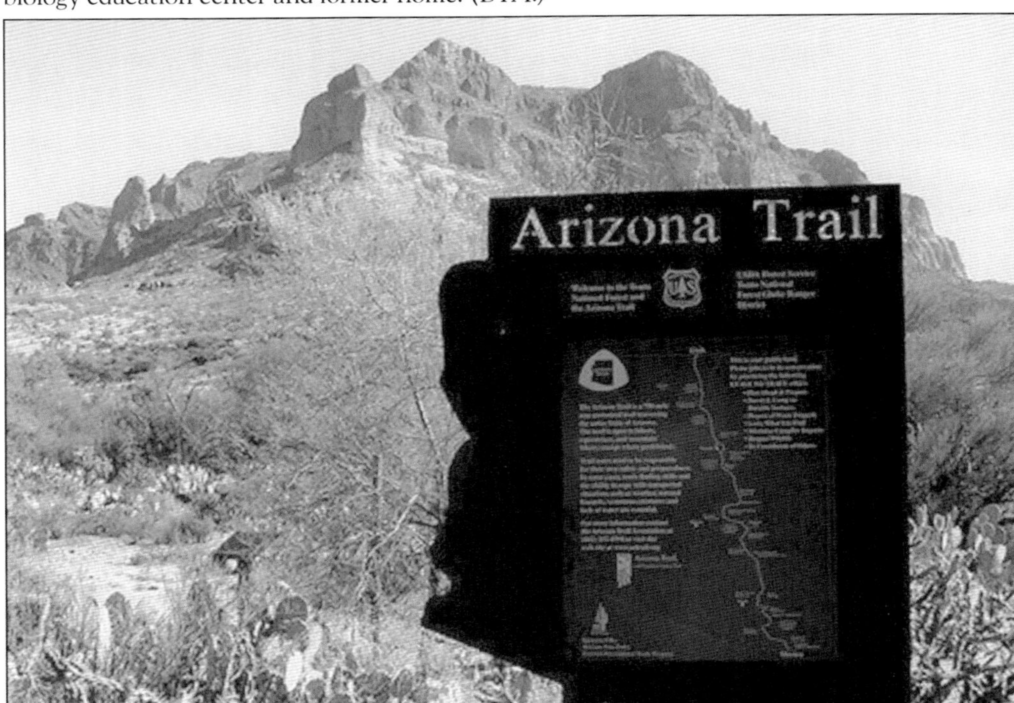

The Arizona Trail is a continuous 800-mile National Scenic Trail that goes across Arizona from Mexico to Utah. It links deserts, mountains, canyons, communities, and people. It passes through the area between Queen Valley and Superior and offers a wonderful opportunity to get to know this historic region intimately.

The Copper Corridor Visitor Center is designed to share information about the history, the businesses, and the economic and ecological benefits of the Copper Corridor. The communities in the coalition, formed in late 2003, are Oracle, San Manuel, Mammoth, Aravaipa, Dudleyville, Winkleman, Hayden, Kearny, and Superior. This group of government agencies, politicians, business owners, educators, and community activists are developing sustainable communities and a prosperous future for Eastern Pinal County.

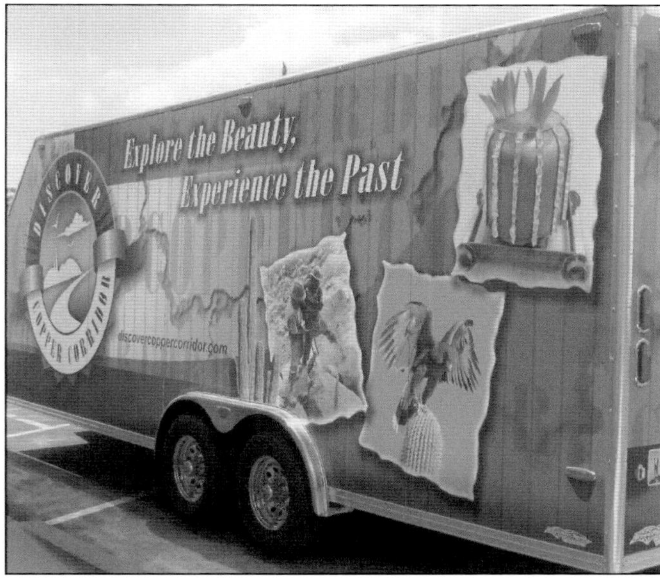

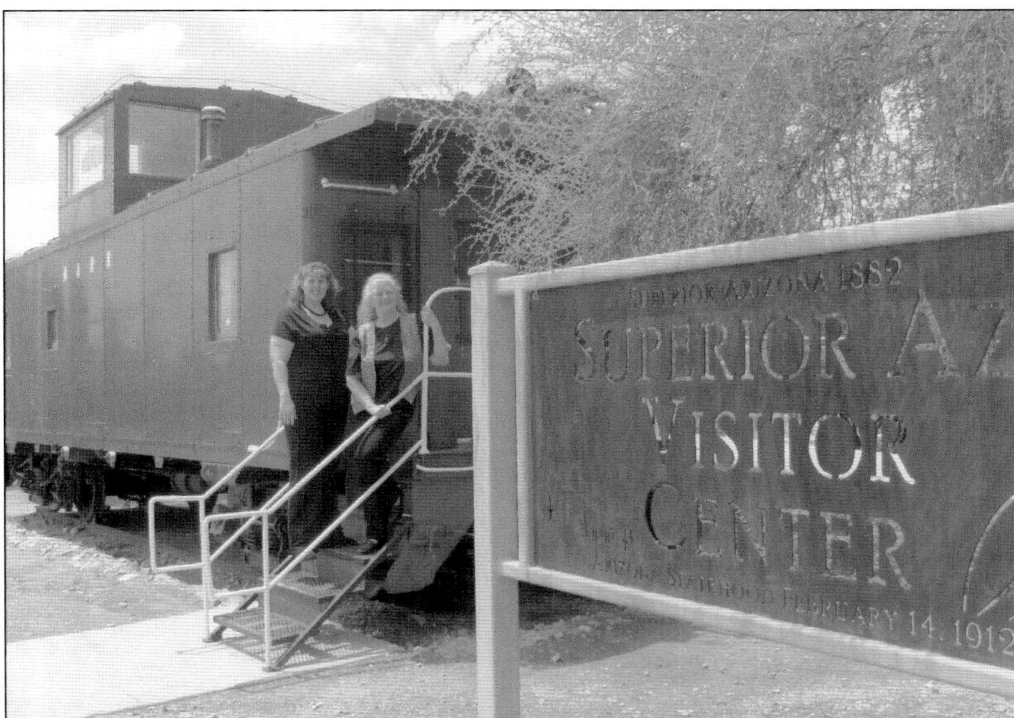

Pictured are authors Danielle Tomerlin, left, and Carol Schumacher at the new Superior Visitor Center caboose. The Superior Chamber of Commerce will staff the only chamber office in Arizona that is located in a train. Visitors will get a warm welcome to the area and be given helpful information about visiting, moving to, or setting up businesses in the area. (Connor Lawrence True.)

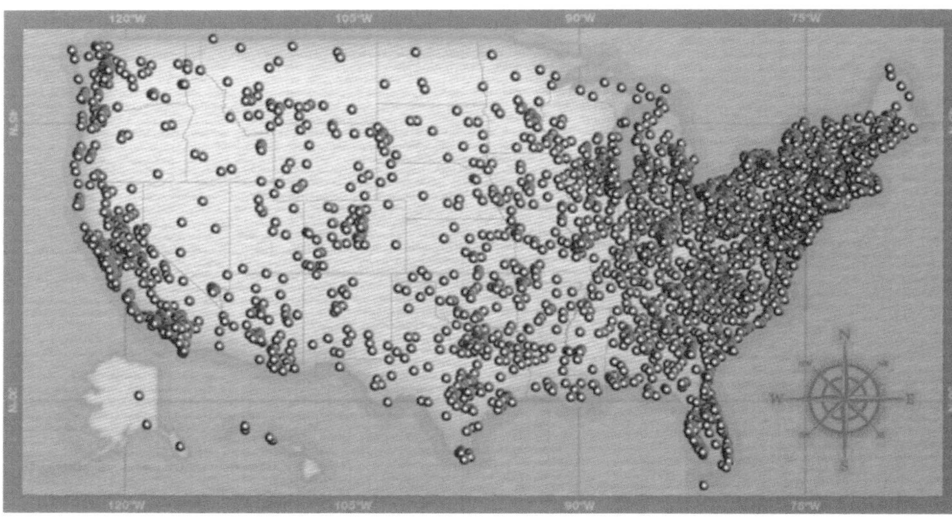